Who Was
That Masked Man?

For over four decades on radio and television, and in movies, books, and comics, the Lone Ranger's "Hi-Yo, Silver" has been a call to adventure for millions of children and adults.

"Come with us now to those thrilling days of yesteryear" for the history of the Lone Ranger as lived and told by many of the people who were there with him.

Who Was That Masked Man?

The Story of the Lone Ranger

David Rothel

South Brunswick and New York: A. S. Barnes and Company
London: Thomas Yoseloff Ltd

A. S. Barnes and Co., Inc.
Cranbury, New Jersey 08512

Thomas Yoseloff Ltd
108 New Bond Street
London W1Y OQX, England

Library of Congress Cataloging in Publication Data

Rothel, David, 1936–
Who was that masked man?

Bibliography: p.
Includes index.
1. The Lone Ranger (Radio program) I. Title.
PN1991.77.L6R6 791.44'7 75-41887
ISBN 0-498-01914-4

PRINTED IN THE UNITED STATES OF AMERICA

to
Michael, Christopher, and Laura

Contents

Preface

The Lone Ranger—he was what so many of us wanted to be when we grew up. (Can you imagine having him for an uncle as Dan Reid did?) The very sound of his voice told you that here was a man of authority who would protect the weak, who would see that justice and fair play always prevailed. He was always firm (he hardly so much as chuckled in forty years) but you knew he would always be fair. He never lied, carried on with women, or cheated anyone. No matter what the problem, he always had a plan. No guns in all the West ever spoke with more thunderous warning, but they never killed anyone.

Oh, Dan Reid, we envied you your summers riding down those dusty, Western trails with your uncle and his Indian companion. You were the lucky one; you actually got to be with him. But we were lucky, too, even if we did have to close our eyes (shutting out that golden glow from the radio eye) to be with the three of you.

Author's Note

In the process of conducting interviews with persons who were on "The Lone Ranger" scene when important decisions were made and/or creative developments took place—particularly the events surrounding the creation of the character—I occasionally found very conflicting views of the same events. I firmly believe that the eyewitnesses or participants have not intentionally misinformed me—they just remember differently.

Therefore, I have reported all of the evidence I have at hand—even when it conflicts directly with something else that has just been presented—so that the reader can see all of the versions of the story as they have been told to me.

Many times in the text I have let the discrepancies between two participants' versions stand without comment; other times, when the urge was too great or when confusion might result, I have added a note in comment or explanation. A result of this reporting technique is occasional repetition of certain bits of information. I ask the reader's indulgence when this occurs.

Acknowledgments

The author wishes to express his sincere thanks and appreciation to the following who provided assistance in the preparation of this book and/or shared their memories of "The Lone. Ranger." Only with the assistance of these guides could the author hope to find his way down the obscure dusty trails that the Lone Ranger and Tonto traveled so many moons ago.

Barbara Avram
Don Burrows
Director's Guild of America, Inc.
Fred Flowerday
Mike Healy
James and Marion Jewell
Harriet Livingstone
J. P. McCarthy
Barry O'Brien
Paul O'Brien
Gene Pillot
Harry H. Poppe
Ted Robertson
Howard Rogofsky
Screen Actors Guild
Margaret Scully
George Seaton
George B. Seitz, Jr.
Janet M. (Mrs. Fran) Striker
Jim Townsend
Jack Wrather
Wrather Corporation

Special thanks are in order to Stanley Stunell of Wrather Corporation who was unstinting in his cooperation and assistance throughout the preparation of the book.

Special thanks are also due to my wife, Nancy, whose assistance and support in the preparation of this book were immeasurable.

Most especially, thanks and gratitude must be extended to Charles D. Livingstone, without whose friendship and assistance this book would still only be a good idea.

Photographic Credits

Photographs from the personal collection of James Jewell: Pages 28, 34, 36, 41–46, 48–50, 53, 78, 80–82, 84, 96, 98, 105, 120, 122, 127–28, 163, 220

Photographs from the personal collection of Charles D. Livingstone: Pages 2, 29, 31, 37, 39, 51, 85, 95, 97, 99, 101, 106, 108, 112, 114–15, 118, 125, 129, 131, 138, 165, 194, 204, 206, 208, 210, 213, 215–16

Photographs courtesy of Lone Ranger Television, Incorporated: Pages 59–76, 87, 103, 167, 189, 196, 202–3, 218, 221–24, 226–40

Photograph on page 126 courtesy of J. P. McCarthy.

Photographs from the personal collection of David Rothel: Pages 22–24, 142–44, 146–49, 151–57, 159, 162, 164, 166, 168, 171–75, 177–88, 190, 198–99, 205, 211, 217

The pictures on pages 162, 166, 168, 171–75 were photographed by Don Burrows.

The pictures on pages 91–92, 205, 211, 217 were photographed by Barry O'Brien.

Photo copy work by Barry O'Brien and Don Burrows.

Proprietary Notice

Lone Ranger Television, Inc., a subsidiary of Wrather Corporation, is the owner of all rights, title, and interest in and to the Lone Ranger property, including but not limited to all copyrights and trademarks pertaining thereto, all Lone Ranger radio programs, and recordings thereof, all motion pictures and television programs, all publications, comic strips and comic books, and all rights to commercial usage of the names and images of the characters and all other related identifications of the property.

Permission has been granted the author by Lone Ranger Television, Inc. for the inclusion of certain pictorial and literary material in this book, which material is protected by its copyrights in and to the Lone Ranger property. Such permission does not convey any interest in the material to the author, publisher, or any other person or firm.

Lone Ranger Television, Inc. assumes no responsibility for the accuracy of the facts and statements contained in this book, and the opinions expressed therein are those of the author and not Lone Ranger Television, Inc.

Who Was
That Masked Man?

1

"From Out of the Past Come the Thundering Hoofbeats . . ."

"THE Lone Ranger" radio program started in early 1933, but I didn't come along until 1936, and didn't take much interest in radio my first three or four years. My mother, father, three older brothers, and I lived in North Eaton, Ohio, in a small frame house that was attached to my father's source of income—a general store-tavern. We never called it a general store or tavern; to us it was just "the store," and it was important and I liked spending my first five years there. The store was bounded on the north by the Yager Lumber Company across the highway, our attached house on the west, an outside privy on the south, and Mr. Preachy, a kid-hating neighbor, on the east. The railroad tracks were within baseball throwing distance, west from the store. There were two gas pumps outside and two entrances to the divided building: the left entrance was to the tables and chairs, jukebox, bar, beer, and wine; the right entrance led to the grocery store portion, which was backed by the pool room that could be entered from either half of the store. There was no Muzak, or even a radio for that matter, in the store. It didn't need either.

It's curious how certain early images are indelibly burned onto the visual memory tracks of our minds. Two in my mind reveal me in the store standing precariously on a small stool that has raised me high enough so that I can maneuver the cue stick to hit the white ball, causing it to hit the other ball, causing that ball to move into a pocket located in one of six areas of the felt-covered table. In the second image I'm riding my tricycle (which is really the cabin on a steam locomotive) in a large circle in front of the store's jukebox (we called it a ju*t*ebox) singing "The Wabash Cannon Ball" to the accompaniment of the juke and the amazement of all the Major Boweses in my audience.

The first radio program I became conscious of was "Tom Mix and His Ralston Straight-Shooters." Either I or one of my brothers (I don't remember which) sent for our first radio premium from Tom Mix. For our Ralston box top we got two or three rather poorly printed Tom Mix comic books. But that didn't matter, they came through the mail from Tom Mix; they had actually been where he was, and it was almost too much to be believed. They had been sent personally by Tom Mix. Now you may think I'm making a lot out of this, but to five-year-old me in 1940, it was a big event to receive comic books from Tom Mix.

The author adorned in his first store-bought cowboy outfit and astride the only steed he possessed at age five, his tricycle.

Sometime late in that year's Ohio winter the store burned down leaving only the house and the connecting passageway which now, frighteningly, led to only charred ruins. That summer we all moved one mile east down the road to our new home—a farm—where I was to spend the next twelve years. There were a big two-story house, a barn, a grainery, a chicken house, a milk house and forty-two acres just made for radio-and-movie-induced-fantasy-filled-cowboys-and-outlaws playing.

These were the peak years for cowboy outfits; cap pistols and holsters (Lone Ranger or Gene Autry embossed genuine leather); caps that never quite produced the "bang" you wanted or expected; cowboy boots; a ten-gallon hat, white, of course. And this, too, was the time for a lucky kid like me to have my very own horse. He wasn't white, so I couldn't call him Silver; Champion was the name of this bay horse, and I'm afraid it was something of a misnomer—he was anything but a champion, but I didn't know that, so what did it matter? It was easy to fantasize him into "The Wonder Horse" of Gene Autry, but it wasn't easy to fantasize my old cavalry saddle with the hole in the middle into a tooled leather western saddle. In all those years I dreamed of having the beautiful western saddle I used to see each Saturday at Sears Roebuck in the nearby town of Elyria, but it never

Scout. And there were sounds: horse's hooves galloping on hard-packed dirt trails or stepping cautiously on rocky creek edges just before wading through to the cave under the mountain waterfall; stagecoach wheels passing over that old wooden bridge as the driver cracked his whip urging the horses on; the saddle leather straining as the Lone Ranger hoisted himself up onto the back of the neighing, prancing Silver ("Steady, Silver, steady, big fellow"); crickets seeming to echo each other somewhere off in the distance from the campsite fire of the Lone Ranger and Tonto; the sound of mighty fist connecting with beard-stubbled outlaw chin. You say it's impossible to tell it's a beard-stubbled outlaw chin? (Years later I was to hear about one of the performers becoming so engrossed in the action that a slightly ad-libbed line came out—"Listen, I hear a *white* horse coming!") Anyway, I might not be able to identify the Lone Ranger's fist encountering a beard-stubbled chin now, but I sure could at ten years of age (with, perhaps, a little help from the narrator) as I stared transfixed into that green eye of the Zenith console.

Sometime around my ninth year we became a two-radio home. The Zenith remained in our living room and a Philco console (I don't think it was new) became a fixture in the corner of our dining room. It didn't have a green eye like the Zenith, but it did have a most fascinating recessed station indicator in the middle of the set, up near the top. Whenever that set was on it exuded a warm golden glow that made me want to turn off all the other lights so that I could stare deep into that golden glow and become lost in whatever adventure was emanating from the giant twelve-inch speaker hidden behind the carved grillwork and cloth. I can't stress enough that it wasn't just a yellow light coming from that station indicator—it was a warm golden glow—that's the only way to describe it. A couple of years ago my wife bought me a replica of the old Philco table model radio and it has that same glow that I hadn't seen for over twenty years.

During those years from, let's say, six until late in my twelfth year, I constantly played cowboys and outlaws—good guys and bad guys—with two neighbor friends. They were a couple of years younger than I, so I always got to be Gene Autry or, if I had a mask, the Lone Ranger. They got to be the outlaws. (I often wondered in later years how this might have affected their little psyches.) Often, however, we were all the good-guy cowboys and then the outlaws were better performed because they were imaginary. You see, my neighbor friends didn't really want to be the outlaws; they wanted to be Roy Rogers, Hopalong Cassidy, Rocky Lane, or some equally thrilling hero. (For some reason they never challenged my claim to Gene Autry and the Lone Ranger. I guess there were enough heroes to go around in those days.)

And heroes were important in those days. They were something you thought about consciously. You talked about them or at least thought about them every day. You pretended that you were them when you could, certainly when you were alone. I'm sure I didn't analyze my hero worship for the Lone Ranger or Gene Autry during those years; I just accepted that they were what they were to me, and I wanted to grow up to be just like them. Oh, I don't mean the adventure part of it, I knew that could never be—I mean the personal characteristics of my heroes: the honesty, friendliness, bravery, kindliness, integrity—all of those things we value so highly, but rarely talk about in connection with our adult selves for fear of embarrassment, or, perhaps, melancholia.

In case you haven't noticed, they're gone—those heroes we had in the thirties, forties, and early fifties. But then, so are the "mom and pop" stores, and the small Ohio farms, and the Lincoln Theatre, and the console radios—all gone. Except, perhaps, they're not gone—in the sense that all that we experienced is stored somewhere in the memory tracks of the brain and with a little jogging it can, bit by bit, be remembered and enjoyed.

And so a few months ago, with the cooperation and assistance of many people who were "there," I started to assemble the many pieces of the gigantic jigsaw puzzle called the Lone Ranger. The Lone Ranger, of course, became real through the people who created him—who wrote, produced, directed, and acted his adventures—and of equal importance through those of us who listened, and later listened and watched, and gradually as time passed, built an aura around him that the creators could never have done alone. I have, therefore, attempted to talk with all of the people I could who have had some tenable connection with the character over the years. I have also talked with others (like yourself and myself) who had a hand in creating that aura that affected the thinking and behavior of over four decades of youngsters.

Many pieces of the Lone Ranger puzzle are missing and may never be found. People are dead or two minds remember the same thing in two entirely different ways. (When that happens, both versions are given in their entirety.) Regardless, there are enough of the pieces left to examine and appreciate the entire picture.

2
Enter the Lone Ranger

I see him as a sort of lone operator. He could even be a former Texas Ranger.

—George W. Trendle

IT was just after Christmas in the winter of 1932, when the twenty-nine-year-old radio writer put aside a completed script of "Warner Lester, Manhunter" to receive a telephone call from Detroit. George W. Trendle, the boss of WXYZ radio, was calling Fran Striker in Buffalo, New York.

This was the first of many calls that Striker would receive during the next few weeks from the former lawyer, former vaudeville house owner, former designer and operator of ornate movie theatres—current Detroit radio station owner in trouble. Trendle was down to his last million. When he and his partner, John H. King, purchased the Columbia Broadcasting outlet, WXYZ, in 1929, Trendle had in mind creating local programming for the evening hours that would be locally sponsored and would, he felt, fill the WXYZ coffers with far more money than they were receiving carrying the Columbia Broadcasting fare. When he informed CBS of his intent, a storm ensued that raged until June of 1932, when the rebellious little giant, George W. Trendle, cut line with the mother ship and set sail as an independent in the choppy waters of the Great Lakes.

During the months between June and early December of 1932, WXYZ was losing four thousand dollars a week as an independent station and time was running out for the now slightly frantic Trendle to prove his contention that he and his scrambling young staff at the station could create programs with the same high quality and showmanship as their big brother stations in New York and Chicago. In addition, Trendle had long talked of a Michigan radio network of seven stations. If he could just find the right program, all of his dreams for the station could come true. But what kind of program should it be?

Trendle kept his own counsel until he had formulated certain "givens" for the new program that he hoped would turn the tide for his waning fortune. In mid-December he called his staff together and delivered the "givens" within which they were to work with him in the creation of the new program.

The first "given" was that the program had to be a drama, because drama was inexpensive, required no name stars, and could be produced and cast from current staff members who had been doing "Warner Lester, Manhunter" in recent months—namely director James Jewell and his "Jewell Players."

The second "given" was that the program

This early photograph of George W. Trendle was taken during the year (1929) that he and John H. King (at the time his name was Kunsky) purchased WXYZ.

must be aimed at kids because they were less critical. Playing to a less critical audience would mean that the program would not have to be so elaborate (translation: less expensive) and, besides, kids could be counted on to coax their parents into buying a potential sponsor's product.

The third "given" was that the program should be a Western. At first Trendle was torn between crime stories and Westerns, but finally decided against crime stories because he felt it was more difficult to make them completely wholesome and, by golly, this was going to be a wholesome program. In addition, Trendle had checked other kid's programs and had found that radio premiums from prospective sponsors could be a lucrative sideline. He felt that the Western offered practically unlimited possibilities in this area. If his game plan worked, Trendle wanted to be able to touch all financial bases.

Trendle was continuing with his list of "givens" as his assembled staff listened patiently, perhaps wondering about the degree of "wiggle room" that would be left to them once the "givens" were out of the way. The program was to take place in the 1880s because a contemporary Western, he felt, would restrict the writers too much.

There must be a hero, of course. He was to be mature rather than young because "it is better to respect than to envy." But what kind of hero should he be? Trendle was still a little unsure of this as he met with his staff. He had spent a great deal of time thinking about the problem in the quiet of his study at home and had repeatedly gone to the shelves to inspect books from his childhood that had inspired him during those early years of avid reading: novels by Zane Grey, James Fenimore Cooper, Horatio Alger; the adventures of such fiction characters as Nick Carter, Robin Hood, Zorro. Yes, he told his staff, these last two especially—Robin Hood and Zorro—most closely possessed the qualities he was looking for in this new Western hero. In his enthusiasm Trendle couldn't resist recalling the thrill and excitement of seeing the great Douglas Fairbanks in "The Mark of Zorro" on the silent screen. Yes, this fictional prototype should serve as the model for the new creation.

At this point the exuberant Trendle fell silent for the response and brainstorming of his staff. Yes, they liked the basic idea of the character and felt that a Zorro-like mask was a necessity along with the "benevolent outlaw" aspects of both Zorro and Robin Hood. Someone pointed out that motion picture cowboys quite often had magnificent horses that became almost as well-known as their riders. Different types of horses were discussed until the staff agreed upon a white Arabian. Trendle, who fancied himself quite a horseman, vetoed the Arabian horse idea because they were too small; however, he agreed that the white horse idea was good because, "He'll stand out at night as well as by day." Trendle suggested to the staff that they do a lot of thinking and talking together about this new program during the next few days and that they would all get together one week later to firm up details of the program.

At the second staff conference, which fell between Christmas and New Year's, Trendle started by reviewing what they had decided at the first meeting or informally since that meeting. "Well," Trendle said, "this guy is decent, athletic, and 'up on the bit'—you know: alert and enterprising. Maybe he has been unjustly banished and is waiting to come into his own again. Anyhow, he goes around righting wrongs against tremendous odds and then disappearing immediately afterwards. I see him as a sort of lone operator. He could even be a former Texas Ranger—."

"There's his name!" spoke up a staff member, "The Lone Ranger."

Trendle and his WXYZ staff felt they had done all that they could do to develop their new radio hero. Now they needed someone to bring him to life, to develop his character, to make him believable—they needed a scriptwriter. It was at this point that George W. Trendle got on the phone to Buffalo.

As he waited for the long-distance operator to complete the call, Trendle was excited; he felt he was on to something. This Lone Ranger character might be the ticket to the renewed success and prosperity that he had been searching for. He hardly knew this free-lance script writer by the name of Fran Striker, but his "Warner Lester" series was not bad and he could tell from the scripts that Striker understood character development and how to sustain a program with a proper mix of suspense and adventure. Yes, he'd give this man Striker a chance.

Striker listened as the ebullient Trendle outlined what he had in mind for this new program. The usually mild-mannered and unassuming Striker was slightly taken aback that the prominent George W. Trendle would personally call him to seek his assistance on a new radio program. Striker, who had never been west of Buffalo, assured Trendle that he would drop everything and get right to the business of developing this adventure of the old West. Trendle stressed that no time was to be wasted since he wanted this new program on the air within a month.

Fran Striker was one of those individuals who, once the challenge had been made, surged forward possessed by the fascination of the work before him. He had been developing a Western radio series on his own called "Covered Wagon Days." Looking back over the scripts he saw that with changes they could be the partial basis for the new program for George W. Trendle. The words came quickly to his mind; his fingers snapped at the typewriter keys and the Lone Ranger evolved.

Striker saw the Ranger as slightly over six feet with a weight hovering close to 190 pounds—this seemed about right for a Western hero. He remembered a program he had once written about Robin Hood where Robin's arrowheads were tipped with silver so that all would know the archer with the distinctive trademark. Why not bullets of silver for this new hero . . . and silver shoes for his horse? Silver bullets, silver shoes, a white horse—wait, call him Silver. It works! And so the creation continued.

Trendle, never an easy man to please, now became as obsessed as his new loyalist, Striker, that this program must be right! Rewrites were repeatedly called for. On the fifteenth go around, it was decided to give the script an on-the-air try-out late at night. Trendle still wasn't happy with certain aspects of the program, but thought it might shake down more quickly if they actually started trying it out with a cast.

Fran Striker, the head writer for "The Lone Ranger" radio program during its long run on radio.

The director, James Jewell, started rehearsing his cast.

Striker had been struggling to come up with a personal signature for the Lone Ranger that would clearly identify him to the listening audience. He buttonholed everyone he could to listen to one of his latest attempts. "Hi-Yi, Yippy, Silver, away." No, it still wasn't right, but he knew the last syllable had to be a long one so that the actor could sustain it in a shout, and so the search continued.

In early January the first try-out program was broadcast with little fanfare. Trendle wanted only a few friends and the staff at the station to listen and provide a critique the next day. The reaction was mixed, but Trendle knew for certain the changes *he* wanted. For one thing the Lone Ranger was far too cheerful. This masked avenger had no business being so happy. He was supposed to be righting wrongs, protecting the poor and weak from ruthless outlaws, bringing peace and justice to the Western frontier—this was no laughing matter! Striker got the message; rarely from that time on would the Ranger so much as chuckle.

The other thing that had bothered Trendle was that awful closing: "Come along, Silver! That's the boy! . . . Hi-Yi (hearty laugh) . . . Now cut loose, and awa-a-y." He felt the idea of a closing signature was right, but it must be shorter, more to the point.

After a few more late-night try-out programs, Trendle instructed Striker to prepare a backlog of twenty-four scripts. They would aim to get the program on the air by the end of the month. Striker got to work immediately on this formidable task and soon found that he had a new problem—the Lone Ranger was too alone. This was radio. Either a narrator had to tell the listener everything the Lone Ranger was doing or else the Lone Ranger had to talk aloud to himself (or Silver) explaining just what he was doing; otherwise, the listener wouldn't understand what was going on. The Lone Ranger needed someone to talk to—a confidant, but who?

It had to be someone who could assist him in his battles for justice, but not someone who would steal the spotlight. It couldn't be a woman because the Lone Ranger moved from place to place and a woman companion was out of the question. A comic sidekick would never do for the sober masked man. This companion must possess the same outdoor knowledge and survival skills as the Lone Ranger. He must be able to track outlaw trails and hunt for the wild game that would make up much of their diet when traveling. He must understand the making of nature's medicines from the herbs, roots, and plants that the wilderness provided. No mere cowboy would possess these skills. The description would, however, fit an Indian—a faithful Indian companion. Striker, remembering a savage character named Gobo from one of his old radio mystery scripts, changed the name by selecting a new set of consonants. The result was Tonto and he first appeared in the tenth script.

It was only six weeks from the time of conception until this man of mystery, this masked rider of the plains, this champion of justice—this Lone Ranger—began his forty-plus year ride into the hearts and minds of millions of people around the world. The date was January 30, 1933: "Hi-Yo, Silver, Away!"

What you have just read is the basic story of how "The Lone Ranger" program came to be—according to George W. Trendle. Current writers have two prime sources of information covering the Trendle version: a 1939 *Saturday Evening Post* article that extensively quotes Trendle, and the authorized biography of George W. Trendle by Mary E. Bickel. Some individuals through the years have claimed that the Trendle version is not entirely accurate—that others in the Trendle staff had a much greater hand in the creation than Trendle wished to acknowledge. Some say that Trendle had practically nothing to do with the creation. It has been said that Trendle was a man with a well-developed ego. He owned the company and what was created by his company belonged to him—was created by him in his eyes.

Some have said that the original director, James Jewell, deserved much of the credit for creating the Lone Ranger. It is interesting to note that Jim Jewell, who directed "The Lone Ranger" program from preorigin try-outs in January, 1933, through June of 1938—directing almost five full years of programs, fifty-two weeks a year, three programs a week from creation to the beginnings of international fame—is never mentioned even once in the authorized George W. Trendle biography.

There are others who believe that Fran Striker deserves the major credit for the creation of the Lone Ranger as a full-fledged, meaningful character. A fairly good case can be made for this contention; after all (according to Trendle), he was the writer hired to color in and give detail to the line drawing of the character that Trendle and his WXYZ staff had provided. (However, this version of the creation requires you to ignore the contribution of director Jim Jewell who it is known had a hand in at least some of the writing on the program while it was being created.)

It has been suggested by someone very close to the scene that "they [Trendle and Striker] had a pleasant enough working relationship, perhaps because each wanted to keep it so. There was always a feeling as to who created 'The Lone Ranger,' each believing he did." Few, however, would argue that Striker was the one who wrote the scripts that helped to make the character an American legend.*

In 1932 at the time of the creation of "The Lone Ranger," Ted Robertson was a teenage assistant to the chief sound effects technician at WXYZ. Later he was to become chief sound technician, then assistant director of "The Lone Ranger" prior to leaving WXYZ in 1940. In correspondence with the author, Mr. Robertson commented on the creation and early years of "The Lone Ranger" program.

DAVID ROTHEL: Do you know who the participants were at the initial brainstorming meetings which resulted in the creation of the Lone Ranger character?

TED ROBERTSON: I was nineteen years of age and the assistant to Bert Djerkiss, the chief sound effects technician at radio station WXYZ (I was also an actor and announcer), and was not invited to the brainstorming session at which the Lone Ranger was created. My opinions are, therefore, second hand and may not necessarily be fact. I know George W. Trendle was definitely there, as was Jim Jewell. Harold True, the manager of station WXYZ, was there and I suspect Allen Campbell, the financial brain of WXYZ, was also there, and possibly Ray Meurer, who was the firm's attorney. Brace Beemer was, at the time, the chief announcer at the station and I would doubt he would be included.

DAVID ROTHEL: Do you have any personal knowledge as to who was responsible for specific contributions to the creation of the program? It has been written, for example, that Brace Beemer was responsible for the idea of the silver shoes for Silver and that Fran Striker was responsible for the silver bullets.

Pictured above is Ted Robertson, who worked his way up from assistant to the chief sound effects technician to the position of assistant director during the years he was with "The Lone Ranger." (circa mid-1930s)

TED ROBERTSON: I was always led to believe that the idea of a Western hero (a former Texas Ranger) was the idea of George Trendle. Harold True once told me *he* had the idea for an Indian companion but I always accepted that with a grain of salt—as I would accept Beemer's contention he was responsible for the silver shoes. I would suspect that Jim Jewell (who had a marvelously active and fertile mind) contributed a great deal and Fran Striker must also have contributed his share.

DAVID ROTHEL: Do you have any idea how fully created the basic Lone Ranger character was when Fran Striker came on the scene to write the series?

* Though "The Lone Ranger" was Fran Striker's most famous and profitable writing venture, "The Green Hornet" was personally his favorite program.

TED ROBERTSON: Fran Striker was based in Buffalo, New York, and was hired to write the scripts. [Author's note: Striker and his family moved to Detroit in December of 1933, almost a year after "The Lone Ranger" went on the air.] I have no way of knowing for sure, but I suspect he was given the basic character of the Lone Ranger, his horse, Silver, and his faithful Indian companion, Tonto. Fran Striker was given a contract to write the show and was paid five dollars per script (which escalated to seven dollars and fifty cents). Fran typed the scripts himself and the number of legible scripts the carbon paper would yield determined the total amount he received for each episode. He usually averaged seven copies, which gave him a profit of thirty-five dollars (minus postage). The sound department always worked from the seventh copy, which probably is the reason my eyes are so bad.

DAVID ROTHEL: Several people have expressed the feeling that Jim Jewell contributed considerably more to the creation of the Lone Ranger than he is given credit for. Could you give your assessment of this?

TED ROBERTSON: I am probably the world's leading authority on Jim Jewell because I was in the theatre with him beginning in 1930 and was hired by him shortly after he became the dramatic director for WXYZ the same year. When I first went to work for Jim and WXYZ it was in the depths of the depression and there was no money for a salary for me. I kept coming to the studio and working for free because I realized how much I had to learn and because of Jewell's charisma. To get to the studio was a long streetcar ride and it cost six cents plus a penny for a transfer. The day came when I just did not have the money so I didn't report for work. Jewell telephoned the house and spoke to an aunt with whom I lived. She told him in no uncertain terms why I did not report for work. The end result was that I began receiving $2.50 per week which a short time later escalated to $7.50, and by the end of a year became $17.50 (when I became chief sound technician). About a year later the company had no money available for its payroll and we were given pink promissory notes which were eventually paid off at the rate of fifty cents on the dollar.

[Author's note: The following is the form letter that George W. Trendle sent to all WXYZ employees during the time of the financial crisis that Mr. Robertson refers to. The employee's name was written by hand next to the word "EMPLOYEES" at the top of the page and the amount of the newly tabulated salary was written at the appropriate places in the text. The letter was neither signed nor initialed by Mr. Trendle.]

BULLETIN:—ALL EMPLOYEES

FROM: MR. TRENDLE

I wish it were possible for me to tell each one of you *personally* how we all appreciate the wonderful spirit of cooperation you have shown in the present financial stringency, and also how grateful I am for the many evidences of sympathy expressed in connection with the losses I have taken through the failure of the Union Guardian Trust Company.

We all want this organization to continue to function with as little curtailment in personnel and efficiency as possible. We feel you all know that the present banking condition is such that it is impossible for us to continue to take the huge weekly losses we have assumed ever since last spring, particularly in view of the fact that hundreds of thousands of dollars of both Mr. Kunsky's money and mine are tied up in our local banking situation. We have, therefore, worked out a scheme which has probably been discussed with you, and under which your weekly salary for the present will be $______. We want you to know that we realize this amount must, of necessity, be more or less temporary, and when conditions right themselves, Station WXYZ will gradually come back to normal, and *that* condition will again be reflected in the payrolls.

Our operating losses during the past several months have run well into six figures, and it is our endeavor to try and operate the station with the smallest possible loss during the next few months, in order that we may be able to meet these losses weekly with cash. As soon as the turn in business takes place, we are confident that the Michigan Radio Network, and WXYZ will go places. We have a sound organization, a sound plan, a loyal staff and a proposition which is far better than any other radio station can offer.

The enclosed remittance of $______ will be construed by us to be your acceptance of the present wage scale, which, we assure you is highly appreciated, and I, personally, want to express my thanks for your kindly cooperation.

I definitely agree that Jim Jewell contributed considerably more to the creation of the Lone Ranger than he is given credit for. I suspect this is the reason he eventually parted company with George W. Trendle. The program was highly successful and made an enormous amount of money. Jim wanted to be paid a salary commensurate with the success of the show. Trendle was not inclined to do so and the parting took place under a cloud of bad feeling.

In the event any of my words find their way into your book (which I hope is a huge success) I feel compelled to make the following observation: It is my considered judgment that Jim Jewell was a dedicated genius. As it is with most geniuses he was eccentric, at times irascible. and very difficult to work for. He drove himself unmercifully and made outrageous creative demands on his actors, engineers, and sound technicians, but somehow he forced them to deliver. I remember being in constant battle with him (I was forever quitting or being fired), but I always returned because I understood his dedication to perfection and had enormous respect for his talent. There was nothing Jim Jewell couldn't do . . . if Fran Striker's scripts didn't arrive in the mail (that happened several times) he was able, at the last moment, to write a script and get it on the air . . . if an actor showed up in an inebriated condition (that happened to one of the early portrayers of the Lone Ranger) Jim was able to (and did) take over the role . . . if he got into a battle with the sound department and the chief sound man went home in a huff (I did it many times) he was capable of handling the turntables. He was a producer-director-creator who dealt successfully in comedy, drama, musical variety, and documentaries. He was a writer, composer, actor—a genius of many talents—and his contributions to the success of "The Lone Ranger," to many other programs, and to the success of station WXYZ has never been properly appreciated and I am delighted to be able to set the record straight. He was a giant.

DAVID ROTHEL: Do you happen to know who decided on the "William Tell Overture" as the theme for the program?

TED ROBERTSON: It is strange I do not know the answer to this question. I later was responsible for a great deal of the music chosen for the show and spent hours at Grinnell Bros. music store listening to records and making my choices, but I never got it clear in my mind who made the memorable choice of the "William Tell Overture." The evidence would indicate Jim Jewell and Bert Djerkiss. Jim was knowledgeable about music (he even composed songs for an earlier puppet show) and Bert was a singer who left WXYZ a short time later to pursue a singing career.

DAVID ROTHEL: In what year did you leave "The Lone Ranger" program? What job did you assume when you left the program?

TED ROBERTSON: I was asked to leave "The Lone Ranger" program (and station WXYZ) in November 1940, and moved to Chicago. The reason for my departure was an ideological difference I had with Brace Beemer—a story of little importance to anyone but me. In Chicago I was hired almost immediately to fly to St. Louis and handle the radio campaign of a man aspiring to become the mayor of that city. The campaign was won and I joined the production staff of WBBM, Chicago, the key Midwest CBS station.

DAVID ROTHEL: Do you have any remembrances of the early days of "The Lone Ranger" program or the people connected with it that you could relate?

TED ROBERTSON: I wish I could authenticate this particular story, or even remember the exact figures, but I simply can not. Maybe somebody else you have talked to could help. I am convinced this story is true—it came from too many sources in a position to know: Fran Striker (who had a very large family) was finally brought to Detroit from Buffalo and given an office and a contract to write for the station. (At one time he personally wrote in one week, three "Lone Rangers," two "Manhunters," one "Dr. Fang," and a show about World War I.) His contract was in the neighborhood of a hundred to a hundred and fifty dollars a week and it contained a clause which said he would receive an additional ten dollars per station, per week, for any additional stations who signed to carry "The Lone Ranger." One day he was informed his work was so outstanding and management was so pleased, his salary was to be increased approximately fifty dollars per week. Fran was ecstatic and the following day the old contract was torn up and he signed a new one containing the increase. In the new contract the extra-station clause was deleted and a few days later Campbell announced that 120 new stations would be added to "The Lone Ranger" line-up.

John Todd, a marvelous actor who played Tonto, was a charming, witty, and virile Irishman who was quite attractive to women. During my tenure as assistant director under Chuck Livingstone we did three broadcasts a night—one at 6:30 P.M. for the Detroit and Michigan area, one at 7:30 P.M. for the East and Midwest states, and a final broadcast at 10:30 P.M. for

Good Luck Always
The Lone Ranger

This is one of the early promotional pictures that was sent to young fans of the Lone Ranger.

the West coast. The time between 8:00 and 10:30 P.M. was usually devoted to poker, Ping-Pong, snooker or pool at the local pool parlor, or, for those of a romantic nature, it was an opportunity for a little hanky-panky.

One memorable night we began the final broadcast and I failed to check the personnel. The first scene concerned a meeting between the Lone Ranger, Tonto, and the local sheriff. When Tonto's first line came up there was a horrifying silence . . . John Todd was nowhere to be seen (or heard). Earle Graser (the Lone Ranger at the time) and the actor playing the sheriff (probably Fred Reto) somehow stumbled through the scene improvising as they went along to cover the absence of the (un) faithful Indian companion. Todd arrived shortly thereafter in a state of complete dishevel and with his prominent bald spot covered with lipstick. The lovable bachelor had been dallying with a damsel in a nearby hotel and had lost all sense of time. John never revealed the identity of the lady friend, and I learned to count noses five minutes before the final broadcast.

Fred Flowerday (who replaced me as chief sound technician when I moved on to directing) constructed a large box on wheels which contained an automobile storage battery which connected to several auto horns mounted in the box which were activated by buttons mounted on the outside rear of the box. These were used for contemporary dramas such as "The Green Hornet." We were short of storage space so Fred's box was kept in the corner of the studio and the battery deactivated when not in use. One night the sound crew failed to unhook the battery. On the 10:30 P.M. broadcast Tonto was sent to watch the horses as the Lone Ranger crept up on a line cabin where a young girl was held captive. Dear old John Todd (tired after a long day at the microphone) repaired to the rear of the studio, sat on a chair and went to rest his feet on the horn box. Suddenly a klaxon horn honked across the prairie drowning out the sound of the crickets. From then on the storage battery was *removed* from Fred's horn box.

On one broadcast we had a scene in which somebody was chopping wood. For this effect we had a sound man with a Boy Scout hatchet chopping on an old log we kept for the purpose. In the sound effects studio (which was back of the director) Ernie Winstanley and Jim Fletcher (two excellent sound men who later became actors) were working the wood chopping, the footsteps, and the horse hooves (bathroom plungers pounded in a large box filled with gravel). On the 10:30 P.M. show (where everything seemed to happen) Ernie was handling the wood chopping and became involved in some horseplay with Fletcher. He was distracted for a fraction of a second and the miscalculation drove the hatchet deep into his shin. The spurt of blood caused Fletcher to hustle Ernie out of the studio immediately and to a nearby doctor. We finished the broadcast without the services of the sound guys and the horses stole silently into the remaining scenes.

Forty years (and more) is a long time ago but I have tried my best to answer your questions honestly.

✣ ✣ ✣

Very late in the preparation of this manuscript, when I had begun to suspect that there was little hope of including the reminiscences of Jim Jewell, the original director of "The Lone Ranger" radio program, I was pleasantly surprised one Sunday evening to receive a call from him from Chicago. He explained that he had not been able to respond to my letters because he had been in the hospital. Though still quite ill, he stated that he would agree to talk with me about the early days of "The Lone Ranger" if I could visit him in Chicago.

There was little question about my going to Chicago. I was not about to miss the opportunity to meet and talk with the man that Ted Robertson described as "a giant" in the radio industry. Here was the man who not only was responsible for "The Lone Ranger" from 1933 to 1938, but who had also directed "The Green Hornet" from its inception until 1938. This was the man who later originated, wrote, and directed "The Black Ace" radio series, which among other distinctions introduced Danny Thomas in his first running comedy role in radio. Mr. Jewell had also taken on the writing and directing chores for "Jack Armstrong, the All-American Boy" from 1943 to 1951. His final network radio creation was "Silver Eagle—Mountie," which was the last network children's adventure program. It left the air in March of 1955. By this time Mr. Jewell was recognized as the "Dean of Radio Adventure Stories."

Within the week I was knocking at the door of Jim and Marion Jewell's seventeenth-floor apartment overlooking Lake Michigan. During the next two afternoons Mr. Jewell, who was certainly one of the closest persons to the scene

James Jewell with Chicago in the background.

Upper left: George W. Trendle, president; right, John H. Kunsky, vice-president Kunsky - Trendle Broadcasting Corporation.
HOWARD O. PIERCE
Secretary and Director of Broadcasting
H. ALLEN CAMPBELL
Director of Sales

Pictured above are the four men who guided the fortunes of the Kunsky-Trendle Broadcasting Corporation in 1933. Upper left and right: George W. Trendle, President; John H. Kunsky, Vice-President. Lower left and right: Howard O. Pierce, Secretary and Director of Broadcasting; H. Allen Campbell, Director of Sales.

when "The Lone Ranger" program was incubating and hatching at WXYZ, told a very different story from the one presented by George W. Trendle.

DAVID ROTHEL: When did you start with WXYZ?

JIM JEWELL: My brother brought me in there in 1930. Ralph was a musician—a very fine trumpet player—and he was with the orchestra at WXYZ. I suppose he got sick and tired of paying his brother's bills and decided I better get a job. He told Fred Jenks, program director, that I was a writer. Howard Pierce (Trendle's right hand man who held many titles with the organization over the years) heard him say this and said, "Send him around; we need writers." I was in the next morning. Pierce said, "Are you a writer?" I said, "Yes." He asked, "What have you written?" I said, "Well, I've written two or three vaudeville skits. One called 'Two Women' and another called 'The Foolish Mrs. Wise.' " He said, "Oh, wonderful, wonderful! We'll give you twenty-five dollars a script, but you'll have to be under contract." I thought, "What kind of a nut is this I'm talking to? He doesn't even want to see a script."

The following day I signed my first contract with George Trendle, Howard Pierce, and John Kunsky for twenty-five dollars a script. The contract was for three months. Later they found out that that was a tremendous amount to be paying for a writer and eventually broke my contract.

DAVID ROTHEL: Tell me about the creation of "The Lone Ranger" radio program.

JIM JEWELL: I was building a seven-days-a-week series called "The Manhunters" on WXYZ in the early 1930s. Out of this "Manhunters" framework came a program called "Curly Edwards and His Cowboys." The program played one night and George Trendle, Howard Pierce, and the then station manager and announcer, Harold True, heard the show. There had been a lot of talk around that Trendle liked the idea of a Western. In discussing the "Curly Edwards" program they had heard, everyone thought it was a good idea, a great idea, and I should go ahead and develop it, but nobody liked the damned title. I didn't blame them; I didn't like it either. Harold True said, "The thing needs a mystery name for the leading character. How about 'The Lone Star Ranger'?" I said to him that it would be wonderful if a fellow didn't already have it and have it copyrighted—Zane Grey. So Harold said, "Aha then, 'The Lone Ranger.' " Well, we all thought it was pretty good. I, truthfully, thought it was kind of corny but that was because it was not my idea; anything that wasn't my idea was kind of corny. (laugh) Well, I went ahead and wrote it up.

DAVID ROTHEL: When did the discussions about starting "The Lone Ranger" program begin? Trendle says they began sometime in December of 1932.

JIM JEWELL: Only because that was when I was doing the "Curly Edwards" show. No. Harold True threw the title out on the table, I would say, around January 18th.

DAVID ROTHEL: And the program went on the air January 30th.

JIM JEWELL: That is not right. It was January 20th. I'm positive.

DAVID ROTHEL: Was Fran Striker in on it at this point?

JIM JEWELL: At that stage of the game, no. He had, of course, written some of "The Manhunters" by this time, but I had never met him.

DAVID ROTHEL: He would just send his scripts in from Buffalo.

JIM JEWELL: That's right. He sent me the syndicated scripts for the "Warner Lester" program, which I put into "The Manhunters" series.

DAVID ROTHEL: So you wrote the first scripts of "The Lone Ranger" program?

JIM JEWELL: I wrote the first ones, yes. For probably two or three months the first "Lone Ranger" shows were just "Manhunters" stories. They were not listed in the newspapers as "The Lone Ranger" stories at all. I don't know exactly when Fran's first "Lone Ranger" script went on. I know it was after that time, of course.

DAVID ROTHEL: I understand that the first "Lone Ranger" script did not have "Hi-Yo, Silver" in it.

JIM JEWELL: No, it did not and for this reason. George Seaton was the actor playing the Lone Ranger. In rehearsal we came to the line, "A fiery horse with a speed of light, a cloud of dust, a hearty . . (laugh) . . The Lone Ranger!" He couldn't laugh. Here we were about to go on the air and the guy couldn't laugh and we needed it. So we went up to the elevator penthouse of the Maccabees Building amid the straining whine of cables and the clatter of relay switches. We tried every shout you could think of: Hi-Yi! and Yippee! and all the rest of them. Finally I said, "Let's try the one the English do, 'Heigh-Ho.' Let's shout it instead of politely doing it." So he tried a few of those and finally in complete

Director Jim Jewell talks with authoress Vera Brown about a new program she has written for WXYZ. Performers Jack Marvin, Beatrice Leiblee, and Charles Livingstone look on. (circa mid-1930s)

and utter disgust he said, "One more and that's it! Hi-Yo, Silver!" And that's the way that was born. That is the honest to God's truth.

DAVID ROTHEL: And Fran Striker had nothing to do with it?

JIM JEWELL: Nothing whatsoever. But I'll never demean Fran's performance. He was too good a man. Fran Striker was in my estimation the greatest hack writer that ever lived. Now, I'm not casting any crumbs to the man when I call him a hack writer, because a hack writer was a person who could hack it out day after day after day. When you figure that that man was in there writing—I mean actively writing—for twenty-five years, you don't demean a person like that. That's a great job.

DAVID ROTHEL: Did Striker come to Detroit at all during the first few months of "The Lone Ranger" program?

JIM JEWELL: No, he did not.

DAVID ROTHEL: How long after "The Lone Ranger" went on the air did Fran Striker start writing the scripts and sending them to you in Detroit?

JIM JEWELL: I can't give you an exact answer. I would have to say early in the series, but I don't remember how early. From time to time as I wanted changes made, I would write Fran letters telling him what I wanted. You see, he had no way of listening to the program.

DAVID ROTHEL: Yes, it was only broadcast on the Michigan Radio Network at that time. Did George Trendle contact Fran Striker?

JIM JEWELL: Trendle (I learned later) called my secretary, Miss Helen Hall, and asked for Striker's address and surreptitiously he wrote to him, called him, and made arrangements for him to come to Detroit.

DAVID ROTHEL: What did George Trendle have to say about the new program?

JIM JEWELL: When Trendle heard the program his comment was, "All that damned shouting in the front part, I don't know whether I like that or not." This was his comment and critique. Mr. Trendle had nothing whatsoever to do with the creation of "The Lone Ranger." He never wrote a word. He never put anything on paper but his signature to a check.

DAVID ROTHEL: Did he read the scripts while you were director?

JIM JEWELL: No. He never read a one.

DAVID ROTHEL: Did the Lone Ranger speak perfect English in the beginning?

JIM JEWELL: No, he spoke Jim Jewell English.

DAVID ROTHEL: What other original elements of "The Lone Ranger" program were you responsible for?

JIM JEWELL: Let's look at "kee mo sah bee"—trusty scout. [Author's note: The spelling of "kemo sabe" has been rather capricious over the years. "Kemo sabe," "kee mo sah bee," "kimosabi," "kemo sabay" are just a few examples that I have discovered. Except where context demands otherwise, I will use "kemo sabe."] That's the only thing it has ever meant or ever will mean. "Kee Mo Sah Bee" was a boys' camp established in 1911 at Mullet Lake, Michigan, owned by my father-in-law. I think it was sort of a natural thing for me to use it on a program when I knew no other words of Indian. Chief Thundercloud (no relation to the Indian actor) was an Indian from Cross Village (which was either a mission school or a reservation) who we used to call over to the camp in the summertime to tell tall stories to the kids. For example, he would come over and tell them how he'd dug the straits of Mackinaw with nothing but a wooden spoon. Occasionally Chief Thundercloud would have a few too many drinks and would become rather rambunctious. When this happened the other Indians would call him a "Tonto"—meaning a "wild one," or words to that effect. It was a word said in derision. Well, I just liked the sound of the word "Tonto" and decided to use it for the Lone Ranger's companion.

DAVID ROTHEL: You told me you were responsible for selecting the "William Tell Overture" as "The Lone Ranger" theme. How did this come about?

JIM JEWELL: Many have speculated as to whether there was a philosophic or psychological reason for choosing the classics for the musical content of the show. Nope! Just a personal liking for great dramatic scores and the fact that we had a fine record library of Victor Red Seal, Columbia, and Brunswick recordings by outstanding orchestras. I had been using this library on other series I had written and produced prior to "The Lone Ranger" and had become very familiar with it.

We were fortunate to have a young man named Bert Djerkiss working as a record turner and sound effect assistant at the beginning of "The Lone Ranger." He had been brought up in a musical environment and he had a natural aptitude for recognizing the dramatic potential of various selections or musical phrases which by themselves would not be identifiable, but in

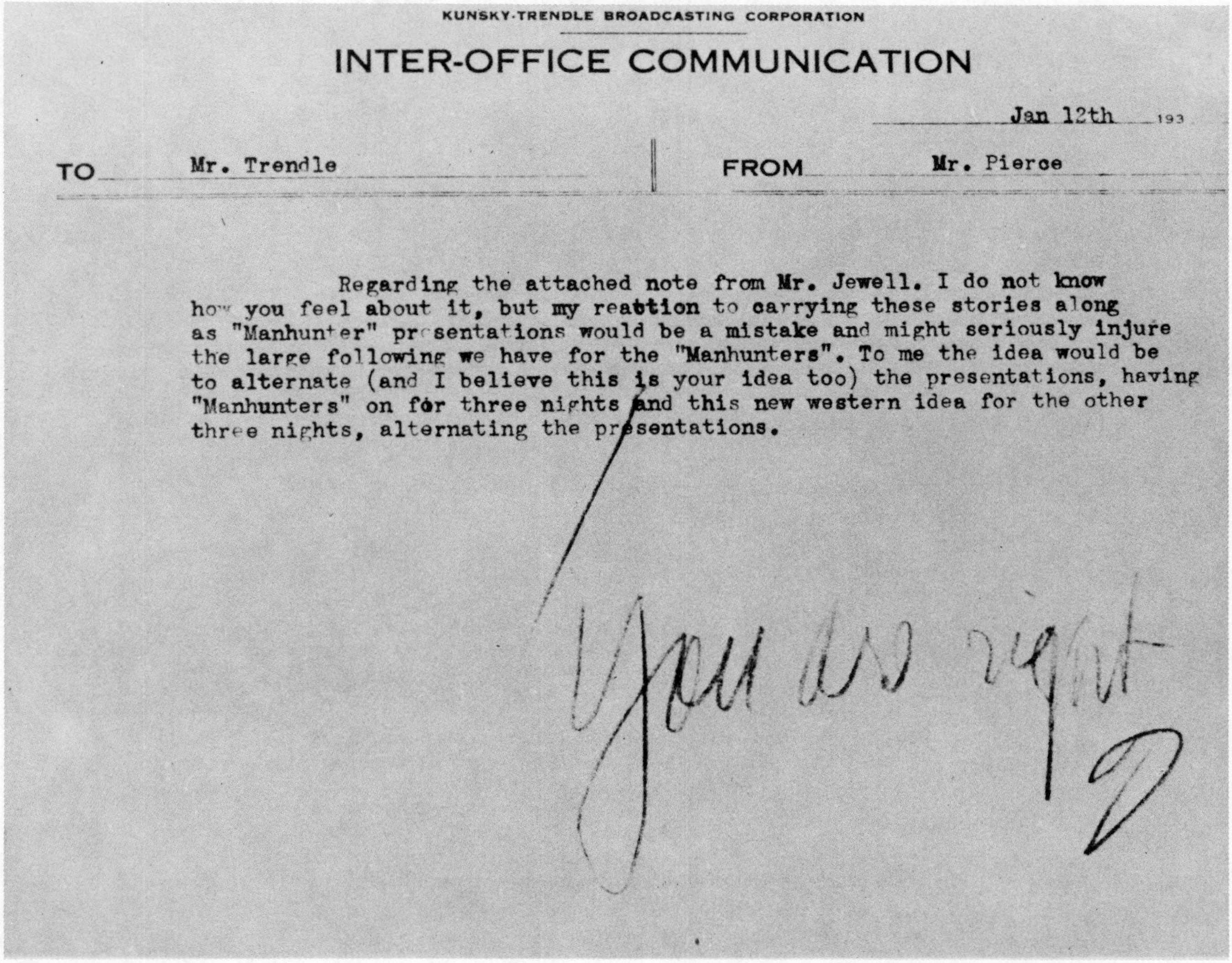

KUNSKY-TRENDLE BROADCASTING CORPORATION

INTER-OFFICE COMMUNICATION

Jan 12th 193

TO Mr. Trendle FROM Mr. Pierce

Regarding the attached note from Mr. Jewell. I do not know how you feel about it, but my reaction to carrying these stories along as "Manhunter" presentations would be a mistake and might seriously injure the large following we have for the "Manhunters". To me the idea would be to alternate (and I believe this is your idea too) the presentations, having "Manhunters" on for three nights and this new western idea for the other three nights, alternating the presentations.

You are right

J

The content of this interoffice memo pinpoints the year as 1933. It is apparent that neither Howard Pierce (Director of Broadcasting at WXYZ and possessor of various other titles), Trendle, nor Jewell realized the potential of "this new western idea" that was to alternate with "Manhunters." The fact that the program is called "this new western idea" instead of "The Lone Ranger" would tend to confirm Jewell's contention that the title did not come along until about January 18th. The handwriting is Jim Jewell's.

, received from one announcement on the Michigan Radio Network, im-
›adcast of an episode of the Lone Ranger adventure series.

›ntribution

little country gal—
did milking go
s turned to mike-ing
he radio.

little country gal—
her voice, and so
has no voice at all
the radio.
By "Mike Rophone"

ATIZED WS EVENTS

A. Fitzsimmons, Presi-
Michigan Mutual Lia-
any of Detroit, finds
d profit in a quarter
ast Sundays at 6:30
inging to the audience
igan Radio Network a
led Michigan Mutual's
e.
tainment is an electri-
ption, which was first
XYZ. Its instant suc-
arked by enthusiastic
ise, caused its being
ie Network.
amatized news events
ully portrayed and
illing interlude to the
Michigan who admitted
this pleasing break in
r less standardized con-
icture type of Sunday
tainment.
the home of the Mich-
al Liability Company,
branches in Michigan,
na and elsewhere. This
pecializes in all types of
insurance protection.

JAMES JEWELL
Playwright for WXYZ

James Jewell, actor, playwright, dramatic coach, and most of all affable, unobtrusive highlight of WXYZ's studio staff.

"Jimmy" creates, writes, directs and plays in the famous "Manhunters" and "Lone Ranger" dramas, and what a whale of a job that is when you add to it conducting, managing, coaching juvenile players and taking part in the Kiddies' Karnival every week day.

James Jewell's requirements are many and varied for his work for WXYZ and the Michigan Radio Network, but fortunately he has a wealth of imagination which always "clicks" at the right moment.

This picture appeared in the "Michigan Radio Network" PR newspaper, which was printed in the summer of 1933.

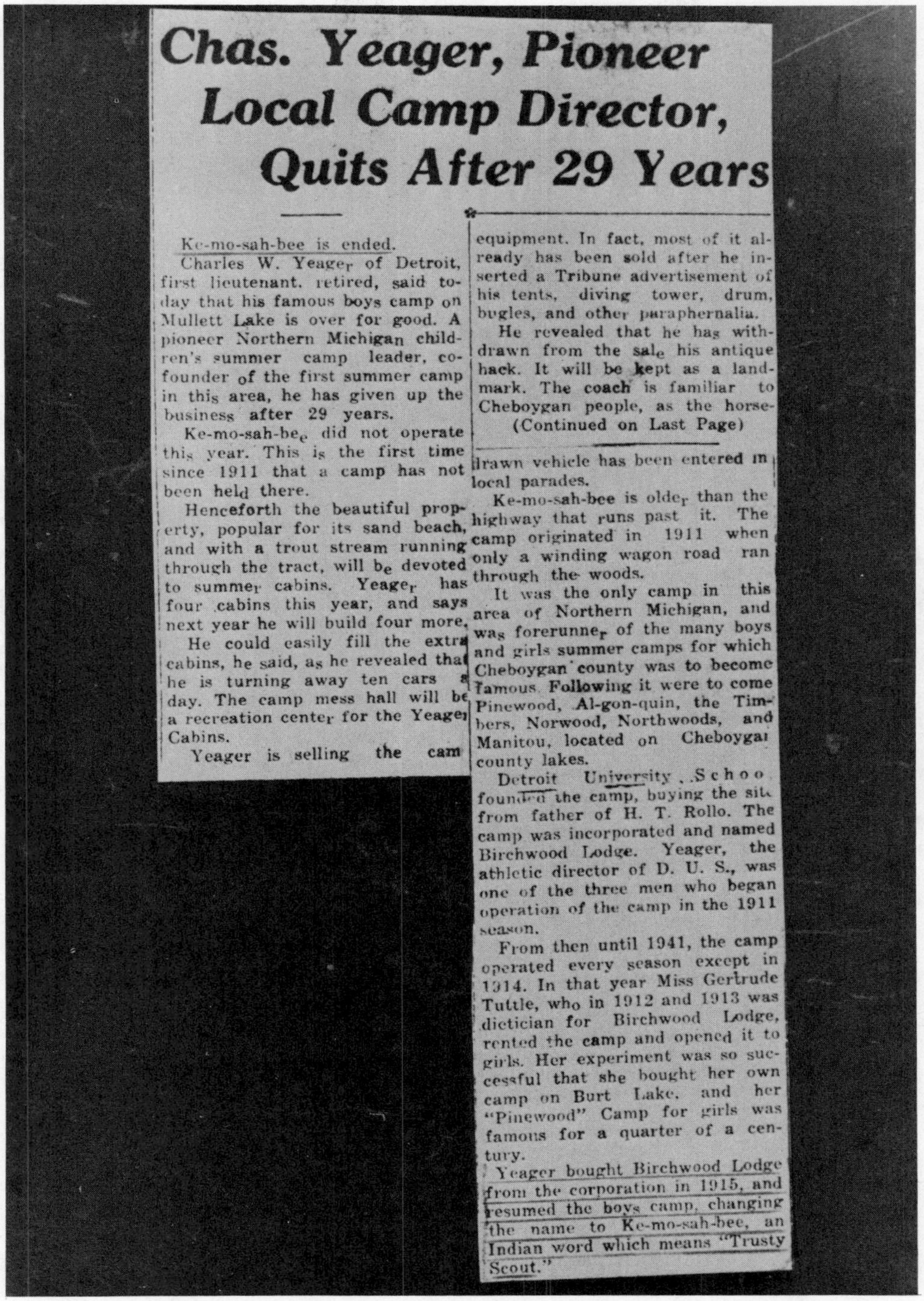

Chas. Yeager, Pioneer Local Camp Director, Quits After 29 Years

Ke-mo-sah-bee is ended.

Charles W. Yeager of Detroit, first lieutenant, retired, said today that his famous boys camp on Mullett Lake is over for good. A pioneer Northern Michigan children's summer camp leader, co-founder of the first summer camp in this area, he has given up the business after 29 years.

Ke-mo-sah-bee did not operate this year. This is the first time since 1911 that a camp has not been held there.

Henceforth the beautiful property, popular for its sand beach, and with a trout stream running through the tract, will be devoted to summer cabins. Yeager has four cabins this year, and says next year he will build four more.

He could easily fill the extra cabins, he said, as he revealed that he is turning away ten cars a day. The camp mess hall will be a recreation center for the Yeager Cabins.

Yeager is selling the camp equipment. In fact, most of it already has been sold after he inserted a Tribune advertisement of his tents, diving tower, drum, bugles, and other paraphernalia.

He revealed that he has withdrawn from the sale his antique hack. It will be kept as a landmark. The coach is familiar to Cheboygan people, as the horse-

(Continued on Last Page)

drawn vehicle has been entered in local parades.

Ke-mo-sah-bee is older than the highway that runs past it. The camp originated in 1911 when only a winding wagon road ran through the woods.

It was the only camp in this area of Northern Michigan, and was forerunner of the many boys and girls summer camps for which Cheboygan county was to become famous. Following it were to come Pinewood, Al-gon-quin, the Timbers, Norwood, Northwoods, and Manitou, located on Cheboygan county lakes.

Detroit University School founded the camp, buying the site from father of H. T. Rollo. The camp was incorporated and named Birchwood Lodge. Yeager, the athletic director of D. U. S., was one of the three men who began operation of the camp in the 1911 season.

From then until 1941, the camp operated every season except in 1914. In that year Miss Gertrude Tuttle, who in 1912 and 1913 was dietician for Birchwood Lodge, rented the camp and opened it to girls. Her experiment was so successful that she bought her own camp on Burt Lake, and her "Pinewood" Camp for girls was famous for a quarter of a century.

Yeager bought Birchwood Lodge from the corporation in 1915, and resumed the boys camp, changing the name to Ke-mo-sah-bee, an Indian word which means "Trusty Scout."

This clipping about Charles Yeager, Jim Jewell's father-in-law, would seem to support Jewell's contention that he was responsible for "Ke-mo-sah-bee" on "The Lone Ranger."

Kamp Kee-Mo Sah-Bee was almost entirely a tent camp in 1919.

During the mid 1930s "Lone Ranger Camp" was held at Kamp Kee-Mo Sah-Bee.

The WXYZ studio from which "The Lone Ranger" was first broadcast. (circa early 1930s)

many cases would be ideal for bridge transitions. Djerkiss deserves a great deal of credit for cataloging a hundred or more such cuttings. It was he who auditioned twenty-five or thirty such examples before I finally decided on Rossini's "William Tell" as the opening and closing theme for "The Lone Ranger."

It was actually a tossup between the "March of the Light Brigade" and the "William Tell" with its inspiring fanfare and ominous galloping movement suggested by the storm scene. Of course, Rossini won out and the rumbling, ever-increasing cadence and roar of the brewing storm became a gallop whether or not it was intended as such. The perfect fanfare with its tacit beats allowed for the stirring opening copy: "A fiery horse with the speed of light, a cloud of dust and a hearty Hi-Yo, Silver, Awa-a-ay!" It all fit so perfectly. It was as simple as that. I heard the selection and I could almost hear those thundering hoofbeats involved in the accelerated pattern of the storm scene of "William Tell." Then and there the music for the opening and closing was set. Only one very minor change has been made throughout the many years it was broadcast; a whistle following the "Hi-Yo, Silver" was deleted because when I left WXYZ I took the whistle with me. I *was* the whistle.

Amusingly, that cry of "Hi-Yo, Silver" almost stopped the heartbeat of Leopold Stokowski. The "William Tell Overture" was the opening selection of a symphony concert he conducted in the Westwood Gardens in Detroit a few months after "The Lone Ranger" went on the air. When the orchestra struck up the fanfare, Stokowski was struck down in disbelief as the entire audience roared out a hearty "Hi-Yo, Silver!"

DAVID ROTHEL: You had the "William Tell Overture" on that very first "Lone Ranger" program.

JIM JEWELL: Oh, yes, sir.

DAVID ROTHEL: Well, you selected the right composition.

JIM JEWELL: I think so. (laugh)

DAVID ROTHEL: It's hard to imagine "The Lone Ranger" without the "William Tell Overture," and if anybody can listen to the "William Tell Overture" without thinking of "The Lone Ranger," he certainly has missed an exciting bit of Americana for over the last forty years. Did you ever have the feeling during those first few years that you were working on a program that was going to become a classic?

JIM JEWELL: No. Nobody who is in anything ever knows *that* at the time.

DAVID ROTHEL: I asked George Seaton if he was the first Lone Ranger and he said he was to the best of his knowledge.

JIM JEWELL: Of course he was. Now he was not the first to play the Curly Edwards part. That was a man named Jack Lawrence. When I decided to put this "Lone Ranger" on the air, George Seaton was available and he got the job. Dave, my budget for "The Lone Ranger" and all the shows I had on the air for the week—I didn't say for five minutes, I said for the week—was seventy-five dollars. That was for *all* the players. Now that meant that George Seaton, who for directing his last motion picture I think I can safely say got $225,000, made $2.50 a performance as the Lone Ranger.

DAVID ROTHEL: He's come up in the world. Was George Seaton a good actor in the role of the Lone Ranger?

JIM JEWELL: Oh, yes. George was a fine actor. I hated to see him leave the role even though I was somewhat responsible for his going. George came to me one day and said, "Here are some tickets for a little thing I've written. They're going to present it down the street here." I said, "What do you mean, George?" He said, "Just a little play I wrote." I said, "Fine. I'll try to get to see it." I got through work and thought I'd go down and look at it. I went in and saw three delightful one-act plays; two of which George had written. I don't know how much of this George remembers, but I remember it very clearly. I called him and asked him to come and see me the next day. When I saw him I said, "George, why do you want to waste your time doing what you're doing here? I saw those plays and they're beautiful." By golly, he went home and thought it over and said, "You're right." So there I was left without a Lone Ranger. I thought it would be a simple job to replace Seaton because I truthfully didn't know the size of our audience. I didn't know that there were a lot of "sleepers" out there—that so many people were listening to us; I had no idea in the world. That's why we would seldom audition anything in those days. We would audition on the air; who the hell was going to hear it? If you wanted to hide something, audition it on the air. (laugh) I don't know how much of that George Seaton remembers.

DAVID ROTHEL: You mentioned to me on the phone that about 111 people have said that they appeared in the first "Lone Ranger" program.

The control room of radio station WXYZ. (circa early 1930s)

The music studio of radio station WXYZ. (circa early 1930s)

JAMES JEWELL

The Lone Ranger is going into the movies. Much of the succes of the Ranger as a radio playlet, is due to James Jewell's fin direcion. Jewell is shown here in the control room giving the ca the "go-ahead" signal as Fred Flowerday, control man, prepar to start the turntable on which a recording of the "William T Oveture" rests.

This picture appeared in newspapers in early 1938 at the time the Republic Pictures' movie serial based on "The Lone Ranger" was announced. In later years Fred Flowerday (at record turntable) eventually became assistant director and, finally, in 1954, director of "The Lone Ranger" radio series.

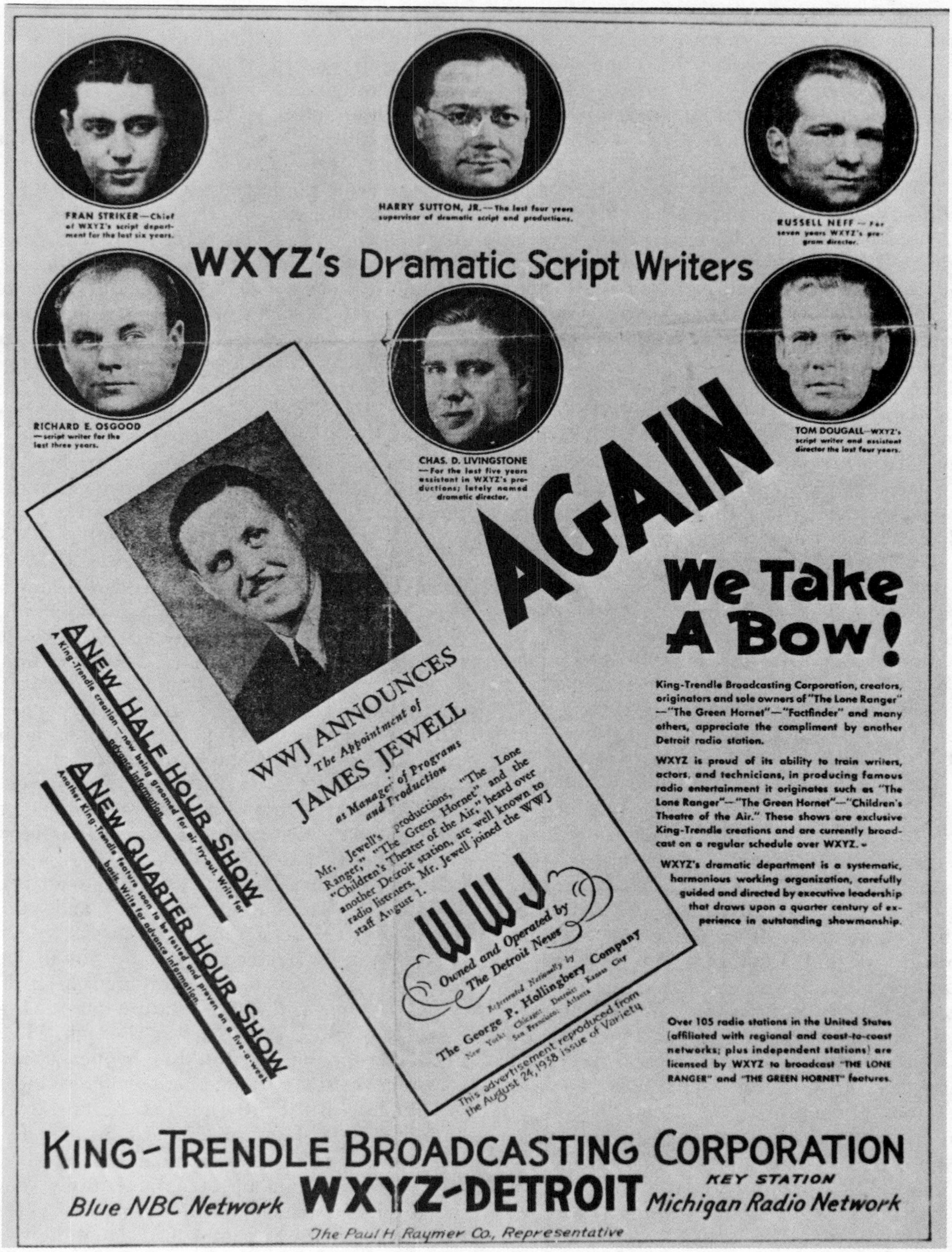

The above advertisement appeared in Variety *on August 31, 1938, at the time James Jewell, the original director of "The Lone Ranger," left the program. Charles D. Livingstone (center picture of second row) assumed the directorship of "The Lone Ranger" and remained with the radio program until 1954.*

JIM JEWELL: That's right. They've come in and told *me* that they were on the program. Sixteen of them claimed to be the Lone Ranger on the first program.

DAVID ROTHEL: I've read that an actor by the name of Jack Deeds once played the Lone Ranger. Can you verify this?

JIM JEWELL: Jack Deeds was the second Lone Ranger. I think he played the role for two days. After the first day we had people calling us saying, "He doesn't sound any more like a cowboy than I do." They were right! I fired him after the first performance and told him that if he didn't show up for the second one I'd put some bumps on his head. (laugh) I had no actor to replace him with. I finally called for all the men in the dramatics class of Wayne University to come over and audition for me. That's how I found Earle Graser who played the role for many years after that.

DAVID ROTHEL: Did Brace Beemer [who played the Lone Ranger years later] have anything to do with creating the elements of "The Lone Ranger"?

JIM JEWELL: The only thing I can think of that might have come from Brace would be some idiotic thing like the horse's shoes being made out of silver. I'll tell you something about Brace. He had a tremendous ego. Brace B. Beemer. We who knew him well, said the middle "B" stood for bluff. But give the devil his due; if he found himself lacking, he would dedicate himself to any task long enough to remedy his shortcomings. That was the amazing thing about the man. Give him enough time and he could do the job. One time a policeman gave him a .38 special which he couldn't hit a barn with, but he went down to the police academy and became deadly accurate. The story about him joining the armed forces at the age of fourteen is perfectly true. Brace was a boy who never grew up. He practically got down on his knees to ask me to allow him to play the Lone Ranger when Jack Deeds went into the program. I refused him.

DAVID ROTHEL: It has been reported that Beemer played the role for a short time during the 1930s, but you say it's not so.

JIM JEWELL: That's right. I would never allow him to play the part.

DAVID ROTHEL: It's ironic that ultimately he was to play the role longer than anyone else on radio.

JIM JEWELL: Why don't you ask me the really important question: Why did I quit WXYZ?

DAVID ROTHEL: Why did you leave?

JIM JEWELL: In 1933 George Trendle asked me for assignment of authorship. He sent it to me at the studio. I looked at it and asked my brother, Ralph, who was an attorney, what I should do. He said, "No, don't sign it. Find out how much he's going to give you for it first." So I said, "Ralph, how much do you think I ought to get?" He said, "Ten percent, at least." I said, "Okay, but Ralph he is such a nice guy." He said, "What the hell, this is not a nice world. Ten percent." I said, "All right, Ralph." So Trendle called me and said, "Where's that assignment of authorship?" I said, "Well, Mr. Trendle, I feel I ought to have some money for that." Trendle said, "Oh, how much, Jimmy?" I said, "At least ten percent." He said, "Ten percent! For heavens sake man, do you know how much that is?" I said, "Yes, I know. It's ten cents on the dollar." He said, "What is it on a hundred dollars; what is it on a thousand dollars?" I said, "Gee whiz, that's a lot of money." Well, I got down to five percent and he said, "Jimmy, sign that damned thing and let me think about the five percent and I'll get back to you. You know I've always treated you well." I said, "Sure, Mr. Trendle." So I signed it and sent it back. A month later I said, "Mr. Trendle, I thought I'd call you today to find out about that assignment of authorship." "What assignment of authorship?" he said. So I don't own and never felt I owned any part of "The Lone Ranger" after that episode. That incident also made me wary of all money-matters at WXYZ.

Brace Beemer became station manager at WXYZ. He came to me one day and said, "I understand I'll be signing your checks from now on." I said, "The second you do you'll need a new boy here. So, my God, if my check didn't come through with his signature on it. I went down and told Trendle I was through. He mollified me and said it wouldn't happen again. At that time I said I wanted more money. He said, "I think we can do it, Jim. Let me talk to Allen Campbell and Howard Pierce." So, I left and went back to the station and later learned through the son-in-law of John Kunsky [one of the original partners in the firm] that Trendle had brought this up and had laughingly said, "Don't worry, we'll protect it [the program], we've got the whole thing copyrighted." During this same time WWJ, an opposition station in Detroit, had been trying to get me to go with them. They offered me a stipend that was about four times as much as I was making at WXYZ. So, those were my reasons for leaving WXYZ. I left there and didn't fight it at all. I just made up my mind that I'm only happy when I'm creating something. I said to myself, "Go out and do another one." This has always been my philosophy. I went with WWJ and created "The Black Ace" series. A few years later I came here to Chicago and wrote and directed "Jack Armstrong," and then in 1951 I created, wrote, and directed "Silver Eagle, Mountie."

DAVID ROTHEL: It's obvious from listening to you talk that you loved those years in radio.

JIM JEWELL: At the age of twenty-six or twenty-seven I was the happiest person in the world. I did everything with the greatest amount of fun you can imagine. It was all there to build with—to build and to keep on building. Those were happy days; there is nothing that I'm commiserating about. I'm not complaining in any part of this conversation because if I had it to do over I would most certainly do it exactly the same way today.

I was so in love with radio—again it was a beginning; it was a new medium that no one had tried on. No one had actually spoiled it yet. I wanted to get in at the beginning of something. Well, it wasn't the actual beginning, but it was close enough to the beginning to allow me tremendous latitude and Trendle was a very generous person in that way. I could do anything I wanted. Of course, he was getting all of this for practically nothing and I was killing myself—no, I was not killing myself; that would be a lie—I was eating it up and having a won-

Director James Jewell and Assistant Director Charles D. Livingstone go over a "Lone Ranger" script prior to a broadcast. (circa 1937)

derful time being able to express myself. So until I left there I had no fault to find with Trendle—not even with the fact that he had taken this one property away from me and I knew I could never regain it. I'd signed it away; I wasn't going to cry over spilled milk. I just wanted to get out of there; I just wanted to get away from the place. I felt I had to go on and originate other things in which I would hold a financial equity. WXYZ had now become a stigma to my progress.

❖ ❖ ❖

And finally this on the creation of "The Lone Ranger": Mike Healy's *Buffalo Courier Express* column of April 14, 1975, entitled "Hi Ho Buffalo! The Lone Ranger Originally Rode From Our City" contains an interview with a man by the name of Corydon (Don) Ireland who has done some research at the University of Buffalo concerning Fran Striker and "The Lone Ranger" series:

On a radio show during the thirties, the final minute would be devoted to something like this:

Question: "Say, who was that masked man anyhow?"

Answer: "Friend, that was the Lone Ranger."

And the William Tell Overture would gallop toward the commercial.

And where was the masked man from? Corydon Ireland, a second year graduate student in English at U.B., knows:

The Lone Ranger was born at a Buffalo radio station in 1929.

Fran Striker, the creator of the Lone Ranger, was born and grew up in Buffalo. Credit for the radio show, which aired in 2,956 segments from 1933 until 1954, has often gone to the show's producer at radio station WXYZ in Detroit, George W. Trendle.

"When I began to find out about Striker and the Lone Ranger in 1973, the credit Trendle got offended me both as a human being and as a mildly chauvinistic Buffalonian," Ireland said in an interview.

The Lone Ranger aired in Buffalo on WEBR as early as 1929.

"The program was called 'Covered Wagon Days' and it was precisely and exactly the same show as the Lone Ranger, except for one detail: The horse's name was Whitey instead of Silver," Ireland said.

Ireland attributes this difference to the fact that the show's sponsor in Detroit was the Silver Bread Company [Author's note: It was Silvercup Bread], and the name change was actually a plug. (It could have been worse. Imagine the masked man shouting a stirring "Hi-ho Pepperidge Farms.")

Ireland has collected a wealth of material on the Lone Ranger since he began his study, "half as a lark" after taking an American Literature seminar in 1973. He is being aided by the U. B. Archives, in which is a collection of Striker's papers, including the first 714 scripts from the Detroit radio shows.

"When I first began looking at the scripts, I nearly jumped out of my skin. There, on page one of volume one of the Detroit scripts were the words "first performed in Buffalo, N.Y.," Ireland said.

Since then he's talked to some of the actual performers in "Covered Wagon Days."

Striker was a radio announcer, advertising salesman and sound effects man for the fledgling WEBR in the 1920's. Ireland has found that Striker invented the sound effects device made up of a sand filled wooden trough and two half coconut shells. He used it as a back up for some Hungarian music, but the Hungarian musician he designed it for suggested that the effect might work better "in an American setting."

The sound he created, of course, is the clopping of a running horse, and Ireland believes this might be the practical genesis of the Lone Ranger—as a setting for a sound effect.

"The character became much more than that. The Lone Ranger is probably as important to American culture as George Washington," Ireland said.

That's not as preposterous as it sounds at first. The George Washington of legend has little to do with the historical Washington—he's a mythological hero of sorts. So is the Lone Ranger.

Ireland says he was reading Edmund Spenser's "The Fairy Queen (*sic*)," for the first time in years the other day, and a strange similarity hit him.

"There was the knight on his horse with his faithful companion, virtuously wandering the countryside of Fairyland, fighting villains and restoring justice. It could have been the Lone Ranger and Tonto in the golden West," he said.

And it could well have been, even though "The Fairy Queen" was written in 16th century England and the Lone Ranger in 20th century Buffalo. It's an old literary tradition Fran Striker was part of. All it took was George W. Trendle's entrepreneurial genius to market it and create an endearing American myth.

❖ ❖ ❖

Unfortunately, time has thinned the ranks of those who remember the details of the creation of "The Lone Ranger" program and the first few years of its existence. Fran Striker, semiretired, working on a novel, and teaching creative writing at the University of Buffalo, died at the age of fifty-nine on September 14, 1962, in a head-on automobile collision near his home in Arcade, New York. George W. Trendle died at the age of eighty-seven on May 22, 1972, of a heart attack. Two weeks after our last phone conversation and four days after my final letter from Ted Robertson, he died suddenly of a massive coronary at his home in Santa Barbara, California. Three months after my visit in Chicago with Jim Jewell, he died of emphysema.

Some who were on the scene when the Lone Ranger first rode the WXYZ airwaves just don't remember the events of the program's creation. After all, it was over forty years ago. Jim Jewell's hard-to-ignore claim for creative credit is in complete variance with the Trendle version. And so the puzzle remains.

In the broad sense, I guess we all had a hand in creating the Lone Ranger.

TONTO: Other Texas Rangers all dead. You only Ranger left. You lone Ranger now.

It was not until a few years after the program went on the air that Fran Striker created the story of the fictional origin of the Lone Ranger for radio listeners. In the telling of the story Striker also explained the background for such things as the mask, the silver bullets, how the Lone Ranger acquired Silver, and how Dan Reid figured in the story. The origin program proved to be so popular that it was repeated each year near the anniversary date in January.

Striker also briefly summarized the origin story in most of his Lone Ranger novels; when the television series came along in 1949, the story was adapted for the visual medium and padded for presentation as a three-part story utilizing the "cliff-hanger" device of the movie serials for the conclusions of the first two thirty-minute segments. The basic story elements were the same for the radio, novel, and television versions, but interesting little variations occurred.

The origin story* as Fran Striker wrote it goes something like this: A pack of outlaws led by the notorious Butch Cavendish is growing rich and powerful terrorizing ranches, towns, and wagon trains throughout Texas. Finally, the Texas Rangers learn where Butch Cavendish and his gang are hiding out. Six Texas Rangers under the command of Captain Daniel Reid are sent to capture Cavendish and his gang. With them is a guide who leads the Rangers through the unfamiliar territory until finally they come to a canyon entrance known as Bryant's Gap. Collins, the guide (in the television version he is called a "half-breed"), suggests that the Rangers camp there until he can scout the canyon rim.

During this pause in the journey the captain speaks to his younger brother, also a Ranger, about the apprehension that he feels. He tells his younger brother that if anything should happen to him he wants the brother to resign from the Rangers and look after his (the captain's) wife and son, Danny, who are on their way from the East. In addition the captain asks that they receive his share of the silver mine the two brothers have staked out. The younger ranger assures his brother that these things will be done. Collins returns and says he has scouted the rim on both sides of the canyon and has found no sign of the Cavendish outfit.

The Rangers break camp and proceed along the rock-strewn canyon floor. They fail to notice that Collins has lagged behind and they don't know that he is really in the pay of Cavendish and has lied to them—that Butch Cavendish and his killers are waiting in ambush on the rim of the canyon. Suddenly shots rain down upon the unsuspecting Rangers. They dismount and return the fire, but soon four of the six Rangers lie dead in the hot Texas sun. Only Captain Reid and his brother fight bravely on. Presently the Captain falls, mortally wounded—and a moment later his younger brother slumps to the ground.

The outlaws wait and watch for any sign of life, then ride away convinced that all six men in Bryant's Gap are dead. (In the television version Butch Cavendish has Collins inspect the bodies. Then he shoots Collins in the back as he

* © Lone Ranger Television, Inc.

goes to mount his horse. Cavendish explains to his men that if Collins would double-cross the Rangers, he might also do it to them.)

Sunset comes and then darkness descends upon the bodies of the ill-fated Rangers. Presently an Indian can be seen through the moonlight moving from body to body. After examining the first five bodies he murmurs, "Them dead." At the body of the sixth man he says, "This man live." The Indian lifts the man tenderly in his strong arms and carries him to a nearby cave where he bathes and tends the wounds. Then the Indian takes a spade from the cave and returns to the canyon where he works steadily until all the dead men have been buried. Returning to the cave he sits watching through the remaining hours of the night. Daybreak finds the Ranger stronger; by nightfall his wounds have become infected, his fever rises, and he lapses into delirium. The Indian calls upon all his knowledge to treat the wounded man; he goes day and night without rest. On the morning of the fourth day the fever breaks, the delirium is gone, and the Ranger slowly opens his eyes. The Indian explains what has happened since the fateful ambush—that the other Rangers are all dead.

"You only Ranger left," he says. "You lone Ranger now."

As his vision gradually clears the Ranger recognizes the Indian—remembers an incident from days long gone. The Indian speaks for the weakened Ranger—"Many year ago, you only boy, you find Indian boy in trouble. You save life of Indian boy."

Remembering, the Ranger says, "Yes. Your name is Tonto. Years ago you called me kemo sabe."

Tonto responds eagerly, "And you still kemo sabe. It mean faithful friend."

(In the television version, as Tonto carries the wounded Ranger into the cave and places him on blankets, he recognizes a piece of flattened metal the Ranger is wearing on a chain around his neck—it is a ring that stirs memories for the Indian of an early childhood tragedy. On seeing the ring, Tonto exclaims aloud, "Why, you, you kemo sabe."

The Ranger, barely conscious, says weakly, "Kemo sabe? That sounds familiar."

Tonto then recalls for the injured Ranger the incident of so many years before: "Long time back when we both young . . . renegade Indians raid settlement when men of tribe away. Kill my mother, sisters. They leave me for dead. You found me, nursed me back to health, saved me from dying. When me well, you give me horse to go find my father. Me take horse only when you accept gift—my ring. It make good luck. Me call you kemo sabe. It mean trusty scout. Me never forget you.")

(That ring looked like a sure bet for a television premium, but to the best of my knowledge and research, it never was.)

The Ranger tells Tonto that the killers know him on sight. If they know one man has escaped they'll look for him.

Tonto explains that the killers won't know—"Tonto bury five men, make six grave. Crook think you die with others." (In the television version it was the Lone Ranger's idea to make six graves.)

Realizing that the outlaws would still recognize his face, the Ranger decides that he will cover his face with a mask and seek retribution from Butch Cavendish and his gang. The mask is fashioned from the black vest of his dead brother.

Now in the Ranger's eyes "there is a light that must have burned in the eyes of knights in armor. A light that through the ages lifted the souls of strong men who fought for justice, for God."

Gaining strength in his determination the wounded man says, "I'll be the Lone Ranger."

(On television the challenge to catch that light in the Ranger's eyes was by-passed for a pledge of service to mankind: "For every one of those men [the dead Rangers] I'm going to bring a hundred lawbreakers to justice. I'll make that Cavendish Gang, and every criminal that I can find for that matter, regret the day those Rangers were killed. Tonto, from this moment on I'm going to devote my life to establishing law and order in this new frontier—to make the West a decent place to live.")

After regaining his strength, the Lone Ranger with Tonto begins anew the battle to bring Butch Cavendish and his gang to justice. One after another the members of the outlaw group are hunted down by the mysterious masked rider and his Indian companion and turned over to the law. With the capture of each member of the infamous gang, the fame of the Lone Ranger spreads across the country from prairie town to ranch to wagon train. The black mask and silver bullets become a symbol of justice to honest people, a cause of fear to the lawbreaker. (An old retired Ranger named Jim Blane agrees to work the silver mine owned by the Lone Ranger and his dead brother. He is the one who fashions the silver into the Ranger's trademark—the silver bullet.)

Finally, only Butch Cavendish himself remains to be brought to justice by the Lone Ranger and Tonto. They relentlessly dog his trail for months until one day they notice that the hoof prints of the outlaw's horse are fresh—that the marauder of the plains, the murderer of the five Rangers, is near at hand. As the Lone Ranger and Tonto round a bend in the trail, a shot rings out and the Lone Ranger's horse falls to the ground, dead. Tonto gallops off on Scout after the ambusher, but his tired pinto horse is unable to catch up with the disappearing Cavendish.

The Lone Ranger and his faithful companion are now forced to travel on foot with the Ranger's saddle, saddle bags, and bridle carried by Scout. They head for Wild Horse Valley where a legendary wild horse, a fiery white stallion, is said to graze with his herd. As they reach the top of a rise leading into the valley, they are halted suddenly by a grisly sight far down in the valley. A great white stallion is in a death battle with a huge buffalo. The mighty stallion bravely lunges, rears, and dodges as the gigantic bison repeatedly charges his smaller, tiring combatant. Convinced that the endangered white horse must be the wild stallion that has been spoken of so often, the Lone Ranger rushes to get within pistol range before the stalking beast completes a final death charge. Its strength gone, its silvery white coat blood and dust soiled, the magnificent stallion's muscles can withstand no more punishment. As the Lone Ranger races to the scene, he witnesses the once seemingly invulnerable steed stagger and then fall.

As the shaggy brown beast draws back, head lowered for the final death charge, the valley echoes with well-aimed, thunderous explosions from the two guns, now smoking in the hands of the Lone Ranger. For a moment the monster stands motionless seemingly bewildered by this intruder, then falls in death.

As Tonto had previously nursed him back to life, now the Lone Ranger works to save the life of the bruised and battered white stallion. Over the next few days the ugly wounds are tended and slowly heal under the gentle care of the masked man and his Indian friend. Gradually the unmatched strength and stamina of the mighty stallion return.

"He's himself again," the Lone Ranger acknowledges. "I wonder if he'll take a saddle? Let's try."

As the Lone Ranger lifts the saddle to place it on the horse's strong back, a shudder runs through the wild stallion's body and he breaks fiercely away from his human benefactor.

"Let him go, Tonto," the Lone Ranger says. "I'd like to have that horse more than anything in the world, but he deserves his freedom; he fought for it. See how the sun reflects from his white coat."

"Yes, kemo sabe," the Indian replies. "Him look like silver."

"Silver, that would be a name for him." The Lone Ranger calls out to the white stallion, "Silver, here Silver!"

The mighty horse pauses on a rise a short way off and appears to study the masked man and Indian. The wild instinct possessed throughout the ages is challenged. This something within the stallion tells him to flee at once to preserve freedom, and yet he stands his ground. Some mysterious bond causes the silvery horse to suddenly bolt and gallop to the side of the Lone Ranger.

The saddle and bridle are quickly placed on the horse and the eager Ranger mounts cautiously, allowing the nervous animal to gradually feel the weight of a human body on his back. The man's voice speaks quietly and gently as the stallion grows accustomed to the saddle and rider. Silver seems to sense the desire of his gentle, yet firm, teacher and does his best to learn quickly. After several days of training the intelligent Silver is ready for the challenges that lie ahead with the Lone Ranger and Tonto. They break camp and once again begin their mission to capture Butch Cavendish.

During the past days Cavendish has gotten far away, but the masked man and Tonto trail him relentlessly with only a minimum of rest. The stillness of the plains is constantly broken by the thundering hoofbeats of the two noble steeds, Silver and Scout. It takes days of hard riding to cut down the outlaw's lead. At long last a desperate horse and rider come into view far ahead on the dusty trail. The mighty Silver responds with a renewed burst of speed perhaps sensing that the climax of the chase of many days is near. As the white horse draws nearer, Cavendish whirls in his saddle and fires wildly over his shoulder until his gun is empty. His horse, though powerful and fast, is no match for the charging Silver. Fear and panic fill the outlaw's face.

The mighty horse closes the gap between avenger and outlaw as the masked man shouts, "I want you, Cavendish!" The outlaw is captured to be tried by law and punished for his crimes.

With Butch Cavendish and his gang behind bars, the Lone Ranger's "avowed mission" is accomplished. He has brought to justice every one of the outlaws who had a part in the murder of his brother and the other four Rangers. Now he must decide what he will do with the rest of his life. He speculates on working the silver mine he and his brother staked out some time before; he considers becoming a rancher, too, but these callings do not appeal to him. During his years as a Ranger and more recently in his search for Cavendish, he has seen so much Western outlawry that he burns with a desire to continue the battle against crime. He knows that it is more than one man can accomplish, but he is determined to do his part by dedicating his life to the service of his fellow man. He will remain the Lone Ranger, the daring and resourceful masked rider of the plains, and with his faithful Indian companion Tonto and his great horse Silver will lead the fight for law and order in the early Western United States.

That's the way the idealistic, romantic Fran Striker ultimately conceived the origin of his radio hero, and his boss, George W. Trendle, loved it. It contained all the heroic elements Trendle wanted for his "Lone Ranger" listeners. As he said, he "intended to give the youngsters a great deal of action and excitement without arousing unwholesome desires and instincts." He also wanted to "teach patriotism, tolerance, fairness, and a sympathetic understanding of fellow men and their rights and privileges."

Emphasis should be placed on the word *ultimately* in the preceding paragraph because it was only after a period of years that the full-blown heroic, romanticized characters emerged. It is almost forgotten today, for example, that the Lone Ranger did not always speak perfect English. In the first Striker novel* (which appears to be aimed at adult readers) the Lone Ranger spoke with a drawl and seemed to fluctuate between rather formal usage and the ordinary colloquialisms of his time. Quite often he even displayed a sense of humor. Example:

"Silver," he laughed, "do you know I haven't had a bit of breakfast, and my belt buckle is knocking against my backbone,—all due to my playing nurse to a bronc who thinks I've played a mean trick on him. Well, here's where I leave you to your happy thoughts, if any, and collect some grub for myself!"

Later he says,

"What evidence we have would be plain to a one-eyed half-wit, but it might not get through a court of law. If you catch a dog with wool stuck in his teeth, you've got evidence that he has killed a sheep, and you can shoot him for it. But when it comes to a man killing another man, you have to rig up so the jury practically sees the killing done before they'll call him guilty."

Probably the greatest surprise to the reader of the first novel is that Tonto is repeatedly referred to as a "half-breed" Indian, and affectionately called "old Smokey-face" by the Lone Ranger. In later years this was conveniently forgotten by the writers, and half-breeds were usually portrayed as outlaws or at least outcasts. Also in this early novel, Tonto still has some of the "savage" left in him. At one point he says to the Lone Ranger, "White man talk, talk, talk. Killer then go free. Me know! . . . You give word and Tonto hunt 'um killer, and dry-gulch 'um before sun come up."

Another thing that is almost forgotten today is that Tonto did not have a horse to ride on the radio series until after September of 1935. In correspondence between director Jim Jewell and the Sehl Advertising Agency, Inc. dated September 17th, Mr. H. W. Sehl asked:

Why can't you get a horse or pony for Tonto? Like all the kids who religiously listen to this program, I myself am getting tired of having Silver carry double all the time. Once in a while it might be all right, but every night Silver has to carry both men and we receive a great many letters from listeners along the same line.

Tonto could have a fleet-footed Indian pony. Of course, he would not be as fast, strong, big and powerful as the great, grand and glorious Silver, but I really believe it would help the play if this could be worked out.

While on the subject of horses—in Fran Striker's first novel (apparently written prior to the

* *The Lone Ranger,* 1936, Copyrighted by Lone Ranger Television, Inc.

Six Texas Rangers under the command of Captain Daniel Reid are sent out to capture Butch Cavendish and his outlaw gang.

The guide, Collins, after supposedly checking the rim of the canyon ahead, lies to Captain Reid that he has seen no sign of the Cavendish gang.

*The band of Rangers enters Bryant's Gap in search of the Cavendish **gang.***

High up on the rim of Bryant's Gap, the outlaws wait in hiding to ambush the Texas Rangers.

Butch Cavendish shoots first, giving the signal to the rest of his gang to "shoot to kill" all of the Rangers.

The Rangers, taken by surprise, fight back as well as they are able. Finally, only one Ranger remains fighting—the younger brother of Captain Reid. Then he, too, falls, struck by the outlaws' bullets.

Hours later, a lone Indian rides up on the scene of the ambush.

After examining the first five bodies he murmurs, "Them dead."

The Indian approaches the body of the last Ranger, the younger brother of Captain Reid, and discovers that though badly wounded he is still alive.

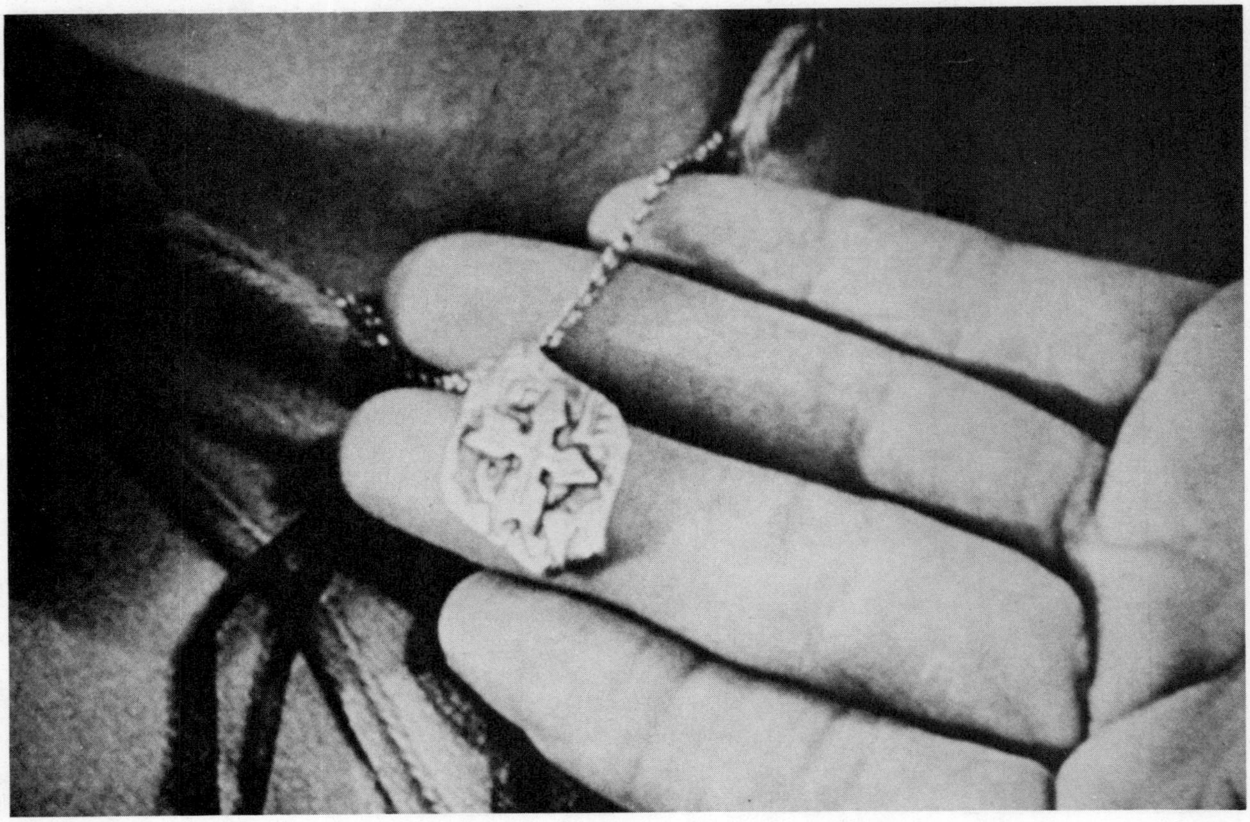

Suddenly the Indian notices a piece of flattened metal on a chain around the wounded Ranger's neck.

The Indian remembers, "Long time back when we both young . . . renegade Indians raid settlement when men of tribe away. Kill my mother, sisters. They leave me for dead. You found me, nursed me back to health, saved me from dying."

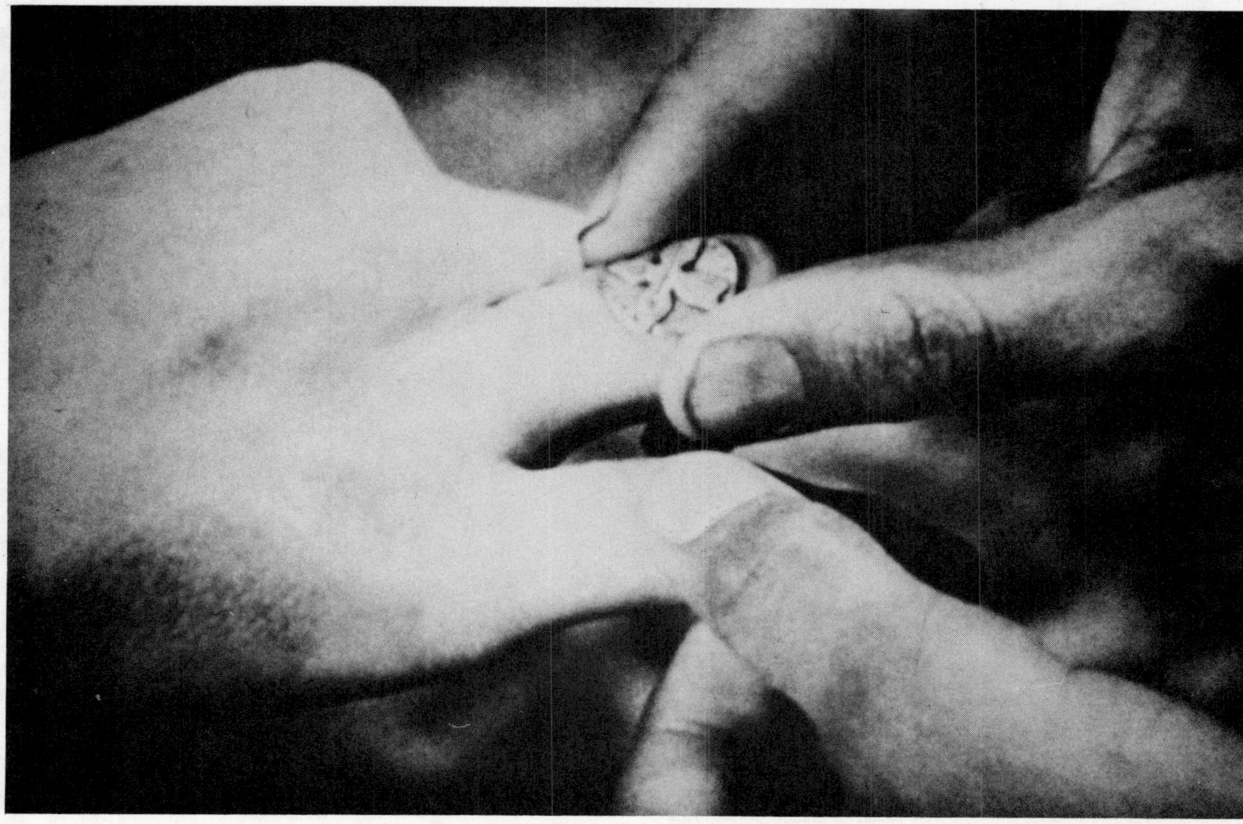

"When me well, you give me horse to go find my father. Me take horse only when you accept gift—my ring. It make good luck."

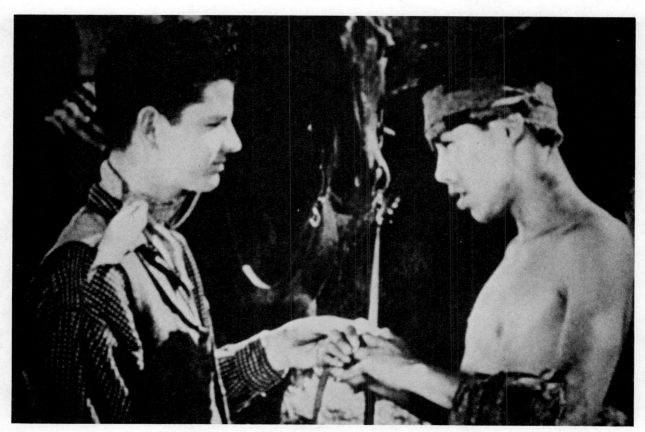

Still remembering the childhood incident, the Indian says, "Me call you kemo sabe. It mean trusty scout. Me never forget you."

Remembering, the Ranger says, "Yes. Your name is Tonto." Tonto tends to the Ranger's wounds and looks after him during his days of slow recovery.

When asked what has happened to the other Texas Rangers in the outfit, Tonto tells the wounded man, "Other Texas Rangers all dead. You only Ranger left. You lone Ranger now."

Finally the wounds heal and the young Texas Ranger regains his strength.

Realizing that the outlaws will still recognize his face, the Ranger decides that he will cover his face with a mask and seek retribution from Butch Cavendish and his gang. The mask is fashioned from the black vest of his dead brother.

Six graves are marked though one is empty so that everyone will think that none of the Rangers survived —thus ensuring the Lone Ranger's anonymity.

"Tonto, from this moment on I'm going to devote my life to establishing law and order in this new frontier—to make the West a decent place to live."

An old retired Ranger named Jim Blane agrees to work the silver mine owned by the Lone Ranger and his dead brother. He is the one who fashions the silver into the Ranger's trademark—the silver bullet. The mine is located beneath an old cabin where Jim now stays.

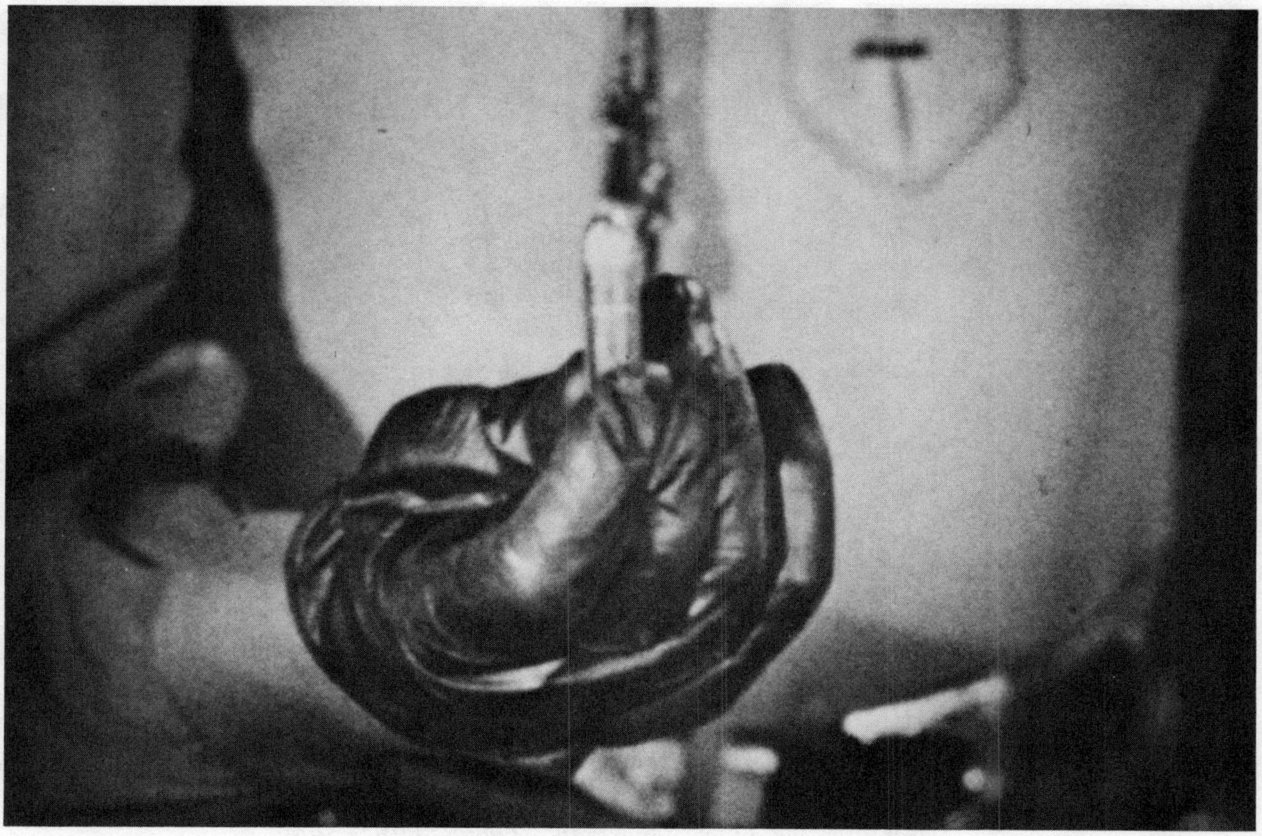

The black mask and silver bullets become a symbol of justice to honest men, a cause of fear to the law-breaker.

The Lone Ranger works with other lawmen to capture the members of the Cavendish gang. Finally, only Butch Cavendish himself remains to be brought to justice.

After the Lone Ranger's horse is shot by the fleeing Cavendish, the Lone Ranger and Tonto journey to Wild Horse Valley where a legendary wild horse, a fiery white stallion, is said to graze with his herd. As they near a rise leading into the valley, they hear the sounds of two mighty beasts engaged in mortal combat.

Approaching closer, they see the exhausted white stallion about to be charged by a gigantic, wounded buffalo. The Lone Ranger's guns bring down the shaggy beast.

The Lone Ranger examines the horse as Tonto checks the now dead buffalo.

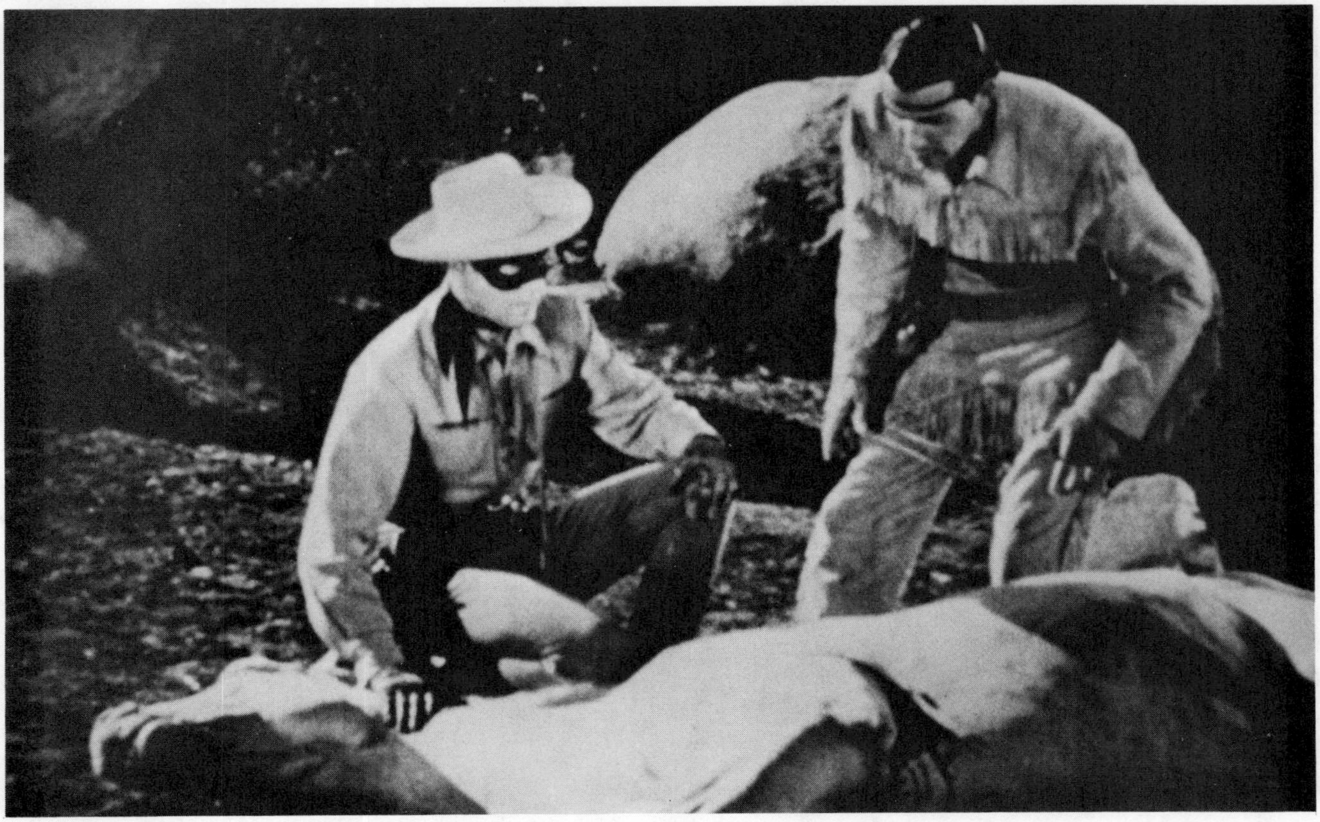

The Lone Ranger and Tonto tend to the wounds of the horse.

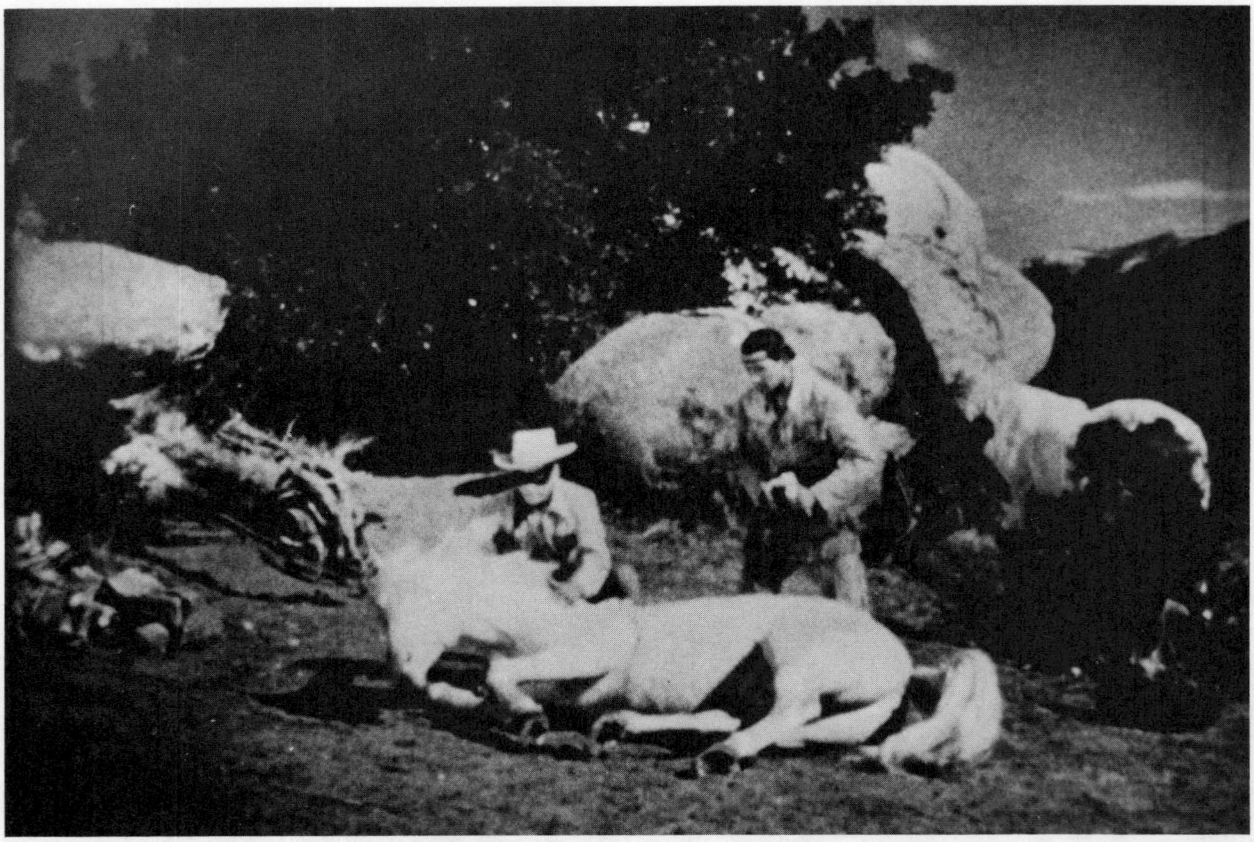

Over the next few days the ugly wounds heal and the unmatched strength and stamina of the mighty stallion return. Finally, assisted by the Lone Ranger and Tonto, the horse rises.

"Let Him go, Tonto," the Lone Ranger says. "I'd like to have that horse more than anything in the world, but he deserves his freedom; he fought for it. See how the sun reflects from his white coat."

"Yes, kemo sabe," the Indian replies, "Him look like silver." The Lone Ranger calls out to the white stallion, "Silver, here Silver!" Some mysterious bond causes the silvery horse to suddenly bolt and gallop to the side of the Lone Ranger.

A saddle and bridle are placed on the horse and the eager Ranger mounts cautiously, allowing the nervous animal to gradually feel the weight of a human body on his back.

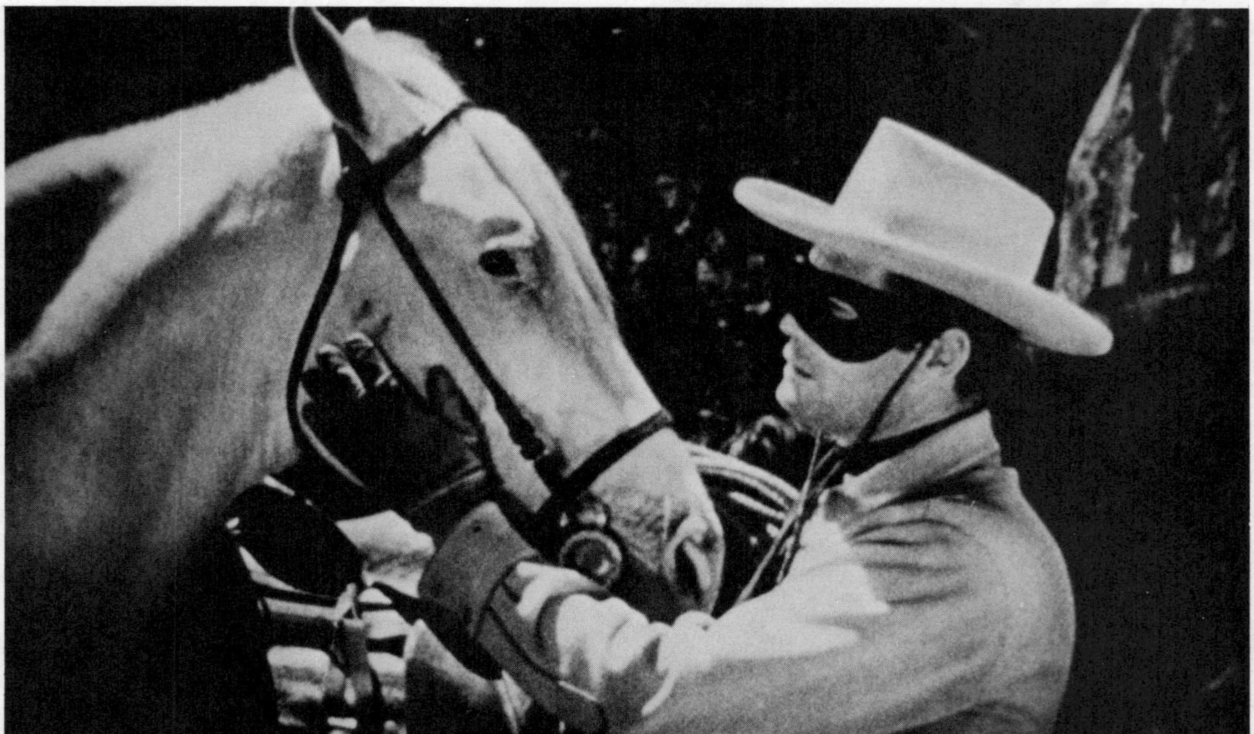

After several days of training, the intelligent horse is ready for the challenges that lie ahead with the Lone Ranger and Tonto.

Days of hard riding cut down the outlaw's lead. At long last a desperate horse and rider come into view far ahead on the dusty trail.

The mighty horse closes the gap between avenger and outlaw.

"I want you, Cavendish!"

The outlaw is captured to be tried by law and punished for his crimes.

radio version of how the Lone Ranger found Silver) the Silver story had the same basic elements except that Tonto is not with the Lone Ranger at the time; and after shooting the buffalo that is charging the wild, white stallion, the Lone Ranger tends to the horse's wounds and then turns him loose with the comment, "You, Silver . . . if I didn't have other business right now, I should like to know you better! Maybe some day,—." With that the Lone Ranger rides off on his "gray mare."

A short time later the gray horse is shot by outlaws and the Lone Ranger returns for the silvery white horse he is then to ride for all time.

To give "The Lone Ranger" adventures even more self-identification for young listeners, the character of teenage Dan Reid, the Lone Ranger's nephew, was developed. With the same thoroughness that marked his story of the origin of the Lone Ranger, Fran Striker now set about writing the "Legend of Dan Reid"—the story of how the Lone Ranger found his only living relative.

Slowly winding through a rugged, boulder-lined valley, a long parade of prairie schooners lumbers westward. Among the pioneers are families challenging the land for survival with all their worldly goods packed into their rickety wagons, and men on horseback who seek adventure in the new frontier. On this particular wagon train there is also a woman with a babe-in-arms who is traveling West to meet her husband, a Texas Ranger.

The sound of the wagon wheels and horses' hooves is suddenly smothered by the blood-chilling shrieks of war-painted Indians who charge out from behind prairie boulders on both sides of the unsuspecting wagon train. A circle of wagons is hastily formed by the surprised pioneers as they attempt to return the fire of the marauding Indians. Though heavily outnumbered, they fight bravely to save their families and themselves—but there is no hope for them. Hours later the battle subsides. The mutilated bodies lie as if in a grotesque mural on the prairie floor, the wagons looted and burned, the embers still smoking. All is still.

It is the morning of the following day when the Lone Ranger and Tonto discover the remains of the wagon train. They draw rein on their horses and examine the bodies carefully to see if a spark of life still dwells in any of the victims.

At last the Ranger speaks the words, "No survivors, Tonto. They must have been the wagon train that was heading for Fort Laramie."

The masked man begins an inspection of the belongings that remain from the ravaged wagon train. Presently he finds a charred nameplate from a burned piece of luggage. Wiping away the soot from a small piece of metal, the Ranger's masked-covered face winces as he reads the name—Reid.

The Lone Ranger recalls for Tonto the words of his brother, Captain Daniel Reid, just before the fateful ambush of the six Texas Rangers in Bryant's Gap, "I want to speak to you, brother to brother. My wife and son are coming from the East. If something happens to me and you survive, well, I know you'll take care of her and Danny. I'm going to count on you to resign and work that silver mine we staked out. See that my son and his mother get my share."

Looking down at the charred piece of metal with the word "Reid" embossed upon it, the Lone Ranger continues, "We were to wait until my brother's wife arrived from the East to see what she wanted done with her share of the silver mine, but now. . . ." The Ranger is unable to continue.

Trying to comfort his friend, the Indian says, "Maybe woman, baby captured. Maybe them live."

With great emotion the masked man says, "It's a faint hope, Tonto. Nevertheless, I shan't be convinced they're dead. We'll always be on the lookout for some clue that Dan Reid and his mother are alive. Meantime, we must help make the West the place where massacres like this can't happen."

Thirteen years pass as the Lone Ranger becomes a legendary character known throughout the West. Countless stories are told of his adventures. He becomes known as a defender of the weak and a champion of justice. Often he seemingly comes from out of nowhere to offer his strength and fighting skill to oppressed people. During the years, he fights with the cavalry in their war against Indian uprisings; saves Western towns buckling under the stranglehold of outlaws; and aids plain, humble folks who seek nothing but a chance to work, live, and raise families on their small homesteads. But wherever his fight for justice takes him, the Lone Ranger is ever alert for proof that his brother's wife and son are dead or, if living, for a clue that might lead him to where they are.

Finally the masked man's adventures take him

'Hi, Yo, Silver! We're on Our Way!'

The Lone Ranger with his trusted Indian friend, "Tonto," shown astride the wonder-horse, "Silver," as they prepare to dash across the plains of the Old West in another thrilling adventure. This is the first picture of the "Lone Ranger" to be released in two years. His identity is kept secret. They are heard each Monday, Wednesday and Friday evenings, over WXYZ.

This faded clipping shows what is probably the rarest Lone Ranger picture. It appeared in Michigan newspapers during 1935 when Tonto still did not have a horse and rode double with the Lone Ranger. Shortly after the picture appeared, the scriptwriters provided Tonto with a horse.

to the high border country in the Northwest where he fights and conquers bandits who seek to rob an old lady known as Grandma Frisby and her adopted grandson, a boy in his early teen years named Dan.

Grandma Frisby's heart falters under the great strain of the fight with the outlaws. The Lone Ranger and Dan are at her side as the dying elderly woman fights to speak a few words before her passing. "I want to be sure that Dan will be all right. I want you to take care of Dan."

The Lone Ranger smiles warmly and says, "I'll take care of him as if he were my own son."

"You ought to know about his past," she whispers, "He's not really my grandson. There's a small box under the bed; hand it to me."

The boy quickly secures the tattered box and puts it in her tired hands while she recounts the story of her trip West many years before. She speaks of a fine lady with a baby boy who was on the wagon train with her. The dying old lady tells about the long-ago savage Indian attack and how she crept away from the massacre with the baby after the mother had been brutally killed.

As Grandma Frisby concludes her story, she removes a locket from the box. "Here's a little gold locket that he wore around his neck. Their picture is inside."

The Lone Ranger opens the locket and looks at the faces of the man and woman as Dan speaks. "I wonder who my parents were?"

Quietly the Lone Ranger speaks to the boy. "I know them. This man, your father, was my brother. He was a captain of the Texas Rangers and one of the bravest men in the country. Your mother was a fine lady from Virginia; her name was Linda. I've been looking for you, Dan, for many years—ever since your father died. From now on, if you're willing, we'll travel together."

The boy says that he would like that very much. Grandma Frisby asks if the Lone Ranger will do one last thing for her. "Would you take off that mask and show me your face?" He does so. "It's a good face, yes, a good face."

The Ranger tells Dan that Grandma Frisby and his father left him a great heritage. He says, "They and others like them have handed down to you the right to worship as you choose, and the right to work and profit from your enterprise. They've given you a land where there is true freedom, true equality of opportunity—a nation that is governed by the people, by laws that are best for the greatest number. Your duty, Dan, is to preserve that heritage and strengthen it. That is the heritage and duty of every American."

The heritage dealing with "the right to work and profit from your enterprise" was certainly one that George W. Trendle could empathize with. Trendle and his "Lone Ranger" staff worked hard during those early years of the program and there were considerable profits from their enterprise.

During the first three months the program was on the air a few fan letters came into the studios of WXYZ, but no flood of mail that would indicate the "Lone Ranger" program had a large following. On the May 16th program it was announced that the Lone Ranger would give a free popgun to the first three hundred youngsters who wrote in to the station requesting one. Two days later on the program it was announced that all of the guns had been given away. On the next program (two days after that) the announcer pleaded with listeners not to send in any more requests. Ultimately, WXYZ was buried under 24,905 letters requesting the popgun. It was an unheard of response to a radio premium for a program that was only broadcast in one state—Michigan.

In July of that same year, 1933, Detroit's Department of Recreation held its annual field day on Belle Isle. This field day was to be like none other the Department would ever schedule for it was announced that the Lone Ranger would appear in person on the great horse Silver. The police were prepared to handle crowds of up to twenty thousand people for the annual event. The twenty thousand figure also represented the most that Belle Isle could handle comfortably. When the unexpected melee concluded, over seventy thousand people had crushed together to get a glimpse of the masked man and Silver. Children and adults broke through police barriers to touch the famous Ranger or to at least get a better, closer look at him. Finally the police had to request that the Lone Ranger himself try to restore order. Brace Beemer, who was the narrator on the program at that time, was portraying the Lone Ranger for the field-day event. When the crowd of youngsters moved in too close to him and Silver and seemed to be getting out of hand, Beemer shouted, "Back, Rangers! Back to your posts!" For years after that, Trendle never let the Lone Ranger make a public appearance for fear of a reoccurrence

MICHIGAN RADIO NETWORK

WXYZ

Volume 1 Number 1 | KUNSKY-TRENDLE BROADCASTING CORPORATION | Madison Theatre Bldg., Detroit

24,905 LETTERS--ONE ANNOUNCEMENT

MAIL RECORD FOR DETROIT

Amazing Mail Response Proves Michigan Radio Network's Home Influence

The Kunsky-Trendle Broadcasting Corporation and owners of associated stations of the Michigan Radio Network feel justified in naming the sensational mail response from one announcement following the Lone Ranger broadcast as radio's most spectacular incident.

The final total of letters received reached 24,905.

In spite of subsequent announcements; immediately following the first 10,000 letters informing children listeners that the supply of Lone Ranger toy six shooters promised to the writers of the first three hundred letters had been exhausted, letters kept pouring in from all parts of Michigan.

This amazing response is interesting because, not only does it prove that the Network speaks to a large family audience, but also admits of the Network's AUDIENCE COVERAGE during the peak of listening hours.

The Lone Ranger free offer to children occurred on the night of May 16th at nine-thirty p. m., following the Lone Ranger broadcast.

Nine-thirty is usually bedtime for children during school term. Nine-thirty is also claimed as full audience time for National network entertainment. Yet the Michigan Radio Network proves itself worthy of distinction by this unprecedented mail response. It certainly establishes the fact that good enter-

Mayor Frank Couzens of Detroit, and Postmaster Roscoe B. Huston, examining the record breaking mail response (24,607 letters in this picture) received from one announcement on the Michigan Radio Network, immediately following the half hour broadcast of an episode of the Lone Ranger adventure series.

NEWSPAPERS AND RADIO

A Contribution

She's just a little country gal—

George W. Trendle saw to it that potential sponsors were made aware of the mail response to the radio announcement about "The Lone Ranger" toy six-shooters.

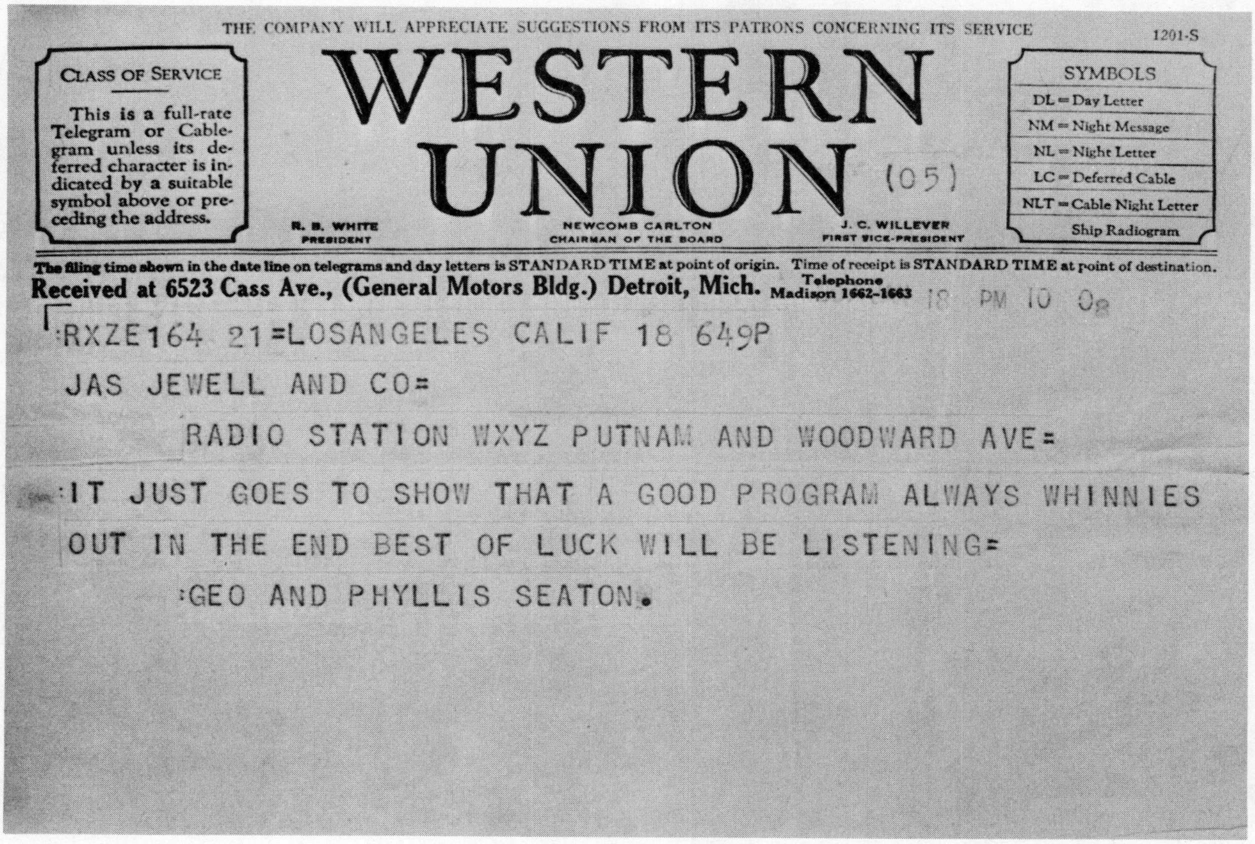

THE COMPANY WILL APPRECIATE SUGGESTIONS FROM ITS PATRONS CONCERNING ITS SERVICE 1201-S

CLASS OF SERVICE

This is a full-rate Telegram or Cablegram unless its deferred character is indicated by a suitable symbol above or preceding the address.

WESTERN UNION

(05)

R. B. WHITE, PRESIDENT — NEWCOMB CARLTON, CHAIRMAN OF THE BOARD — J. C. WILLEVER, FIRST VICE-PRESIDENT

SYMBOLS
DL = Day Letter
NM = Night Message
NL = Night Letter
LC = Deferred Cable
NLT = Cable Night Letter
Ship Radiogram

The filing time shown in the date line on telegrams and day letters is STANDARD TIME at point of origin. Time of receipt is STANDARD TIME at point of destination.

Received at 6523 Cass Ave., (General Motors Bldg.) Detroit, Mich. Telephone Madison 1662-1663 18 PM 10 08

:RXZE164 21=LOSANGELES CALIF 18 649P

JAS JEWELL AND CO=

RADIO STATION WXYZ PUTNAM AND WOODWARD AVE=

:IT JUST GOES TO SHOW THAT A GOOD PROGRAM ALWAYS WHINNIES OUT IN THE END BEST OF LUCK WILL BE LISTENING=

:GEO AND PHYLLIS SEATON.

George Seaton, the first actor to ever play the Lone Ranger, sent this telegram to Jim Jewell near the time of the 1937 anniversary program.

We take a bow

FIRST IN AMERICA!

STATION WXYZ HAS BEEN HONORED WITH THE SHOWMANSHIP AWARD FOR PROGRAM ORIGINATION FOR 1937. THIS "BLUE RIBBON" CITATION TO THE RADIO STATION MOST SUCCESSFUL IN CREATING POPULAR PROGRAMS IS SPONSORED BY VARIETY, THE NOTED THEATRICAL WEEKLY.

KING-TRENDLE BROADCASTING CORPORATION

The Lone Ranger
Now broadcast to 25 stations via special network (coast to coast) each Mon., Wed., Fri., 7:30-8:00 P. M. basic time.

The Green Hornet
The original newspaper story that strikes at "law breakers within the law." Broadcast each Tuesday and Thursday, 7:30-8:00 P. M.

The Factfinder
Little known facts about people, places and things; presented with orchestra and mixed quartet. Broadcast each Monday through Friday, 6:15-6:30 P. M.

Hollywood Impressions
An innovation in exploiting deluxe pictures: Originating use of the entire Michigan Radio Network webbed with major Detroit stations. Half hour broadcasts with orchestra and large variety cast.

Children's Theatre of the Air
Musical comedy radio show presented entirely by boys and girls aged 5 to 14: Forty-five-minute show from the stage of the downtown Broadway Capitol (audience) 12:00-12:45 P. M. each Sunday.

Junior Matinee
Teen age graduates of WXYZ's dramatic school presenting songs and chatter with a musical background. Previously heard three times weekly. Now Sundays only, 5:45-6:00 P. M.

Happiness House
Quarter hour broadcasts each Monday through Friday, 10:30-10:45 A. M.: Featuring foods, diets, menu suggestions and hints for housewives on labor saving methods. After Jan. 3, will be broadcast at 9:30 to 9:45 A. M.

WXYZ · DETROIT

Basic Station N B C Blue Network · Key Station Michigan Radio Network of the frightening experience.

The Belle Isle crowds confirmed Trendle's speculation after the popgun phenomenon—that he had a hit on his hands, a program that should lure wealthy sponsors and be sought by stations throughout the country. On November 27th the first sponsored broadcast was sent out over the Michigan network. Within two months the program was picked up by WGN, Chicago, and WOR, Newark, and WLW, Cincinnati, the nucleus of the Mutual Broadcasting System that was formed later that year, 1934. By 1937 the program made it to the Pacific coast. In February of 1938 the program was first offered to stations in transcription form (on prerecorded disks). By 1939 the program was being heard on 140 stations in and outside of the United States. Newfoundland, New Zealand, Hawaii, and Ontario were among those outside the United States to first listen to "The Lone Ranger" adventures.

During all of this time of rapid development for the program, Fran Striker and his small staff continued to work quietly in the background spinning Western lore into WXYZ gold. In the evolution of broadcasting, radio and then television, writers quickly discovered that it was one thing to create an appealing character or series idea, and it was an entirely different thing to sustain the public interest in the character or series for any period of time. Striker knew this and worked long, hard hours to keep his adventures of the Lone Ranger constantly interesting and exciting.

It was estimated in 1939 that Striker was pounding out approximately sixty thousand words every week of the year. Someone figured that it was the equivalent of the Bible every three months. Each year Striker, with the assistance of his small staff of writers, wrote 156 "Lone Ranger" radio adventures, 365 newspaper cartoon scripts (which he continued to write until his death in 1962, at which time Charles Flanders, the cartoonist, took over as writer), and, in addition to the "Lone Ranger" activities, he wrote 104 "Green Hornet" and fifty-two "Ned Jordan, Secret Agent" radio scripts each year. Over the years he also wrote more than a dozen "Lone Ranger" novels for Grossett and Dunlap Publishers. Striker was putting in fourteen hour work days in 1939 for his ten thousand dollar salary; by 1950 he was making around fifty thousand dollars a year.

"The Lone Ranger" was most lucrative for the Trendle Corporation. The net income by 1939 was approximately half a million dollars a year —and the money machine had only started to function. By the time of the final network radio adventure (#2596, on September 3, 1954, entitled: "Cold Spring Showdown"), many additional millions would flow into the Trendle coffers. No other fictional broadcasting character remained so popular for so long and made so much money for its owners.

But more important than the money "The Lone Ranger" made for its owners was what the character came to mean to his millions of listeners, viewers, and readers throughout the years. On the tenth anniversary of "The Lone Ranger" radio program, the famous Michigan poet Edgar A. Guest gave his friend George W. Trendle a poem he had written to commemorate the decade-long popularity of the masked man of the plains. Much of what the Lone Ranger had come to mean to his followers was caught in the poem.

The Tenth Anniversary of
The Lone Ranger

Ten years of "Hi Yo Silver!" Ten years of riding hard!
Ten years of pistol shooting and still alive, unscarred!
Ten years of horse and rider, of wagon, pack and stage.
Ten years of desperadoes and still no sign of age!
Ten years of "Me-Called Tonto," the masked man's faithful scout—
A thousand times they've shot him, but still he rides about.
Ten years of hooves a-gallop with never a sign of drag—
Ten years of laryngitis for good old Mustang Mag.
Three nights a week I've listened (His devotee am I!)
To hear the Masked Man giving his long-familiar cry:
"Hi Silver, there is danger. It's time to hit the trail!
Beyond the gulch they're waiting to rob the western mail!"
Ten years for good old Silver's persistent chase of thieves
And still no sign of spavin, or bott, or gall or heaves.
Ten years of vice and virtue! Ten years of war with sin
That's fifteen hundred battles—and every one a win!

But now to change the picture. Ten years of scenes like these:

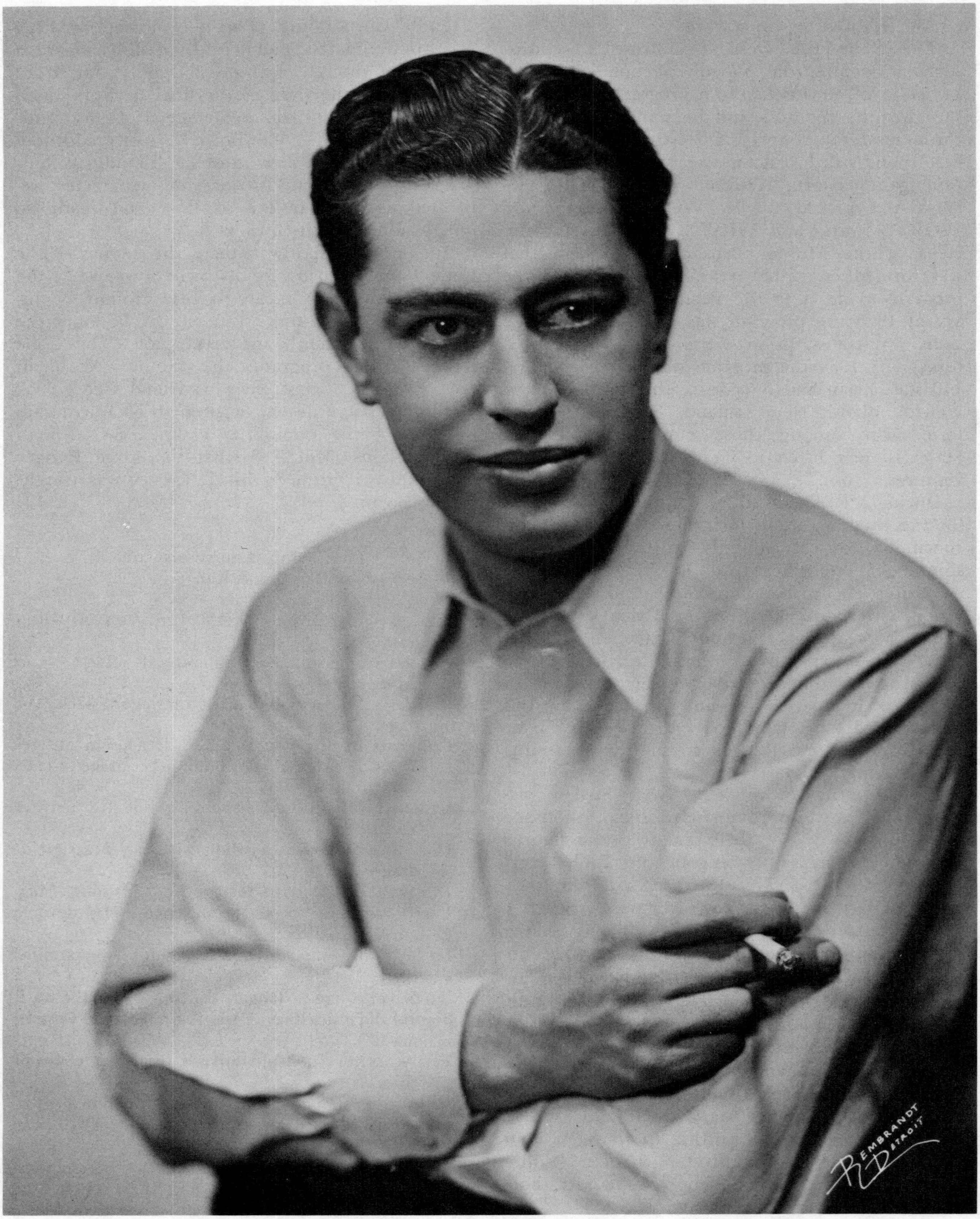

Fran Striker (circa 1938)

"Turn off the radio, Willie, and come to supper,
please!"
Ten years of youth excited, wide-eyed and tousled
brow,
Replying "Just a minute, The Ranger's on right
now!
He's shouting 'Hi Yo Silver, Away! There's danger
grave!
They're holding up the stage coach! There's gold
we've got to save!' "
And still as when he started, the boys on every street
Would rather hear The Ranger, than sit them
down to eat.

Oh, who would trace the glory of ten such golden
years
Would find it all lived over in countless brave
careers!
He'd find it in the jungles, the seven seas and the
skies
For who sets high example sets that which never
dies.

From left to right: Brace Beemer, Fran Striker, George W. Trendle, H. Allen Campbell (who started as sales manager of WXYZ and eventually became a partner in Trendle's firm), and Charles D. Livingstone (radio director from 1938 to 1954). (circa 1943)

Who walks the paths of honor takes many a lad
along—
For boys are quick to follow where leadership is
strong
And though he may not see them—Lone Ranger of
the Air—
His followers are legion at home and everywhere.

Lone Ranger—Phantom Rider! Ten years they've
called him that—
And yet whate'er his journey or what the peril
known
This is the truth about him—He never rides alone!
That cry of "Hi Yo Silver! There's danger now!
Away!"
Calls forth a bright-eyed army to share it, come
what may.
Wherever strength is needed and faith too strong
to fail—
Ten million boys and over, ride with him down
the trail.

Wanting to keep a tight rein on his writers, Trendle prepared a list of rules for Striker and his writers. Among them:

- "The Lone Ranger never smokes, never uses profanity, and never uses intoxicating beverages."
- "The Lone Ranger is a man who can fight great odds, yet takes time to treat a bird with a broken wing."
- "The Lone Ranger believes that our sacred American heritage provides that every individual has the right to worship God as he desires."
- "Play down gambling and drinking scenes as far as possible, and keep the Lone Ranger out of saloons. When this cannot be avoided, try to make the saloon a cafe—and deal with waiters and food instead of bartenders and liquor."
- "The Lone Ranger at all times uses precise speech, without slang, or dialect. His grammar must be pure. He must make proper use of 'who' and 'whom,' 'shall,' and 'will,' 'I' and 'me,' etc."
- "The Lone Ranger never shoots to kill. When he has to use guns, he aims to maim as painlessly as possible." (Striker and his writers must have found "maiming as painlessly as possible" an intriguing rule to follow.)

Because over the years many free-lance writers wanted to submit scripts for the radio series, Felix Holt, a story editor for "The Lone Ranger," was requested by Fran Striker to prepare a "Writer's Guide to 'The Lone Ranger' Program." The guide provides a further insight into Striker's and Trendle's view of the character and is, therefore, reproduced here in its entirety.

WRITER'S GUIDE TO "THE LONE RANGER" PROGRAM

So you want to write a Lone Ranger story?

That's fine, and to help you do a really good job of it, we are going to acquaint you with some interesting things to bear in mind.

First, listen to "The Lone Ranger" program on Monday, Wednesday and Friday evenings over the Blue Network. By so doing you will observe how the simple rules stated in this brochure are applied in the production.

In writing a Lone Ranger story remember that the sole purpose of the program is good, clean entertainment. Although right triumphs, the program does not preach. Neither does it deal in any way with controversial subjects of today and no parallels should be drawn.

The program is a half-hour in length, with the story running approximately 24 minutes. The story is broken in the middle for a commercial. Disregard the standard opening and close, and proceed directly into your story.

We have found that many young writers, when first attempting to write this show, immediately want to change the Lone Ranger, make him different than he is. Don't do that. The Lone Ranger has been a top favorite of the American radio audience for more than ten years, so people must like him as he is.

The Lone Ranger program is NOT written from the juvenile viewpoint, but rather from the adult. Today's boys and girls demand the same high standard of story and drama their elders are accustomed to hearing. Although the show is written from the adult viewpoint, it must not be slow or talky. It is an action show. However, don't write in action unless it plays a part in the story. For instance, the Lone Ranger is leaving the Sheriff's office. If the story calls for no objection on the part of the Sheriff, the Lone Ranger simply walks from the room. If however, the Sheriff objects, the Ranger may kick over the desk and jump through a window. That is logical action.

Do not resort to phony heroics to carry your story. Have the Lone Ranger act and react as nearly normal as possible. Consider him as a highly intelligent, quick-thinking man who is skilled in the ways of the west, particularly with a gun, horse, lariat, etc., but not infallible. For instance, he can miss a shot and generally be subject to the margin of error that confronts (and sometimes confounds) all champions.

This artist's rendering of the Lone Ranger and Silver has been used repeatedly over the years (with minor variations such as the hat blocked differently in the late 1930s version) for publicity purposes. This particular depiction was used throughout the 1950s.

THE PERIOD

The period of the Lone Ranger saga generally lies between the Civil War and 1890. We have used stories which were based upon matters outside those limits, but no dates were mentioned. In fact, it is best to leave all dates out of stories.

The locale is generally the southwest, although he has moved all over the west from the Mississippi to California. However, it is best that your story deal with purely fictional names and people and places.

THE CHARACTERS

There are three regular characters, namely the Lone Ranger, his nephew Dan Reid and their Indian friend, Tonto.

The Lone Ranger is a man of mystery. Aside from Dan Reid and Tonto, nobody knows his actual identity. Of course, many people know of the Lone Ranger by reputation, but few, very few, know him personally as the Lone Ranger. Occasionally it may be necessary from a story standpoint for some one, such as a lawman, or a chief character, to know the Lone Ranger. He is a man of approximately 30 years of age. He speaks perfect English at all times and has no southwest brogue at all. He rides a great white stallion named Silver and wears a mask. Occasionally the mask may be removed when the Lone Ranger assumes a disguise for some particular purpose, though that device should not be used except in extreme cases. Bear in mind that the Lone Ranger must never be put into a position where he can be unmasked and his real identity exposed. Therefore he must not be tied up or knocked out.

The Lone Ranger is never a detective and should not be portrayed in that role. He is a man of direct action, rather than deduction. He will act first and then explain, if necessary. No one gives him orders. It is the Lone Ranger who motivates the action and usually the plot, where possible. He never just goes along for the ride.

The only way he will identify himself, when it becomes necessary, is by a silver bullet. The Lone Ranger does not shoot to kill, though he may wound in an effort to prevent murder or the escape of criminals.

Dan Reid is a boy about 14 years of age whose parents were killed by Indians, and he was later found by his uncle, the Lone Ranger. Dan is just a normal boy. He gets into difficulties, has lots of fun, enjoys excitement and is well mannered and always loyal. He addresses the Lone Ranger as "Sir", though he refers to him as "The Lone Ranger" when not in the masked man's presence. Dan rides a white horse named Victor. It is not absolutely necessary that Dan Reid be included in all stories, though it is desirable.

Tonto is the son of a chieftain of the Potawatomi tribe of Indians. He is about 26 years of age, speaks English brokenly and is usually serious, though he likes a good joke or an amusing situation. He lives to serve the Lone Ranger. He speaks most of the Indian languages, knows all of the lore of the woods, the fields and streams. He rides a spotted horse named Scout.

THEIR ARMS

The Lone Ranger wears two silver six-shooters, specially made for him. He shoots silver bullets. He may use a rifle when necessary, though the rifle is carried by Tonto.

Tonto carries a knife, which he can throw with deadly aim, a bow and arrows, and a rifle carried in a saddle scabbard, usually called a "boot."

Dan Reid carries no weapons at all. He has a hunting knife for woodcraft purposes.

TYPE OF STORY

About the type of story we like on the Lone Ranger program: This is very important. Don't write a story about THINGS such as stolen gold claims, mortgaged ranches, water rights, railroad franchises, etc. Write stories about PEOPLE and their problems. After all, the Lone Ranger is the friend of decent PEOPLE and the enemy of BAD PEOPLE. He is neither the friend or foe of gold claim, mortgage, franchise or water right.

For instance: Fran Striker wrote a story about a United States marshal who rode into Texas to arrest old Judge Roy Bean for interpreting the law his own way. The Lone Ranger showed the officer that Judge Bean was interpreting the law the way the people of Pecos River Valley liked the law interpreted, and that after all justice was done. The Marshal turned his horse around and went back where he came from. Well, there was a claim-jumping angle in the story, but it was only the backdrop for the more human story of Judge Bean and how he administered frontier justice.

Bob Green wrote a story about a mine disaster, but as such it was the backdrop for a story of a little man who wanted to be a big man. The Lone Ranger made it possible to the extent that the little man actually became bigger than he had ever visioned it possible for him to become. It was a story about a man, not a mine disaster.

We place no restrictions, except good taste and good judgement, in the matter of characters you may place upon your stage. The more unusual and colorful they are, of course, the more interesting they will be. They are your brain-children, so *make them live.*

Too many writers make the mistake of having all their WESTERN characters talk like ignoramuses. The West was largely settled by educated people, many of them highly cultured. Of course there were the rough types also, but the Lone Ranger Program is not a stage for the exclusive exhibition of such people. If you need an uneducated person in your story put him in, but unless there is a reason for him to chew tobacco and the king's English, leave him out. In establishing character, it is permissible to use figures of speech, but do not write in dialect. Indicate the type of dialect in your cast sheet. The director and actor will take care of the interpretation.

If you have the Lone Ranger faced with impossible odds, don't have him shoot the guns out of the hands of some 20 men surrounding him. Instead, deliver him by some outside means, such as the Sheriff riding up and demanding that the Lone Ranger is HIS prisoner. It will be more logical for him to escape from the Sheriff than from a posse of 20 heavily armed men who already have the drop on him. In other words, keep the story and action as logical as possible.

It is desirable to get the Lone Ranger into the story as soon as logical. He should make his appearance by page seven, if not sooner, and certainly before the half-way point in your story. This can be done by a competent radio script writer, regardless of the story he is telling.

In plotting your story, eliminate the use of a "gimmick" for your final solution of the problem. For instance, don't get your characters in a tough spot and then have the Lone Ranger find a broken spur which fits the heel of the biggest "heel" in the crowd. That's too easy. Even the kids won't go for that one any more.

When you have outlined your story in your mind or on paper, ask yourself this question: Would I still have a good story if I took the Lone Ranger out of it, or if I moved it to some other locale and in the present day? If the answer is "Yes", then you have a story that will probably ring the bell with the Lone Ranger program.

So, once again, let me stress three points. (1) Write a story with strong characters, strong plot and plenty of action. (2) Make the Lone Ranger motivate either the plot or the action, both if possible. (3) Write about PEOPLE and not about things, such as .... well, if you're a good writer, you know what I mean. (4) Above all, don't write down to your audience. The Lone Ranger has been recognized as Americana, a literary legend. Approach it with that viewpoint and you will probably do a good job.

Felix Holt
Story Editor

Address all manuscripts to the
Story Editor,
King-Trendle Broadcasting Corp.,
Stroh Building
Detroit 26, Michigan

3
"Come with Us Now to Those Thrilling Days of Yesteryear"

I first met Chuck Livingstone in late August of 1968. I had recently been appointed producer-director of The Player's Theatre of Sarasota, Florida, one of the largest and finest community theaters in the southeastern United States, and was about to go into try-outs on my first play. On the Friday before the Sunday casting, I received a phone call from the newly retired Charles D. Livingstone, who felt he might like to keep active by returning to his early (and I later suspected first) love of acting. He asked if he and his wife Harriet might meet with me at the theater, get a copy of the script, and discuss the upcoming try-outs.

The next day shortly after lunch we met at the theater and began a personal and professional relationship that has remained strong ever since. At this first meeting Chuck mentioned that he had been a radio and television director. When I inquired what he had directed, I was intrigued to discover that I was conversing with a man who had lived more than twenty of his adult years in the daily presence of one of my greatest childhood heroes, the Lone Ranger. Not only had he directed both "The Lone Ranger" radio and television series, but he had also directed "The Green Hornet" on radio. In addition Chuck had supervised the radio "Sergeant Preston of the Yukon" and directed many of the programs in the television version. No radio-television child of the thirties, forties, or fifties could fail to be impressed with credentials like those.

While Chuck wished to discuss the about-to-be-cast play, I'm afraid my thoughts were tripping back to "those thrilling days of yesteryear" and conjuring up a ridiculous number of questions about "what it was like back then." Chuck finally got me back to my job; I gave him a script and wished him well at try-outs. I hoped that he really would be a good actor (many times a good director is a lousy actor) and could be cast in the play. I already had visions of occasionally getting him to sit down with me and reminisce about those years with the Lone Ranger. I need not have worried about his acting ability—he was excellent at try-outs and ultimately received wonderful reviews for his portrayal of the frazzled father of the newly married and very expectant daughter in the comedy *Generation*.

During the years I was director of The Players Theatre, Chuck played a wide variety of roles (from Sitting Bull in *Annie Get Your Gun* to the dour New England caretaker, Mr. Kimber,

During an interview taping session, the author and Charles D. Livingstone walk along the beach near Mr. Livingstone's Long Boat Key, Florida, home.

in Moss Hart and George S. Kaufman's *George Washington Slept Here*). Audiences rarely allowed him to make a final exit without the echo of applause ringing in his ears.

Our friendship over the years continued to heighten my interest in the old radio heroes. One day I called Chuck and asked if I could see him about a new project I had on my mind. When we got together a few days later, I told him that like so many other people I had become more and more fascinated with the early days of radio and television and the programs we enjoyed then. I told him I wanted to explore the subject using "The Lone Ranger" program as the focal point since it had been a pioneer in both media fields, and the Lone Ranger character had been a hero to me and to millions of other people over the years. In addition, "The Lone Ranger" had branched out into other interesting areas such as movie serials, features, merchandising, comics, and novels; and I was sure that they would prove to be equally intriguing to explore. Chuck was fascinated by the project and agreed to share his memories and thoughts in any way that would help me.

Over the next few weeks we repeatedly got together with a tape recorder to discuss the masked man and related matters. Little did he or I realize the ambush of long ago ghosts that waited for us at the pass.

DAVID ROTHEL: How did you get interested in show business?

CHARLES LIVINGSTONE: My high school drama teacher, Julia Gettemy, gave me my first push. Then, while a prelaw student at the University of Michigan, I discovered I was much more interested in theater than law. Shortly after I got into the University of Michigan, I was cast in the play *Pygmalion*. A girl who was later a writer for "The Lone Ranger" and "Challenge of the Yukon" radio programs, Mildred Henry, played the lead in the show. During college I played more than my share of leads and character parts. I was president of Comedy Club, the all-campus drama organization, and Mimes, which was the men's dramatic honorary society. I was in three of the Mimes' shows. You know, the musical extravaganzas where men dress up as women. (laugh) We toured all over the Middle West with the shows during Christmas vacation.

DAVID ROTHEL: Chuck, did you have a personal hero when you were a kid?

CHARLES LIVINGSTONE: Yes, I guess so, but it

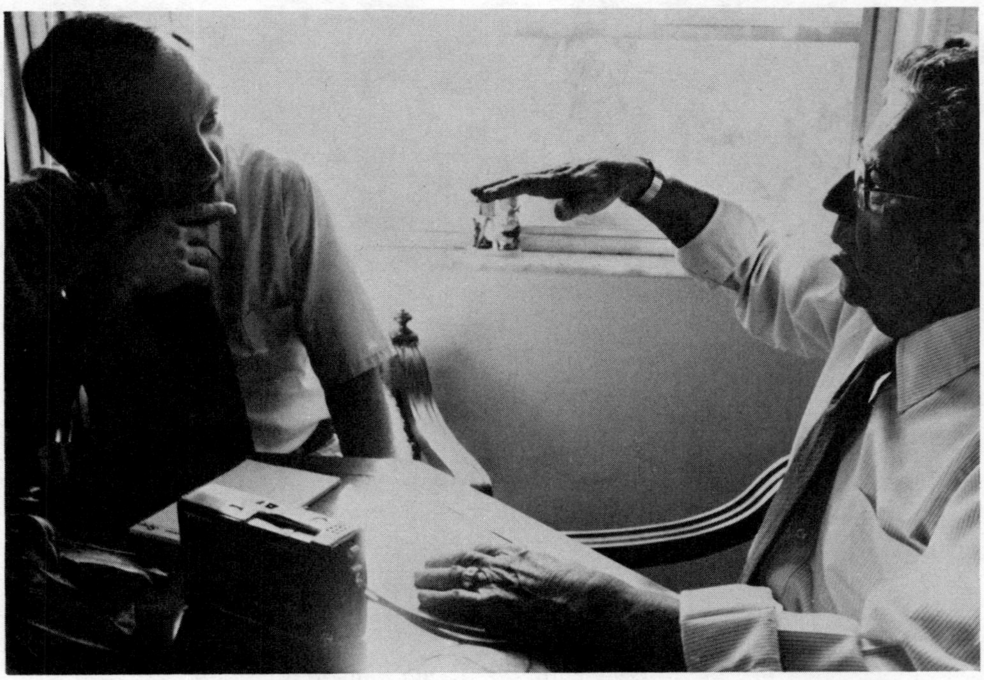

Charles D. Livingstone recalls the early days of "The Lone Ranger" radio program for David Rothel.

wasn't one particular hero; it was anyone who was a cadet at West Point. Being a cadet symbolized all that was adventuresome and exciting in the world. I used to get all the West Point books and read them. A friend of mine in high school went to West Point. I thought he was the luckiest guy in the world. I haven't thought about this in years.

DAVID ROTHEL: The Lone Ranger, of course, was a hero for me when I was a youngster. Did you have any fictional-type heroes?

CHARLES LIVINGSTONE: Not really. Of course, we all had our movie heroes in those days. I particularly liked Bronco Billy Anderson and Francis X. Bushman. Wallace Reid was everyone's hero in those days. But I didn't have the type of mind that settled on any one particular hero.

DAVID ROTHEL: Well, you obviously didn't become a lawyer, but you did become a professional actor and director. How did this come about?

CHARLES LIVINGSTONE: While I was playing in the University of Michigan's Theatre, Adams R. Rice, Jessie Bonstelle's technical director, saw me and this caused me to get the position of "general business" in Jessie Bonstelle's Stock Company.

DAVID ROTHEL: And that came after college?

CHARLES LIVINGSTONE: That was right after college. I was graduated in February of 1928, and went right with Jessie Bonstelle.

DAVID ROTHEL: Jessie Bonstelle was a woman not a man.

CHARLES LIVINGSTONE: Ah, that she was. Miss Bonstelle!

DAVID ROTHEL: What does it mean to have the position of "general business"?

CHARLES LIVINGSTONE: That's the lowest position in a stock company.

DAVID ROTHEL: A spear carrier?

CHARLES LIVINGSTONE: Well, no. You filled in on any type of character that was needed. My first good part was the Dauphin in *Saint Joan.*

DAVID ROTHEL: That's a good part.

CHARLES LIVINGSTONE: Yes, it was, and I got good notices.

DAVID ROTHEL: This was a professional company.

CHARLES LIVINGSTONE: Oh, yes—this was for pay. I got thirty dollars a week. Eventually I played all kinds of roles. In fact, during the second year I became the "juvenile" of the company. The last show I did for Jessie Bonstelle ran for twenty-nine weeks. It was called *After Dark.* It was one of those reverse "mellerdramas" where the audience cheers the villain and hisses the hero, and all that stuff. William Brady, the well-known producer, took over the show from Bonstelle and sent it out on the road. We played in Philadelphia, New York in the Bronx, and Boston. The show closed the same week as the stock market crash in November of 1929. After that I played in vaudeville at the Palace Theatre in New York. We did scenes from *The Merchant of Venice.* Maurice Schwartz, one of the best-known actors in the Yiddish Theatre, played Shylock. I played Solanio, one of the guys who mocked the Jew. Man, I got write-ups in the *New York Telegram* for that! Carl Benton Reid was in that show, too, along with several other darned good actors. We went next to closing on the vaudeville bill.

DAVID ROTHEL: And did they have comics and jugglers and dog acts?

CHARLES LIVINGSTONE: Oh, yes. Horace Heidt and His Musical Knights was the last thing on the bill. I don't remember the other parts of the show. When we closed in that, I went home to Detroit—the first time I'd been home since the Brady show started.

DAVID ROTHEL: This was about 1930?

CHARLES LIVINGSTONE: The first part of 1930. We were in the depression and things were rough. In November I had married a lovely young actress named Harriet Russell and we worked on Broadway, stock companies, and two summers with the Detroit Players, a super summer theater tent show. This was the same tent show that Jim Jewell, Ted Robertson, and Earle Graser were with at one time or another. In 1932 we went to Hollywood. Finally, in the spring of 1933, I had had my fill of traveling here and there around the country acting in shows. Harriet felt the same way. I decided I wanted to try my luck in radio. Jim Jewell, a guy I'd met a few years before doing a puppet act in a tent show, was now a director with WXYZ radio in Detroit. He was directing a number of dramatic programs including a new show called "The Lone Ranger." I talked to him about an acting job in his company of actors called "The Jewell Players." I didn't get a thing. I also did an audition as an announcer for George W. Trendle, the boss, and he couldn't use me either. It was 1933 after the crash and things were just barely coming along. Harriet and I kept busy working in local theaters and industrial film companies.

Wilding's was one; Jam Handy's another—the same Jam Handy that I got connected with years and years later—in fact thirty years later.

DAVID ROTHEL: Well, you obviously got connected with "The Lone Ranger" or at least radio acting around this time.

CHARLES LIVINGSTONE: All right, I'll tell you how that came about. In August of 1933, Wynn Wright, who was director of drama at WWJ, had been called in by all the radio stations to do a combined radio show for some special occasion. Well, I got a part and must have done well because after that Jim Jewell started to use me.

DAVID ROTHEL: Let's see, "The Lone Ranger" first went on the air in January of 1933.

CHARLES LIVINGSTONE: And I didn't get with it until August. Did you know there was just the Lone Ranger at first? Tonto didn't come into the show until about the tenth program. But you'll find out all about that when you talk with other people. You see, I wasn't there at the time of the creation of the Lone Ranger; I came along a few months later. I can't tell you how it was created, but you can rest assured that Jim Jewell was the director, Fran Striker was the writer, and George W. Trendle was the boss. I know there has been some speculation as to who actually created the character of the Lone Ranger, but I don't know for sure. Trendle, according to his biography, was the creator of it, and I sure don't know otherwise.

DAVID ROTHEL: When you started with "The Lone Ranger," then, you started as an actor. What kinds of parts did you play?

CHARLES LIVINGSTONE: I started out playing heavies, but eventually played every type of role. Here's something I'll bet you didn't know. Brace Beemer, who later became the Lone Ranger, was narrator of the program when I started acting in it. Brace was also station manager. Brace and Jim Jewell didn't get along too well, and finally, Brace decided that he was going to start another company of actors in a late night program called "Dr. Fang." I did my first radio directing with that program.

DAVID ROTHEL: How did you happen to become director of "Dr. Fang"?

CHARLES LIVINGSTONE: Well, Brace started out directing "Dr. Fang," but because it was on late at night and he didn't want to hang around, he asked me to be the director. Also, around this time I started to get the title of assistant director to Jim Jewell on "The Lone Ranger." I don't remember how that came about. Jim, at times, would leave after the first rehearsal, which was for the setting of characters and reading through the lines, and he'd let me time the program for him.

DAVID ROTHEL: Did he have anything to do with the "Dr. Fang" program?

CHARLES LIVINGSTONE: No, no.

DAVID ROTHEL: Didn't you tell me one time that "The Lone Ranger" was done on stage as a live production?

CHARLES LIVINGSTONE: Yes, that's right. It was done at the Fisher Theatre and another theater in the Detroit area. I can't remember for sure whether it was in 1934 or '35. The Jewell Players—the radio stock company of actors—performed the stage production of "The Lone Ranger" program.

DAVID ROTHEL: How long did you do "The Lone Ranger" on stage?

CHARLES LIVINGSTONE: It was only performed for a very short time—just a few weeks.

DAVID ROTHEL: Did you have a horse on stage?

CHARLES LIVINGSTONE: We had a great big white horse that the radio Lone Ranger, Earle Graser, could hardly get onto.

DAVID ROTHEL: Earle Graser played the Lone Ranger on stage, too?

CHARLES LIVINGSTONE: One horrible night the show ended as usual with the Lone Ranger shouting, "Hi-Yo, Silver, Away!" and the curtain came down still revealing the horse's hind end—leaving it bouncing up and down in front of the audience. That was the funniest thing I think I ever saw. (laugh)

DAVID ROTHEL: Did Graser do a good job as the Lone Ranger on stage?

CHARLES LIVINGSTONE: He was a little bit short and slim for the part, but he acted it very well. On stage he looked very much like Clay Moore, the television Lone Ranger. They both had similar physical builds.

DAVID ROTHEL: Did you play the villain in the stage production?

CHARLES LIVINGSTONE: That's right. I was always the heavy!

DAVID ROTHEL: During the early years of the radio program was Jewell your boss or was Trendle always overseeing?

CHARLES LIVINGSTONE: Jewell, but Trendle, even though he had a big radio station to run at this time, was always checking the programs to see that they were being produced in the manner he wanted.

DAVID ROTHEL: When did you become direc-

This newspaper photo (circa mid-1930s) shows members of the WXYZ stock company of actors rehearsing for an upcoming broadcast. Pictured (left to right) are John Petruzzi, Margorie Richmond, Charles Livingstone, Beatrice Leiblee, and Malcolm McCoy.

These three stills are from the little-known stage production of The Lone Ranger. *The stage version was the equivalent of a long one-act play and was presented as an "added attraction" to accompany the feature movie that was currently playing the theater. Unfortunately no photographs including Earle Graser, the stage and radio Lone Ranger, could be located. The performers in the photographs are Margorie Richmond (the heroine), Malcolm McCoy (cowhand sitting on ground), and Charles Livingstone (the villain).*

Charles D. Livingstone probably portrayed more villains on radio between 1933 and 1938 than any other actor. As usual, he is involved in dirty work in this still from the 1930s stage production of The Lone Ranger.

tor of "The Lone Ranger" radio program?

CHARLES LIVINGSTONE: In June of 1938. That was when Jim Jewell left to go to WWJ in Detroit where he produced a big radio program—an adventure program for competition with WXYZ. It didn't do too well. I haven't any idea what the name of the program was. [Author's note: The program was called "The Black Ace."] I don't know how long he was with WWJ, but then he went to Chicago and he's been there ever since. He directed "Jack Armstrong" for some years. When Jewell left WXYZ, there was a decision to be made about who was to take over. I had been working as Jewell's assistant director and had been doing a good job, so I was selected. Things had been running smoothly on the program, so I didn't make too many changes in the routine of things when I took over.

DAVID ROTHEL: "The Green Hornet," of course, was another radio program created by the Trendle organization. Did you also take over the direction of that program?

CHARLES LIVINGSTONE: Yes. When Jim Jewell left, I took over both "The Lone Ranger" and "The Green Hornet."

DAVID ROTHEL: "The Challenge of the Yukon" was another Trendle creation, wasn't it?

CHARLES LIVINGSTONE: Oh, yes. I can't take credit for having had a hand in the creation of any of those programs. I started directing them well after they were developed. The programs I did direct right from the beginning were "The American Agent" and "Ned Jordan, Federal Agent."

DAVID ROTHEL: Did a stage or movie actor have to be retrained for radio?

CHARLES LIVINGSTONE: Definitely. The whole technique of radio was to read and sound as if you were not reading. Many stage actors will always say—you've heard them, David—"I can't give a good reading when I get the script the first time. I've got to have it to study so that I can get to know more about the character." This is why those people starved in radio; time was money. You got your script when you got to the studio to do the program. We had to do "The Lone Ranger" and "The Green Hornet" with three hours rehearsal. While "The Lone Ranger" was on the air, every once in a while some stage actors would come to Detroit in a play. Occasionally I'd cast them in a program with the regular stock company of radio actors we had. Pretty soon in the script we'd get to a stage coach robbery or a fight with the Indians. The actors new to radio techniques many times couldn't follow it on the script because the tempo was so fast. They would suddenly find themselves two pages behind. They couldn't follow it on the sheet of script as fast as the regular cast. The regular cast, of course, was part of the reason why the shows were so great. The stock company of actors on the program was melded together into such a team that they could handle the most difficult of scenes with little rehearsal and pull it off beautifully. Even though the audience recognized the same voices playing different roles on the programs week after week, they didn't seem to mind. It was important to keep this company together because you only had three hours of rehearsal for each program.

DAVID ROTHEL: Was radio considered a worthy profession to enter at that time? When television came along people who were in movies, for example, did not want to get into it because it was considered a second-class medium. Was there ever that feeling about radio that you know of?

CHARLES LIVINGSTONE: Well, David, I don't know. Radio came at a time in the economy of the country when any kind of job was wanted. When radio forged ahead stronger out of the depression, there weren't as many stage shows being produced in New York. The stock companies died when the musician's strike started in 1929. That killed stock companies right across the country. The union said you had to have so many musicians on your payroll in order to open a theater, even if you didn't need them. With the death of stock companies, another means of making money for actors was wiped out. Actors were very happy to get radio work during those days even considering the low pay. When "The Lone Ranger" first started, we were getting $2.50 a performance. So, golly, when I was getting $17.50 or $25.00 a week, I thought I was really doing well. This was the 1930s, of course.

DAVID ROTHEL: How much of a budget did you have for "The Lone Ranger"?

CHARLES LIVINGSTONE: I had no set budget. It depended on the size of the cast.

DAVID ROTHEL: As simple as that!

CHARLES LIVINGSTONE: However, many of the actors were under contract.

DAVID ROTHEL: So there were actors under contract, writers under contract—.

CHARLES LIVINGSTONE: And I was under contract. If a good actor came along that I wanted,

A stern-looking Charles Livingstone is about to put his "Lone Ranger" radio cast through its paces prior to a broadcast. (circa early 1940s)

I would get him a contract. I got John Hodiak his first job in radio; he was getting $120.00 a month at General Motors working in the bookkeeping department or something. I think I got him for $130.00 a month. In order to hold this excellent company of radio actors together it was necessary to use them continuously. An actor might play a leading role on one program and a bit part on another, but he would get the same base pay. On each program, of course, there were the Lone Ranger and Tonto, but you also had to have a juvenile lead, an ingenue, a character woman, and several male character parts. These were script characters that you had to have for just about every program. During the war it was rough because so many of our regulars were in the service. I even had to go to New York once to audition some actors and bring them back to Detroit. One young fellow I tried-out, because we wanted an understudy for the Green Hornet, had a heart attack while he was auditioning. He died right on the spot. People were really up tight in those days. That was in 1942.

DAVID ROTHEL: Describe what your radio studio at WXYZ looked like. What was the physical set-up?

CHARLES LIVINGSTONE: Back in the early and mid-1930s the studio was a room about as large as a living room. A mike was hanging in the corner on a thing that we would now call a boom. There was a windowed booth off the studio where the technical man who operated the recordings was located. That was the whole place. No air conditioning. Tubs of ice with fans going kept us a little cooler during the heat of the summers. There were benches along the wall. We did make some changes when I became director. Up until that time the director was always in the studio with the actors. When Jim Jewell was there he was right in the studio. I had a booth built where the engineer, the technical man, and I were located.

DAVID ROTHEL: Technical means sound effects and music?

CHARLES LIVINGSTONE: Yes. Some time in the forties Trendle bought a place on East Jefferson, redid it, and made it into "The Lone Ranger" Studios where the program originated for the next ten years or so.

DAVID ROTHEL: In the early days where were the sound effects men located during a broadcast?

CHARLES LIVINGSTONE: Right in the studio with the actors. They used the same mike as the actors. Such sound effects as horses hooves, gun shots, and fist fights were all done live. In the beginning when there weren't any sound effects records, a car skidding on "The Green Hornet" was done by an effects man pursing his lips and blowing through them. He could really make it sound convincing. Some of the sound effects were taken right on the actor's mike by the actors . . . like striking a match. In later years at the new studios, doors opening and closing were done in a passageway between the sound studio and the actors' studio. That was called the hole. If there was any ad lib talk called for in the script, it was all done in this passageway. There was a mike there that could be opened or closed down depending on how much of the background talk you needed. I think it's interesting how the sound effect of horses' hooves developed over the years. We started with the sound man pounding his chest or knees with his fists; then we went to coconuts on boards or sand; then we went to plungers. Later, when we had recordings of horses' hooves, we would do the starting up of the horses live and then mix to a recording of the horses galloping. When it came time for the horses to stop, we would mix from the recording to the live effects. Another thing, David, that was absolutely wonderful to have in a radio studio for dramatic shows was an echo chamber. We had a tunnel built down in the basement of our new studio. At one end of the tunnel there was a speaker and at the other end a microphone. Depending on the amount of delay you wanted—echo you wanted—you placed the microphone closer or farther away from the speaker. The sound that was happening in the studio came out of the speaker in the tunnel and was picked up by the microphone at the other end of the tunnel and was then sent back into the same system. This process caused a little bit of a lag which resulted in the echo. That's the way we did echos in the early days.

DAVID ROTHEL: When I was a kid growing up listening to radio, there was no question in my mind that the music and sound effects used on "The Lone Ranger" were the best. When the Lone Ranger shot his gun, you knew you were hearing a very special gun.

CHARLES LIVINGSTONE: This was part of the use of the echo chamber. The gun shot effects developed from a rat trap sound to the shot pad to other things. We even tried actual guns, too. They just wouldn't work; there wasn't that re-

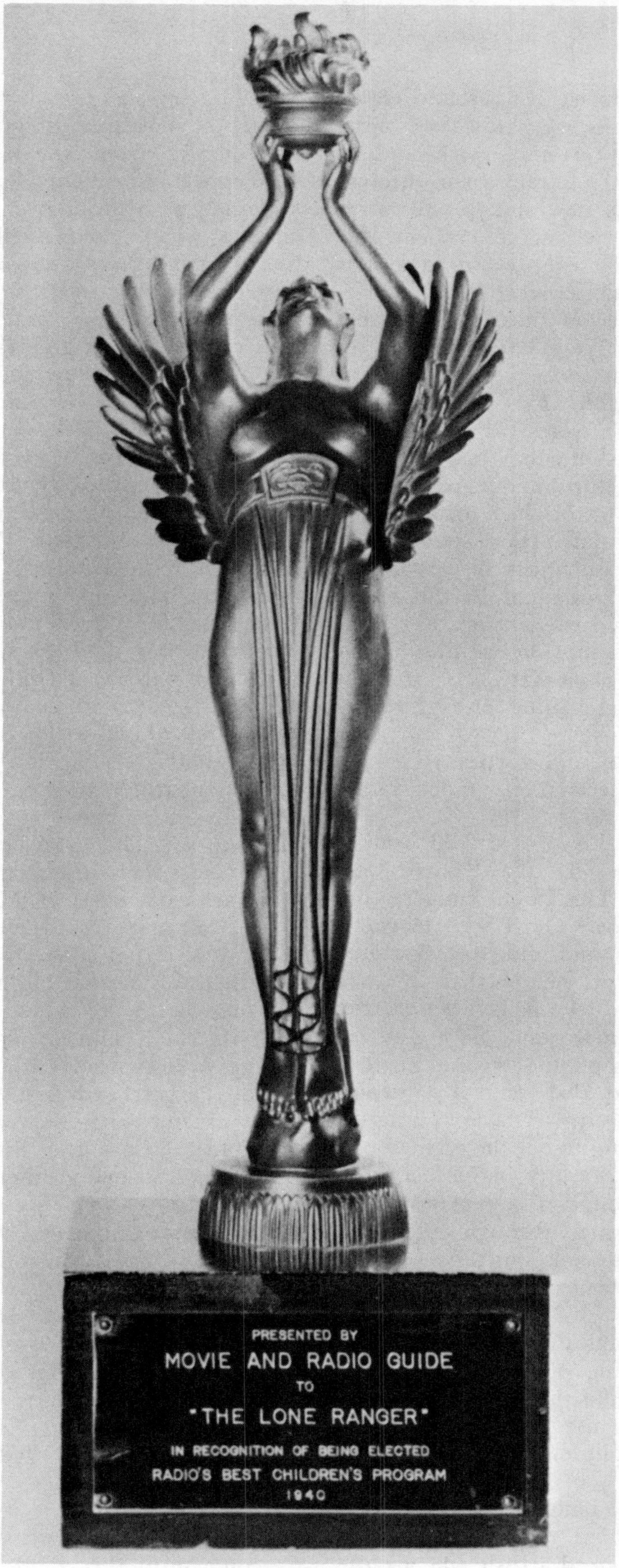

This trophy is only one of many awards "The Lone Ranger" program received during its many years on radio.

verberation we wanted. So we got a sound effects record with the best shots we could find. Fred Flowerday, my head sound man, picked them off the record, and then we ran them through the echo chamber. These new shot sounds were then our own; nobody had any like them. We made a master and when ever we needed new ones, we got them off the master.

DAVID ROTHEL: Didn't you once tell me that some radio people from New York came to see how you were doing gun shots?

CHARLES LIVINGSTONE: Oh, that was while Jim Jewell was still there. We were still using a shot pad at the time. In New York they had great big studios. They had the actors in one part of the same studio. Now, when actors had to talk softly because of a script situation and a sound effect suddenly came in, it wasn't just heard on the effects mike, it was also pulled in by the actors' mike, too. They had very little control over these things. If they had a gun shot, it just didn't have the feeling, the sense of a shot at all. It was due to the fact that they were using one great big studio.

DAVID ROTHEL: By the mid forties were you using recorded sound effects pretty much rather than doing them live?

CHARLES LIVINGSTONE: No, no. We walked footsteps live and things like that. There were no cars, of course, on "The Lone Ranger," but when we needed them for "The Green Hornet," we took our car effects and did special things with them through filters. Now that I think about it, as the recorded effects got better over time, we did use them more and more. But we didn't just use what was on the record, we took it and worked on it so that it really became something that was all our own. For instance, we had quite a time trying to get the right sound for the start of the Black Beauty, the Green Hornet's car. We took the sound of a car and ran it through a filter and then through the echo chamber. What came out was entirely different from what you would hear on a regular sound effects record.

DAVID ROTHEL: What was the sound effect that you used at the beginning of the program that was supposed to sound like the buzz of a bee or hornet? You know, it was used in the stock opening along with the "Flight of the Bumble Bee" music theme.

CHARLES LIVINGSTONE: That sound effect was created by using a Russian musical instrument called the theremin. It looked a little like a radio receiving set. An upright rod projected from the corner of a cabinet and a metal loop extended horizontally from the side. Sound vibrations were produced by moving your hands close to and then away from two high frequency electric circuits which used oscillating radio tubes. At first we tried the sounds of bees, wasps, and hornets in a bottle to get the effect. We had no way of controlling their sounds, so it was no good. You can see the engineers and the sound effects people had to be terrific, too. This was a technique they had to be trained in.

DAVID ROTHEL: Tell me about the stock company of actors that worked on "The Lone Ranger." Did they also work on "The Green Hornet" and "Challenge of the Yukon"?

CHARLES LIVINGSTONE: Yes, except the leads. Although John Todd who played Tonto, also in the early days, sometimes played the older Mr. Reid on "The Green Hornet." When he played Tonto, I also doubled him as an Englishman and other parts that could be played so that he was not recognized as the Lone Ranger's pal. During all those years Todd was also teaching drama in the Conservatory of Arts in Detroit.

DAVID ROTHEL: Did the company change very much over the years? I know the years I spent listening to "The Lone Ranger" it seemed those same voices were there all the time.

CHARLES LIVINGSTONE: That's right. Some of the actors were with the program for many years. Paul Hughes was a popular actor on the show. He was a great big guy with a husky voice, but then he could switch and play the character with the high squeaky voice. Fred Reto was a very gravelly-voiced little fellow. Jay Michael, Rollon Parker, Ted Johnstone, Mel Palmer, Bertha Forman, Ruth Dean Rickaby, Bea Leiblee, Malcolm McCoy, Bill Saunders, and Jack McCarthy and so many others were regulars in the cast.

DAVID ROTHEL: And each one, I'm sure, occasionally got to ask that famous question, "Who was that masked man?"

CHARLES LIVINGSTONE: Do you know that ending to the program wasn't started until after I took over the direction of the program. It was a sort of gimmick thing that Trendle had put into the script.

DAVID ROTHEL: Oh, that wasn't there originally?

CHARLES LIVINGSTONE: No. The "Who was that masked man?/ That was the Lone Ranger!" didn't come until the late 1930s or early '40s.

When the Lone Ranger Rides

This is what happens when someone in the Lone Ranger show gets ready to break up a fist fight with a six-shooter. Gibson Fox (left) is ready to make the sound of a shot by hitting a pillow with a stick; Fred Reto (center). is doing the shooting; Jack Petruzzi is socking Malcolm McCoy on the kisser, and Ernest Stanley makes the sound of a falling body by collapsing to the floor.

This posed publicity picture was an attempt to show what happens in the radio studio "When the Lone Ranger Rides." (circa late 1930s)

Cast, crew, and staff of "The Lone Ranger" radio program. (circa 1943) Front row, left to right: Three women, unknown; Gilbert Shea, actor; Bob Martin, actor, first Dan Reid; John Todd, Tonto; Brace Beemer, Lone Ranger; Charles D. Livingstone, director; Jimmy Fletcher, sound man and actor; Ernie Winstanley, actor; three women, unknown. Back row, left to right: First man, unknown; Rollon Parker, actor; Bertha Foreman, actress; man, unknown; Mel Palmer, actor; man, unknown; Bill Saunders, actor; Paul Hughes, actor; man, unknown; man, unknown; Fred Foy, narrator; Elaine Alpert, actress.

DAVID ROTHEL: Do you know how the "Hi-Yo, Silver" began?

CHARLES LIVINGSTONE: No, I don't. That was before my time.

DAVID ROTHEL: Fran Striker was the head writer on the series. Considering that you did three programs a week, how far in advance was he able to work?

CHARLES LIVINGSTONE: In the beginning, before I was director, I remember we'd sometimes get to the studio and have to wait for the script to come in. You would get a typed script with carbon copies. The poor actor who got the eighth or ninth carbon sometimes had a hard time getting through the script. Later on the scripts were run off on a ditto machine. By the time I became director, the operation was running along pretty smoothly and I'd usually get the scripts well in advance. I would have the scripts about two weeks before air date, so that I could cast for an entire week. Remember, we were doing three "Lone Ranger" programs and two "Green Hornets" each week. I had to do the casting, using the contract actors first and then filling in with other actors as needed to complete the cast.

DAVID ROTHEL: Was Fran Striker also scripting "The Green Hornet" at the same time he was writing "The Lone Ranger"?

CHARLES LIVINGSTONE: Yes, he started it . . . also "The Challenge of the Yukon" and "Ned Jordan, Federal Agent." At first he wrote the scripts for "The Lone Ranger" in Buffalo and sent them to Detroit. He didn't come to Detroit until after I was in the company. Fran started out for something like five thousand dollars a year and was making around fifty thousand dollars near the end of the series.

DAVID ROTHEL: Not too bad by the pay standards for those days, but the amount of responsibility he was assuming is staggering. How many writers did Striker have working under him?

CHARLES LIVINGSTONE: Oh, it would vary, but I would say three or four at any one time.

DAVID ROTHEL: Did one person write a script or did they all collaborate on one?

CHARLES LIVINGSTONE: I don't know for sure. I suspect that Fran would say to them, "Now, here's a plot; go develop it." When I got a script, it was in its completed form.

DAVID ROTHEL: All right, you have the script and you've cast it. Next would come the rehearsals.

CHARLES LIVINGSTONE: Well, we're missing something. I'd get the script and read it. If there were certain things in it I didn't like, I'd go to Fran and we'd get them straightened out. We'd argue back and forth as to whether it was right or wasn't right. I mean things like whether the script was too slow, if more action might be needed. Finally, we'd amicably come to a decision for the good of the program. We'd always laugh and say, "for the good of the program." That's the line Trendle always used with us to end a disagreement. We would have meetings at noon each day with Trendle in which we would talk about the scripts and criticize them. This was later on in the series, of course. Striker would have to take a hell of a lot during these meetings. When the script was finally okayed for production by Trendle, I got it for casting and timing.

DAVID ROTHEL: Did Trendle actually read every script?

CHARLES LIVINGSTONE: Once he sold the station and established his production company for "The Lone Ranger" and the other programs, he read every one of them . . . and so did his wife, a former high school English teacher. She would check to see that the Lone Ranger always spoke perfect English. Fran and I had some good laughs about some stuff. For example, the Lone Ranger might knock on a door and the person inside would say, "Who is it?" Mrs. Trendle would want the Lone Ranger to respond, "It is I." (laugh) Well, you just couldn't have a response like that in a program about the old West. So Fran would have to figure a way to get around the problem and still keep Trendle's wife happy.

DAVID ROTHEL: Now let's go into the rehearsals.

CHARLES LIVINGSTONE: We had four rehearsals during the three hours of rehearsal time we had for each program. All of the rehearsals, of course, were on the performance day. The first hour of rehearsal was for the setting of characters, giving cuts, and things like that. The head sound man was there making notes. Next was the timing rehearsal. This was with the actors. I did, of course allow time for sound effects and music bridges from scene to scene during the timing rehearsal. Meanwhile, the sound people were going over what they had to have ready for the program. During the timing rehearsal I would log the time at the beginning of the first scene and every fifteen seconds during the scene, and

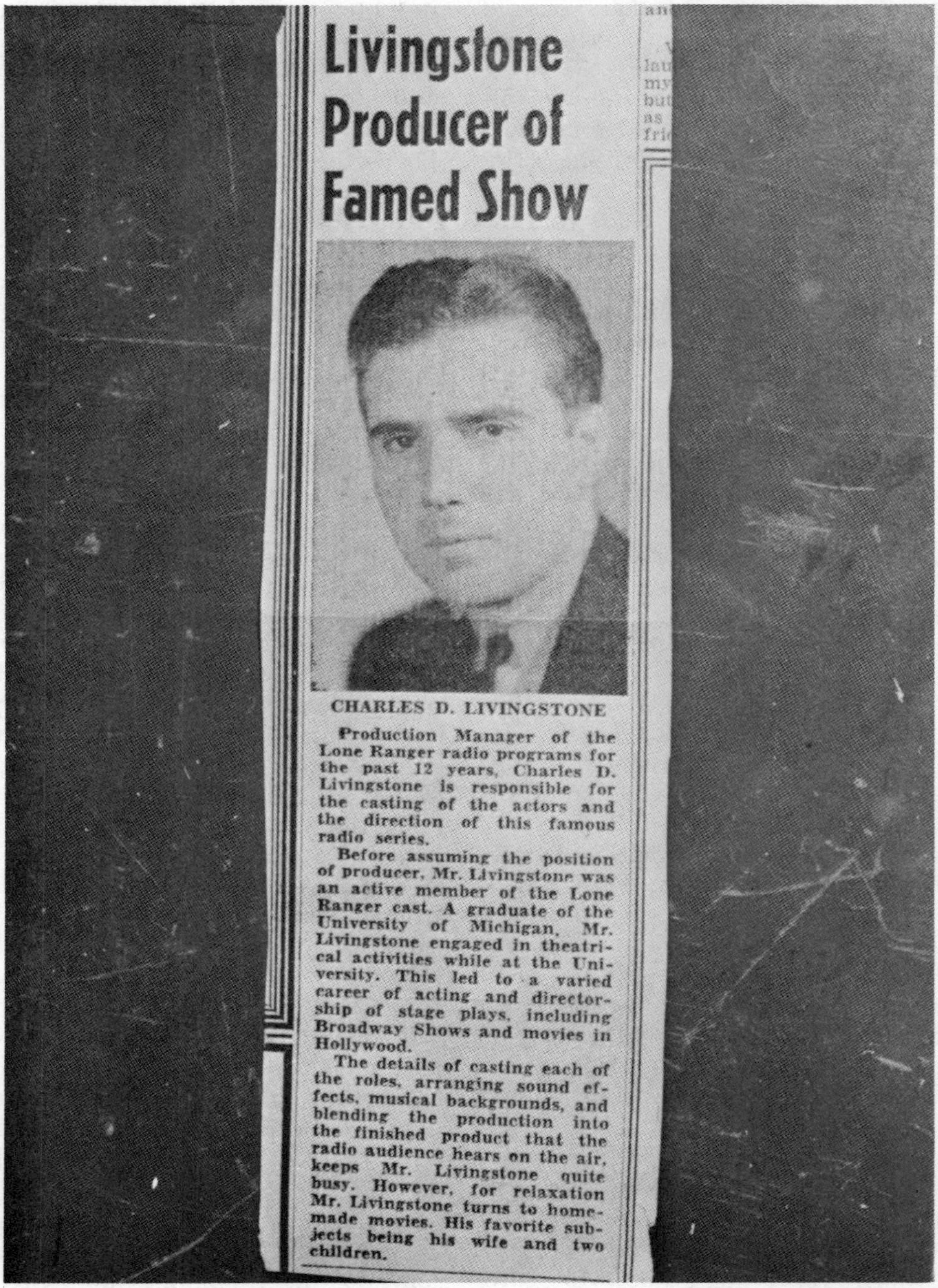

Livingstone Producer of Famed Show

CHARLES D. LIVINGSTONE

Production Manager of the Lone Ranger radio programs for the past 12 years, Charles D. Livingstone is responsible for the casting of the actors and the direction of this famous radio series.

Before assuming the position of producer, Mr. Livingstone was an active member of the Lone Ranger cast. A graduate of the University of Michigan, Mr. Livingstone engaged in theatrical activities while at the University. This led to a varied career of acting and directorship of stage plays, including Broadway Shows and movies in Hollywood.

The details of casting each of the roles, arranging sound effects, musical backgrounds, and blending the production into the finished product that the radio audience hears on the air, keeps Mr. Livingstone quite busy. However, for relaxation Mr. Livingstone turns to home-made movies. His favorite subjects being his wife and two children.

Livingstone was, of course, director of "The Lone Ranger," not producer. But then, people always have had trouble differentiating between the two titles.

at the end of the scene, allowing ten seconds for the music bridge before the next scene. We would continue like that throughout the script. At the end of the timing rehearsal the actors had about an hour off. During this time any cutting or adding to the script would be done. If we had to add anything, which we seldom had to do, we'd rush up to the writers and have them put something in. Also during that hour while the actors were off, the sound department and I got together and worked out the effects for the program. After that we got into our production rehearsal which lasted an hour. The production rehearsal was where you worked with the actors, sound, music, everything.

DAVID ROTHEL: And that was your last rehearsal.

CHARLES LIVINGSTONE: Until the dress rehearsal when the show was retimed. If you had added or cut anything, this was very important. During the dress rehearsal you had your announcer, commercials—the whole darned works. After the dress rehearsal you had about fifteen minutes left before the live network broadcast.

DAVID ROTHEL: So at 7:30 P.M. the broadcast went on the air. During the 1930s and most of the 1940s it went on live.

CHARLES LIVINGSTONE: And the fifties, too. It always went on live at 7:30 P.M. The only time we used tape was for repeats for the Midwest and Far West. We would do the live show at 7:30 P.M. The 8:30 P.M. and 10:30 repeats would be on tape. But that only started well into the 1940s.

DAVID ROTHEL: But during the thirties and part of the forties you had to do three different live broadcasts during the evening. Did the performers get paid for each of the broadcasts or did they just get a set amount for all of them. Now, I'm talking about the actors who weren't under contract.

CHARLES LIVINGSTONE: Well, in the beginning, before it went commercial, they only got a set amount for the three performances. When it went commercial, they got more. I know it developed until finally they were making about seventy dollars a show.

DAVID ROTHEL: For all three performances.

CHARLES LIVINGSTONE: Yes, but there weren't three. There weren't three live performances.

DAVID ROTHEL: Oh, yes. There was the original and the tapes. Approximately how many people were connected with any one program?

CHARLES LIVINGSTONE: Well, let's see. Let's say we have an average cast of actors—eight to ten—let's say ten. There would be the technical director, the engineer, four to five sound men, the narrator and the commercial announcer. With me there would be approximately seventeen to twenty people.

DAVID ROTHEL: This company worked together daily. Would you describe it as a happy company? Did they get along together well?

CHARLES LIVINGSTONE: I was the only person who didn't get along. (laugh) No, I'm kidding. They usually got along very well; there wasn't much trouble. Brace Beemer, the Lone Ranger, was a very temperamental type of guy. He was the star, definitely the star. Just before I left the program and went to Hollywood Brace often wouldn't be there for the first reading. I wanted him there for the timing rehearsal because his tempo was necessary. He'd be there, of course, for the production rehearsal. Paul Sutton was his understudy and would read the lines for the rehearsals that Brace missed.

DAVID ROTHEL: After doing the role for so many years, Brace probably had the feeling that he could do it in his sleep.

CHARLES LIVINGSTONE: Sure. Brace was himself in the role.

DAVID ROTHEL: Was there any rivalry among the three shows—"The Lone Ranger," "The Green Hornet," and "Challenge of the Yukon"?

CHARLES LIVINGSTONE: No.

DAVID ROTHEL: Was there any ego business between the actors and the technical crews?

CHARLES LIVINGSTONE: Oh, hell no. No! No! There was nothing like that. The technical people were just as important as the actors, and the actors knew it. I don't think they were getting paid as much as the actors, at least some of them weren't.

DAVID ROTHEL: How many weeks a year did you do "The Lone Ranger" program?

CHARLES LIVINGSTONE: Fifty-two.

DAVID ROTHEL: You must have had a vacation sometime.

CHARLES LIVINGSTONE: My assistant would take over when I was on a three-week vacation.

DAVID ROTHEL: What about the actors?

CHARLES LIVINGSTONE: They just wouldn't be in it now and then. The leads were always there. Tonto did get sick a couple of times, and Frank Russell or one of the other actors took over for him. You know, John was in his late fifties or early sixties when the series began.

DAVID ROTHEL: Did John Todd, Tonto, live

through the run of the program?

CHARLES LIVINGSTONE: Yes, it was off the air when he died.

DAVID ROTHEL: Did you get much mail on the program?

CHARLES LIVINGSTONE: Oh, yes.

DAVID ROTHEL: Was it in the form of fan mail?

CHARLES LIVINGSTONE: And complaints. There was one very sad letter from a mother who told about her little boy who had been playing the Lone Ranger at the top of a flight of stairs. He got tangled up in a rope, fell down the stairs, and was killed. Trendle always tried to be very careful to avoid things in the scripts that might be dangerous for kids to emulate.

DAVID ROTHEL: George Seaton commented to me about having a bad cold once during the time he was playing the Lone Ranger, and that Striker wrote into the script that the Lone Ranger was wounded and that Tonto dragged him into a cave and attempted to save his life. Seaton says that they got many letters from listeners making suggestions on how to get him well again. This just seems unbelievable; I mean for people (listeners) to take the story line that seriously and to write in. In George W. Trendle's biography he says that while "The Green Hornet" was on the air, people actually wrote in wanting the Green Hornet to come to their communities to rout evildoers. I didn't believe it when I read it in the Trendle biography, but now when George Seaton tells me almost the same thing, I can't deny it, I guess.

CHARLES LIVINGSTONE: I would support Seaton and Trendle that listeners believed these things—absolutely.

DAVID ROTHEL: Let's talk about the actors who played the Lone Ranger on radio. The first one was. . . .

CHARLES LIVINGSTONE: I don't know for sure; I wasn't there at the time. There is some confusion about that.

DAVID ROTHEL: Well, George Seaton says that as far as he knows he was the first.

CHARLES LIVINGSTONE: Trendle in his book, mentions a man named Deeds and also Seaton as being among the first to play the role. The program started, as I mentioned before, in January of 1933, and I got there in August. Now during that time there may have been a number of different actors used. I just don't know. Jimmy Jewell might be able to help you out on that question. George Seaton, though, was one of the first Lone Rangers, if not the first. He is a wonderful man. My wife knows George better than I do; they both attended Jessie Bonstelle's drama school in 1930. His name at that time was George Stenius. [Author's note: In subsequent conversations with Jim Jewell, he confirmed that George Seaton was, indeed, the original Lone Ranger.]

DAVID ROTHEL: What can you tell me about Earle Graser?

CHARLES LIVINGSTONE: Next to Brace Beemer, Earle played the role longer than anyone. He started playing the part just a couple of months before I came with the program in August of '33. I don't know how they found him for the role. He was at first a student at Detroit City College which was right near the studio. He was a relatively slight person in build. He had a deep, resonant voice, a nice personality—very pleasant guy. He and his wife bought a farm house out in Farmington and started to raise horses. He fell asleep driving on his way home from the studio one night and was killed in a car accident.

DAVID ROTHEL: Abel Green and Joe Laurie, Jr. in their book *Show Biz* say that "over one thousand people paid him [Graser] a last tribute in Detroit." Jim Harmon in his fine book *The Great Radio Heroes* says that "ten thousand people attended his funeral." I suspect that someone either dropped or added a zero.

CHARLES LIVINGSTONE: From where he lived in Farmington to where he was buried at the corner of Telegraph Road and Grand River, there was a bunch of kids lined up along the road to see the procession. I don't feel there were ten thousand people, but it was a big funeral.

DAVID ROTHEL: You were there then.

CHARLES LIVINGSTONE: Yes, I was in one of the cars; I was a pallbearer.

DAVID ROTHEL: Let's see, that was in 1941 when Earle Graser died and Brace Beemer took over the part of the Lone Ranger.

CHARLES LIVINGSTONE: Now there's a story about that. When I started in 1933, Brace was station manager and narrator on "The Lone Ranger." Then Brace left the program to go to an advertising agency. Sometime after 1938 when we were interested in finding a new voice to play the lead in "Challenge of the Yukon," I suggested Brace as a possibility to Mr. Trendle. We contacted him and he was interested. It was a stroke of luck for us, because when Graser was killed, we had our experienced leading man who made a switch from Sergeant Preston to the Lone Ranger.

DAVID ROTHEL: *Time* magazine, in a story it ran at the time of Earle Graser's death, indicated that Brace Beemer played the Lone Ranger immediately after George Seaton, before Earle Graser started. *The Big Broadcast* by Buxton and Owen shows that Brace Beemer was the narrator at one time, but does not indicate that he played the Lone Ranger prior to the death of Earle Graser. What is your knowledge of this? Did Brace play the Ranger prior to taking over at Graser's death?

CHARLES LIVINGSTONE: Now remember, I was not there, but I never heard of Brace playing it prior to Graser's death. As I said, Brace was the narrator when I arrived in August. Seaton told you he played the part for four or five months starting in January. This means that Brace would have played the Ranger and done the narration in a period of just a couple of months. It seems highly unlikely.

DAVID ROTHEL: Chuck, what kind of a person was Brace Beemer?

CHARLES LIVINGSTONE: Well, he was a mixture of a lot of things. Physically, he was a handsome, big man. When he walked into a room, you knew he was there. He was a John Wayne type in this sense. If he liked you and you did the things he wanted, he'd give you the shirt off his back. But if he wanted something and you wouldn't give it to him, he was tough. In any gathering you could be sure that he would be the center of attention. He was it! He had charisma!

DAVID ROTHEL: Was he a wealthy man?

CHARLES LIVINGSTONE: I think he had a background of money. He certainly had a lot more money than we did.

DAVID ROTHEL: Did Beemer have any children?

CHARLES LIVINGSTONE: He had two wonderful boys and a daughter. One of his sons became "Justice Colt" on a radio program on another station.

DAVID ROTHEL: Billy Bletcher, the performer and voice animator, says that Trendle brought him (Bletcher) to Detroit in 1950 for three hundred dollars a week to understudy Brace Beemer. In *The Real Tinsel* by Bernard Rosenberg and Harry Silverstein, Bletcher says that he stayed in Detroit for about eight months covering for Beemer who was sick a lot. When Beemer was there, Bletcher indicates he played character parts on "The Green Hornet" and "The Lone Ranger." Chuck, what can you tell me about this?

CHARLES LIVINGSTONE: Well, it's a long time ago, but I certainly can *never* remember having Billy Bletcher play the Lone Ranger on the air. I don't remember any time that Brace was so sick he couldn't play the part.

DAVID ROTHEL: But Bletcher was an understudy.

CHARLES LIVINGSTONE: Yes. You see, I was having auditions in Detroit for an understudy when unbeknownst to me Mr. Trendle hired Bletcher. I didn't know at the time that Bletcher had done some voice dubbing of the Lone Ranger role in the 1930s movie serials. Bletcher did have a very similar voice to Beemer's, but I do not remember ever having him play the Lone Ranger on the air.

DAVID ROTHEL: It's sort of incongruous to imagine little 5 feet 2½ inch Billy Bletcher riding the mighty Silver and shouting "Hi-Yo, Silver, Away."

CHARLES LIVINGSTONE: Did you know that the "Hi-Yo, Silver, away" signature at the end of the radio program wasn't Brace's voice much of the time.

DAVID ROTHEL: It wasn't?

CHARLES LIVINGSTONE: It was the recorded voice of Earle Graser. Brace never did get it down as well as Earle. Graser's voice was also used for the endings of the television programs. Brace did say it, of course, within the radio scripts. But he said, "Hi-Yo, Silver" a lot more times than he said, "Hi-Yo, Silver, away." He had difficulty getting that "away" shouted with the proper inflection. Near the end of the radio series we put in Brace's voice more of the time for the closing, but a lot of the time we just rolled in the recording of Earle's voice.

DAVID ROTHEL: You told me one time that the Lone Ranger and the Green Hornet were related. Could you go over that genealogy again?

CHARLES LIVINGSTONE: Nobody ever knew the Lone Ranger's first name despite the fact that some writers claim it was John; his last name was Reid. You know the story of how the Lone Ranger came to be—the Cavendish Gang ambushed the six Texas Rangers and only one survived who became the Lone Ranger. Well, in that same ambush the Lone Ranger's brother, a captain in the Rangers, was killed. The brother had a son, Dan. Later in the radio series the writers developed the character of Dan Reid,

Director's Young Son His Guide on Thrillers

A director of children's radio dramas not only must be a director but a child psychologist, says Chuck Livingstone, who directs "The Lone Ranger" and other children's serials, at WXYZ. Chuck finds the reactions of his own son, Russell, a good guide.

Livingstone

Recently a script had a small boy calling from the second floor of a house to the Lone Ranger and his Indian friend, Tonto, who were supposed to be on the building's ground floor. The Ranger urged the boy to hurry down the stairs, but Tonto suggested he could get there quicker by jumping. Tonto's line was cut, and the Ranger's advice left intact.

"Too suggestive for youngsters," explains Director Livingstone.

Another time, a mother, leaving her young son for the night, reminded him to wash his face and ears before going to bed, and the boy replied:

"I promise to wash—TOMORROW."

The line was cut to, "I promise!"

Too many juvenile listeners might have followed the actions, or words, of the boy in the radio drama too literally.

New WJLB Announcers

There have been several additions at the WJLB announcing staff recently. Charles Layton and Bill Morgan are new, Morgan being a WCAR Pontiac alumnus. A junior announcer, from Wayne University speech class, Merrill Wared, is doing part-time work for the station.

the Lone Ranger's nephew. "The Lone Ranger" series took place in the 1880s. "The Green Hornet" was a contemporary series in the 1930s. Dan Reid was the father of Britt Reid who was the Green Hornet. So that means that Britt Reid, the Green Hornet, is the Lone Ranger's grand nephew. See if this doesn't boggle your mind: John Todd who played Tonto on "The Lone Ranger" also played Dan Reid (father of the Green Hornet, Britt Reid) on "The Green Hornet." Therefore, besides being the Lone Ranger's faithful Indian companion, he was also the Lone Ranger's nephew grown old. (laugh) Have you got that?"

DAVID ROTHEL: Trendle and Striker planned this relationship, then.

CHARLES LIVINGSTONE: Yes, they wanted the Green Hornet to be the modern-day counterpart of the Lone Ranger, so what better way to do it than to make them relatives.

DAVID ROTHEL: The characters on "The Lone Ranger" were so interestingly named. Butch Cavendish . . . Thunder Martin. . . .

CHARLES LIVINGSTONE: There was a character I played for years called Black Bart. There was a popular female character named Mustang Mag. A lot of them I've forgotten.

DAVID ROTHEL: Did you have ratings to contend with in those days?

CHARLES LIVINGSTONE: Ratings? They were important, but I never heard too much about them. Nobody ever said, "Look, Livingstone, we dropped down to here and something must be done." There came a time when "The Lone Ranger" reached a peak and then started to gently go down. But this was happening to radio. When television came up in the 1950s, we knew things weren't as good as they had been.

DAVID ROTHEL: You said, "when it reached its peak." Which were those peak years in your mind?

CHARLES LIVINGSTONE: Well, I would say—not because I started directing it in 1938—that the peak years were from 1938 to 1945.

DAVID ROTHEL: To what would you attribute the gradual decline after that?

CHARLES LIVINGSTONE: Gee, I don't know for sure. I suppose television coming in. I don't think the radio programs really declined in quality. The stories remained good; the production remained the same.

DAVID ROTHEL: Were you ever concerned about cancellation during the run of the radio series?

CHARLES LIVINGSTONE: No. It was always firmly sponsored right up until 1955. If we were in any danger of cancellation, I didn't hear about it. I only worried about the possible cancellation of my contract as director with Trendle. I worried about that every two years; I had a two-year contract. I could have made three times what I was making with Trendle, but, David, why did I become a director rather than stay an actor? It was because I wanted security for my family—for my kids and wife. An actor's life was sort of a gypsy existence. That's why radio when it came along was a blessing for me. It enabled Harriet and me to settle down in one place and to have a family.

DAVID ROTHEL: Did you ever feel that you were directing a program that was becoming a classic?

CHARLES LIVINGSTONE: Not that it was becoming a classic. But you could tell by the ratings how it was going up by leaps and bounds. Probably an even better index of the program's popularity was the greatly increased response to each new give-away. Of course, Trendle had publicity starting to build it up and up to something greater than it probably was. No, if we had thought it was going to become a classic, we'd have saved all those silver bullets and some of the scripts. In the early days they pretty much ignored us in New York on radio ratings. "The Lone Ranger," which was coming from a little station out in the provinces, wasn't talked about as being big-time radio. As "The Lone Ranger's" popularity grew, it forced them to recognize us. I think "The Lone Ranger" became—like a lot of things in life—far more important as we looked back on it, as you're doing now.

DAVID ROTHEL: Was there a sense of doom around the radio studios during the late forties and early fifties?

CHARLES LIVINGSTONE: Not in the late 1940s; it was in the fifties. I started to wonder what I should do. There were whisperings about the fact that radio drama was dying. One day Trendle came to me very quietly for a meeting. He said, "Look, radio has about reached its end as we've known it. How would you like to go to the Coast and supervise the television production of "The Lone Ranger" and be the television coordinator?" I said I was very interested in the job. I told Mr. Trendle that I had always been interested in motion picture direction and asked him if I might eventually be able to direct some of the television programs, assuming I was able

Russell Livingstone (the director's son) at six years of age in 1944, wearing the official Lone Ranger outfit.

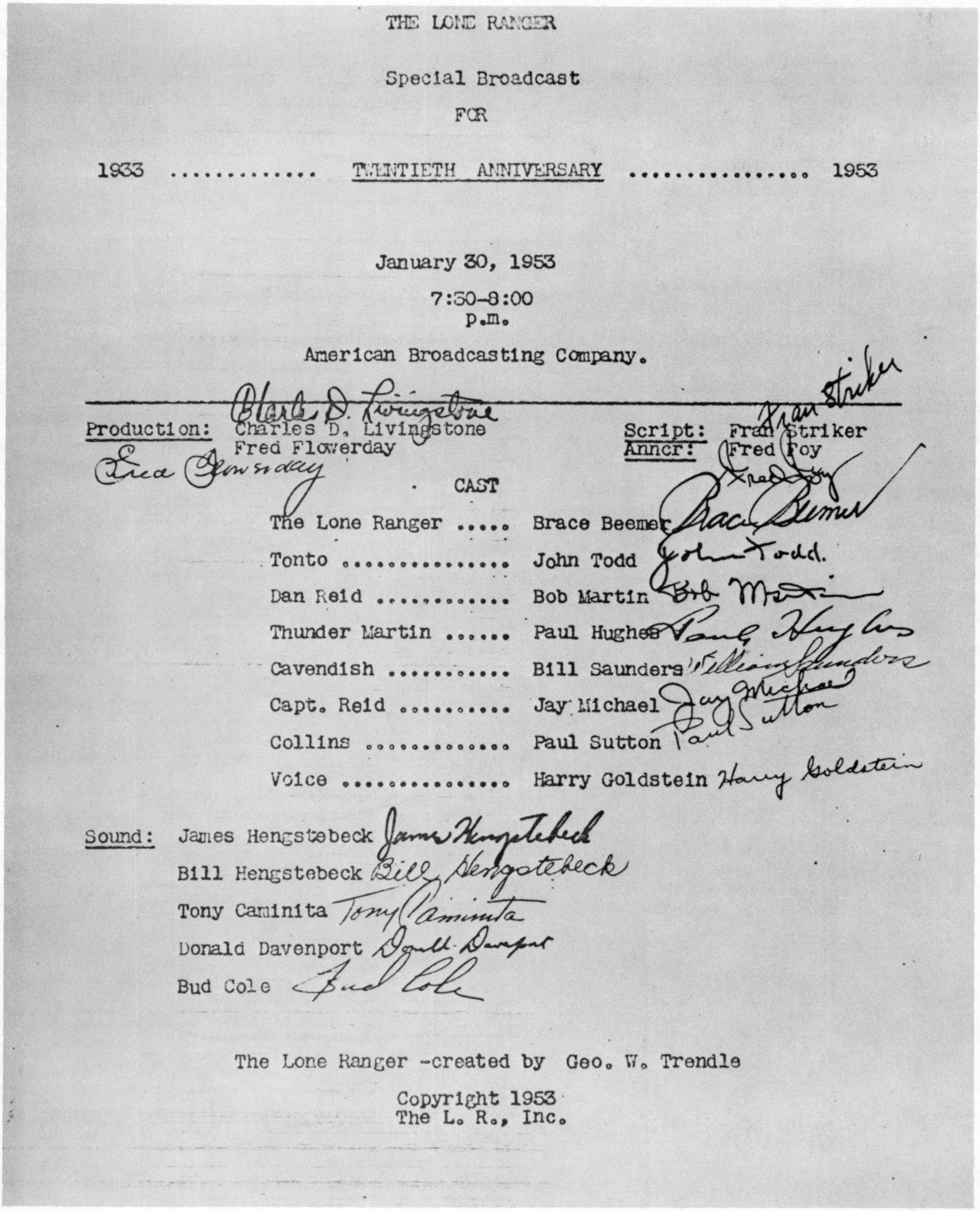

THE LONE RANGER

Special Broadcast

FOR

1933 .... TWENTIETH ANNIVERSARY 1953

January 30, 1953

7:30-8:00
p.m.

American Broadcasting Company.

Production: Charles D. Livingstone
Fred Flowerday

Script: Fran Striker
Anncr: Fred Foy

CAST

The Lone Ranger	Brace Beemer
Tonto	John Todd
Dan Reid	Bob Martin
Thunder Martin	Paul Hughes
Cavendish	Bill Saunders
Capt. Reid	Jay Michael
Collins	Paul Sutton
Voice	Harry Goldstein

Sound: James Hengstebeck
Bill Hengstebeck
Tony Caminita
Donald Davenport
Bud Cole

The Lone Ranger -created by Geo. W. Trendle

Copyright 1953
The L. R., Inc.

The above twentieth anniversary souvenir "Call Sheet" was autographed by all of "The Lone Ranger" cast and crew.

to soak up enough information and had the ability. He said he was sure he could arrange it with Jack Chertok, the producer.

DAVID ROTHEL: How long did the radio show last after you left and went to Hollywood?

CHARLES LIVINGSTONE: I left in early 1954, and the program was over in 1955. I don't know what part of 1955. My assistant, Fred Flowerday, became director when I left and he stayed with the show until it ended. [Author's note: Actually the live program only lasted until September 3, 1954.]

4
"Why, *He's* the Lone Ranger"

GEORGE SEATON— THE FIRST LONE RANGER

IN a long and prestigious career George Seaton has successfully touched most show business bases: acting, writing, producing, and directing. He has put these talents to use in the theater, radio, and motion pictures. He is, of course, most famous for his film work. His pictures range from the madcap *A Day at the Races* with the Marx Brothers (he had a hand in writing it) to writing and directing the delightfully sentimental *Miracle on 34th Street*. For *Country Girl* with Bing Crosby and Grace Kelly he wrote the screenplay, co-produced with William Pearlberg, and directed Miss Kelly to her Academy Award. In 1969 he wrote the screenplay for and directed a goldmine called *Airport*. Now in his mid-sixties and still active, Mr. Seaton responded to my queries from his office at Universal studios.

DAVID ROTHEL: Mr. Seaton, were you or Jack Deeds the first to play the Lone Ranger?

GEORGE SEATON: This Jack Deeds is a mystery man to me as well as to many others. Strangely enough I never heard of Jack Deeds until a few years ago when others engaged in the same research as you are mentioned his name. During the time I played the Lone Ranger, I never once heard him referred to either by the production staff or the other members of the cast who were engaged before I was. Since similar inquiries have come to me in recent years, I talked to James Jewell, the originator, producer, and director of the show to try to settle the question. He told me that Deeds was one of the actors who had auditioned before I did but never played the part in a broadcast. I also checked with Ruth Rickaby who played the women's parts and was hired before I was. She had no recollection of anyone named Deeds. Unfortunately, Ruth died recently so that source of information is no longer available. I understand that Deeds might have done a "pilot" for management to listen to, but so far as I know, I was the first to play the part on the air.

DAVID ROTHEL: How did you happen to be cast in the role?

GEORGE SEATON: I auditioned. Having worked in Jessie Bonstelle's stock company in Detroit, I was known by those who were working in the local entertainment field. Consequently I was contacted among many others to try out for the role.

DAVID ROTHEL: How long did you play the part?

GEORGE SEATON: About six months, maybe seven or eight. [Author's note: It could not have been quite that long because Earle Graser took over the role on April 16, 1933; the show began on or near January 30, 1933.]

DAVID ROTHEL: Do you remember what your salary as a radio actor was in those days?

During the early years of the radio series there were only a few photographs distributed of an actor playing the Lone Ranger. Instead, this painting and others similar to it were often used for promotion of the program.

GEORGE SEATON: I certainly do. I received fifteen dollars a week. For that amount I not only played the Lone Ranger three times a week but played parts in "The Manhunters" and in an afternoon show called "Tee Time." We had sort of a radio stock company and were subject to call for any program on the air.

DAVID ROTHEL: *The Filmgoer's Companion* by Leslie Halliwell states that you joined the MGM writing staff in 1933, the same year you played the Lone Ranger. Could you relate the circumstances surrounding this seemingly sudden change in your activities?

GEORGE SEATON: If memory serves me correctly (and many times it doesn't) I was hired for "The Lone Ranger" in late 1932. During 1931 I was acting in the road company of *Elizabeth, The Queen.* I returned to Detroit for Christmas of that year to be with my family. Jessie Bonstelle asked me to return to the stock company, which I did. During 1932 I also wrote a play entitled *Together We Two* which I directed and produced in The Little Theatre. After its run I sent the play to my agent, Leah Salsbury in New York. Nothing happened for quite a time. Feeling that the play was a dead duck, I took the Lone Ranger job at WXYZ. In June or July of 1933 I heard from Leah Salsbury that a producer had become interested in *Together We Two* and advised me to come to New York the first part of August. A Broadway production of the play fell through but Sam Marx who was head of the Story Department at MGM read it and offered me a contract to write for that studio under the personal supervision of Irving Thalberg. On August 23, 1933, I left for Hollywood.

DAVID ROTHEL: Do you have any remembrances, anecdotes of those early radio days, Lone Ranger or otherwise, that you would care to mention?

GEORGE SEATON: Oh, yes, I remember many things about the early days. At that time there were no union rules. Consequently, we didn't have any sound effects men. All of us in the cast had to do our own sound effects, with a script in one hand and paraphernalia in the other. The sound of the horses hooves I supplied by banging coconut shells on a rubber mat. The sound of a raging fire was supplied by crinkling a piece of cellophane close to the microphone, and every time the Lone Ranger fought with anybody I was pounding my fist on my chest. After a time we all became pretty secure in our roles (often I played other characters on the program by changing my voice) and we used to merely run through the script with one quick rehearsal and then go on the air immediately following. One thing that might be of interest to you was how we discovered we had an audience. You must remember in those first months we were not sponsored and we didn't know whether anyone was listening to us or not. On one occasion I developed a heavy cold so the script was changed to have me shot by an outlaw and dragged into a cave by Tonto. For two performances I was monosyllabic and the cold seemed to exude a feeling of pain. To our great surprise the studio was soon flooded with flowers, candy, letters, and telegrams wishing me well. The audience was not only there, but obviously they took the whole thing rather seriously. Some of the letters went into great detail as to how I could be cured; many contained home remedies of certain kinds of applications which would draw out the infection from the wound. It was then that the studio realized that they had a viable show on their hands and began to search for a sponsor. It took a little time because in those days companies still thought the best advertising was newspapers. However, Silvercup Bread became the sponsor and I was implored to stay on. The enticement was a raise of five dollars a week. However I had had enough of "Hi-Yo, Silver" and went on to New York.

EARLE W. GRASER—
THE IMPROBABLE LONE RANGER

The rich, vibrant voice comes out of the radio speaker into homes around the country. Each person who hears the voice has his own mental image of the face and body that belong to the voice—and no two images are the same. Since the first human voice was sent through the air as if by magic to a distant radio speaker, radio listeners have expressed surprise, disappointment, and, sometimes, outright disbelief upon first seeing their radio favorites in person or in photographs. What the voice has caused the mind to conjure seldom resembles the actual physical person. The phenomenon almost always occurs and we are almost always surprised at ourselves for allowing our minds to trick us again.

George W. Trendle realized the game the human mind plays each time it hears a new voice on the radio; he knew that each set of ears

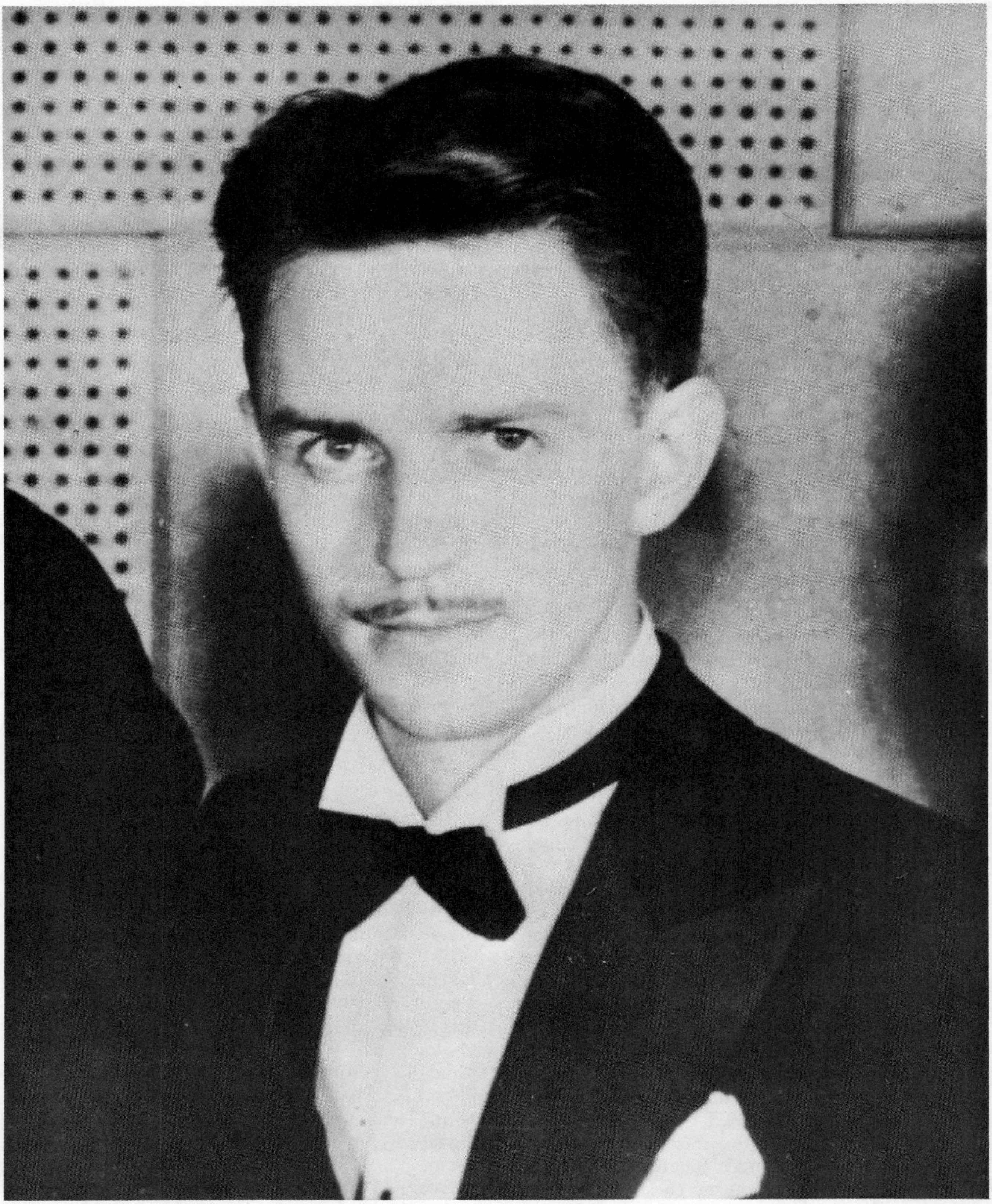

Earle Graser, the improbable Lone Ranger, who played the role for eight years on radio.

would be absorbing the words of the radio actor playing the Lone Ranger, and the mind between those ears would be creating a mask-covered face and a body for that voice. Trendle rightly felt that there should be an aura of mystery about the Lone Ranger, that the actor playing the part on radio should sublimate himself to the part and receive no personal publicity so that the listener would have only the illusion created by his own mind. Trendle felt that this illusion would be dissipated if the actor as a person were too familiar to the listener.

So it was that when George Seaton left the program in April of 1933, George W. Trendle looked for the right voice for the Lone Ranger and worried little about the appearance of the actor. According to Trendle, he tested the voices of some of the men in the regular company of actors at the station. One of the voices pleased him very much. It was rich, deep, vibrant, and rang with authority. Surprisingly, this extraordinary voice was housed in the twenty-four-year-old body of an inexperienced actor named Earle W. Graser. Even though no one had paid much attention to young Graser up to this time, Trendle felt that he could play the part and immediately cast him as the Lone Ranger. (Jim Jewell in his account, remember, maintains Graser was not a member of the Jewell Players at the time and that he [Jewell] found Graser in a Wayne State University drama class and cast him in the part.)

Earle Graser's background bore little hint that he would someday portray a western hero. Born in Kitchener, Ontario, Graser and his family moved to Detroit where he attended high school. After high school he went to Detroit City College, which is now Wayne State University, where he studied drama, oratory, and interpretive reading. He graduated with a bachelor of arts degree. (During the time he played the Lone Ranger he continued his studies at the graduate level in the field of law. He really didn't plan to become a lawyer, but found the study fascinating as a hobby.)

Graser made his first professional appearance on a stage in 1928 at the Michigan Theater. He had three responsibilities for each performance: to usher the audience to its seats, to announce each organ selection as it came up, and to play an Alpine shepherd boy for each stage show. An ironic coincidence was that the musical theme for the stage show was the "William Tell Overture." For fulfilling these varied responsibilities the young neophyte was paid the sum of eighteen dollars a week.

By 1931 he was doing two-night stands throughout Michigan with a tent show. *Your Uncle Dudley* alternated with *The Haunted House* as the stellar attractions. But the gypsy life did not appeal to Graser so he drifted back to Detroit, and in April of 1933 was selected to play the Lone Ranger.

Certainly an unlikely candidate to portray the Lone Ranger, Graser had never been west of Michigan, had shot a pistol only once, and didn't know how to ride a horse. His one affiliation with horseflesh up to that time got him a nickname that stayed with him over the years. There was a horse by the name of Barney that pulled a grocery wagon past the family home when he was young. Graser, who had always wanted a nickname, told his father to call him Barney after the plug horse. His father did—from then on!

Physically, Graser bore little resemblance to the character he played. He was relatively slight of build and did not appear to be athletically inclined, although he did enjoy swimming and badminton. Instead of riding the range on a mighty stallion, Graser preferred gardening and looked forward to the day when he could afford to buy a farm in Connecticut. (Portraying the Lone Ranger may have spurred an interest in horses because around 1940 he did buy a farm in suburban Farmington, Michigan, and began to raise horses as a sideline and hobby.)

In his personal life Earle Graser was to the Lone Ranger what Clark Kent was to Superman—a mild-mannered, likable, unassuming counterpart who did not reveal his other, more colorful existence. Over the years Graser's natural shyness and quiet manner sometimes caused strangers or casual acquaintances to feel that he was somewhat aloof. Most of his neighbors hardly knew him, much less knew that millions had begun to listen to his now-famous voice on three nationwide radio broadcasts each week. Probably his closest friend was the much older character actor, John Todd, who played Tonto on the broadcasts. Quite often after the West Coast broadcast, the two of them would get together at one or the other's home for a game of cards, a smoke, and a drink.

It was the good life for Earle Graser—he was the star of a popular radio program, but he was able to avoid the bothersome aspects of fame because he had no great wish for personal recognition. He and his wife, Jeanne, lived very

This was an often times misleading photograph (circa 1934) of some of the members of the "Jewell Players." The picture is misleading in that Brace Beemer (wearing mask) was not playing the Lone Ranger at the time. The shorter man to Beemer's left with the mustache, Earle Graser, was the voice of the Lone Ranger and would remain so for many years. Ironically, Beemer ultimately succeeded Graser and played the role longer than any other actor.

According to Jim Jewell, the picture, which was taken in fun during a picture-taking session, was only meant to be a joke on Brace Beemer who was taking very seriously the business of the hat, mask, and gun much to the dismay of the others. Jewell also maintains that the original concept of the Lone Ranger called for a kerchief mask that covered the bottom portion of the face. This mask, which just happened to be around the studio, was used for the "joke picture" with no thought that people would take it seriously as the Lone Ranger mask.

Others pictured from left to right are: Jack Lawrence, who played the lead in "Curly Edwards and His Cowboys," out of which (according to Jim Jewell) "The Lone Ranger" evolved; John Todd, Tonto; Ruth Rickaby (seated left); Bruce Gregory; Beemer; Graser; Fred Reto; Leonore Allman (seated right); Malcolm McCoy.

comfortably on the $150 a week he eventually made as the Lone Ranger. He was well-liked by the studio personnel and his fellow actors. He was dependable—in well over three thousand broadcasts he never missed a performance. He was a quick study in the part and usually had his lines under control after the first rehearsal. Fran Striker knew his one verbal weakness—the word *probably*—and avoided it in scripts since Graser invariably stumbled over it.

In his own quiet way he had a self-effacing sense of humor and enjoyed telling stories on himself. One of his favorites concerned the time he and his wife attended a performance of Horace Heidt and his orchestra at a nightclub. During the show Heidt offered a prize to the person in the audience who could shout the Lone Ranger's cry of "Hi-Yo, Silver" most nearly like the radio Lone Ranger. Graser didn't even come close to winning. (Interestingly, as noted elsewhere, Graser's recorded "Hi-Yo, Silver, away!" was used for years after his death as the final signature on the radio *and* television series because future actors in the part never could get the inflection on "away" as well as Graser did.)

As the founder of the Lone Ranger Safety Club, Graser had broadcast many appeals for safe driving. (A few years earlier he had been greatly embarrassed when the day following a particularly vigorous appeal for careful driving he had been arrested for speeding.) It was, therefore, sadly ironic that while driving home near dawn on an early April morning in 1941, as his car passed the Methodist Church in Farmington, he apparently dropped off to sleep, allowing his car to crash head-on into the back of a parked truck. As *Time* rather callously reported: "So died a rootin', tootin', shootin', hell-for-leather buckaroo—radio's Lone Ranger."

Because the actor behind the mask, Earle Graser, was so little known, many of the obituaries were made to sound as if the Lone Ranger had died rather than the actor who portrayed him. Even the *New York Times* took note editorially of the passing of this relatively little known man, but stated their words in a sort of "the king is dead; long live the king" manner:

> The Lone Ranger, under that name, came into being in this generation for a radio public, but under various names he has been alive for many centuries. He was Ulysses, William Tell and Robin Hood; he was Richard the Lionhearted, the Black Prince and Du Guesclin; he was Kit Carson, Daniel Boone and Davey Crockett; he was honest, truthful and brave—and so he remains.

The sudden death of Earle W. Graser posed an immediate and serious problem for the program. The sudden shock of a new voice for the Lone Ranger could be alarming for the huge listening audience and had the possibility of doing long-term harm to the program. After hurried meetings of the staff at WXYZ it was decided that the Lone Ranger would be seriously wounded by an outlaw and for a couple of weeks would be unable to speak. Tonto would carry the program and take care of the Lone Ranger. After that, for another week or two, the Lone Ranger would speak in only a whisper. Then gradually his full, rich voice would return.

The actor selected to play the Lone Ranger was Brace Beemer, who had for a short time in 1933, during the first few months of the program, been the announcer for the show. Now he was back with the program and perfect for the part in just about every way. His voice was amazingly like Earle Graser's; he looked the part (handsome, six feet two inches, two hundred pounds); and his personal interests corresponded with the part (excellent horseman, a marksman with pistol and rifle, and handy with a thirty-five-foot bull whip).

There was an orderly transition, as we like to say in the United States.

5

"Adios, Kemo Sabe"

A TRIBUTE TO BRACE BEEMER

DIED: Brace Bell Beemer, sixty-two, the last of radio's Lone Rangers (1941–1954), a six-foot two-inch mellow-voiced actor whose "Hi-Yo, Silver" thundered onto the air thrice weekly to the accompaniment of the "William Tell Overture," thrilling youngsters of all ages as he, his faithful Indian companion Tonto, and his fiery horse Silver fought for peace and justice in the early West; of a heart attack; in Oxford, Michigan, March 1, 1965.

Brace Beemer was the most famous Lone Ranger of them all. He was to the Lone Ranger what Johnny Weissmuller has always been to Tarzan—the quintessence of the character. When Brace Beemer died in 1965, J. P. McCarthy, Detroit's top-rated radio personality for WJR and long-time fan of "The Lone Ranger," contacted people who had been associated with Beemer during his halcyon days as the Lone Ranger—a number of the series' actors, the radio narrator, two of the former directors, and others—and scheduled a radio tribute to this most famous of the Lone Rangers.

I heard that program back in March of 1965 and was very moved by what the friends and co-workers had to say about Brace Beemer and the years of their association with the program. A few months ago I was able to secure a tape of that 1965 radio program and to listen again to those reminiscences. The radio tribute offers a rare opportunity to get behind the scenes (microphones?) of one of the most famous radio programs ever with the people responsible for much of its success, and to listen to them recall their days with the Lone Ranger and Tonto.

Recently I contacted J. P. McCarthy, who is still with WJR in Detroit (and in recent years has received the Gavin Award and *Billboard Magazine*'s award as the number-one radio personality in America), and received his permission to include the text of the program in this book.

A TRIBUTE TO BRACE BEEMER*

J. P. McCarthy, Host

("William Tell Overture" up and then under voice.)

J. P. MCCARTHY: This is a tribute, a tribute to

* Broadcast March 7, 1965, by WJR Radio, Detroit, Michigan.

Brace Beemer (in a Lone Ranger outfit of the early 1940s) and Silver posing for a publicity photo.

J. P. McCarthy, Detroit radio personality, who planned and hosted the radio "Tribute to Brace Beemer."

This profile study of Brace Beemer was autographed to Jim Jewell. (circa 1934)

He's the Studio Chief

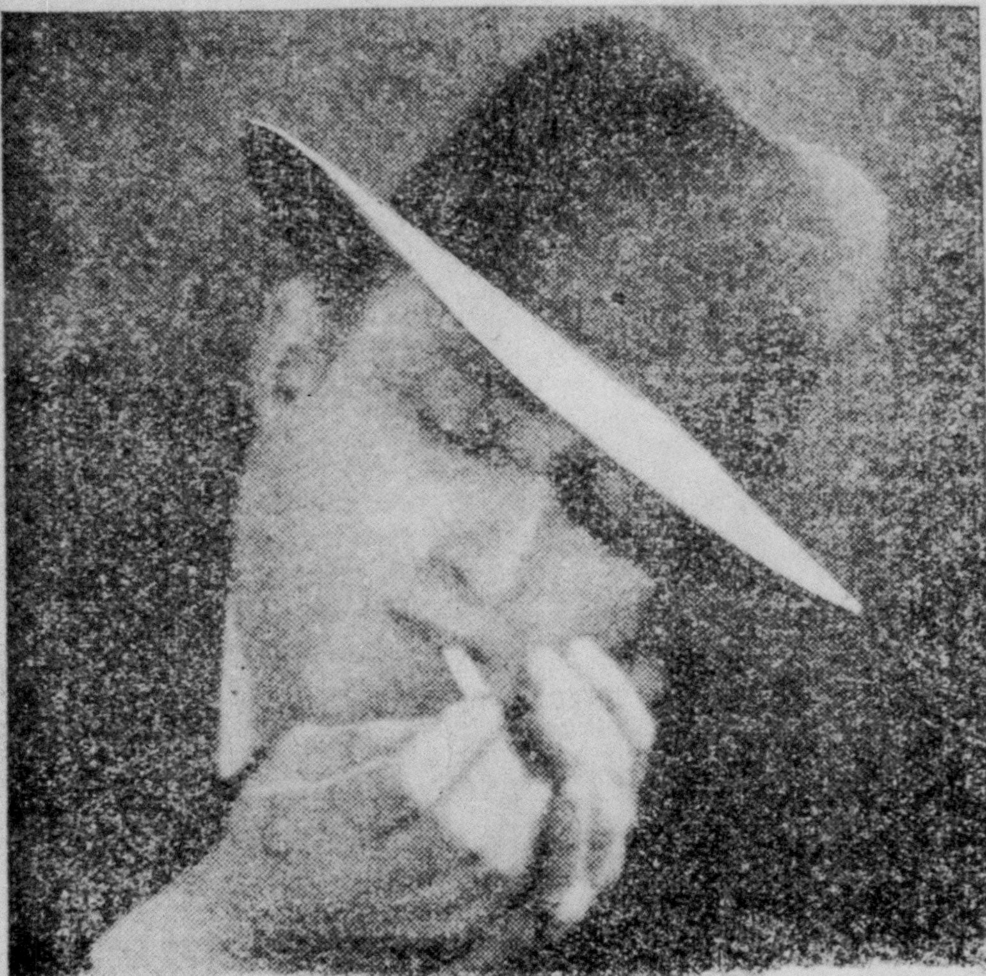

Although identified with character parts in various sketches on WXYZ, and known as the poet-philosopher of the Sears-Roebuck "Wandering Vagabonds" program, Brace Beemer's chief role is that of studio supervisor, his task in that capacity being to see to it that all details of studio production run off smoothly.

This faded photograph is from the second issue of the WXYZ PR newspaper called Michigan Radio Network, *which was published in late 1933. Beemer played many roles during his years at WXYZ. He posed for all promotional pictures for the Lone Ranger from the beginning of the series in 1933, but did not play the role on the air until 1941.*

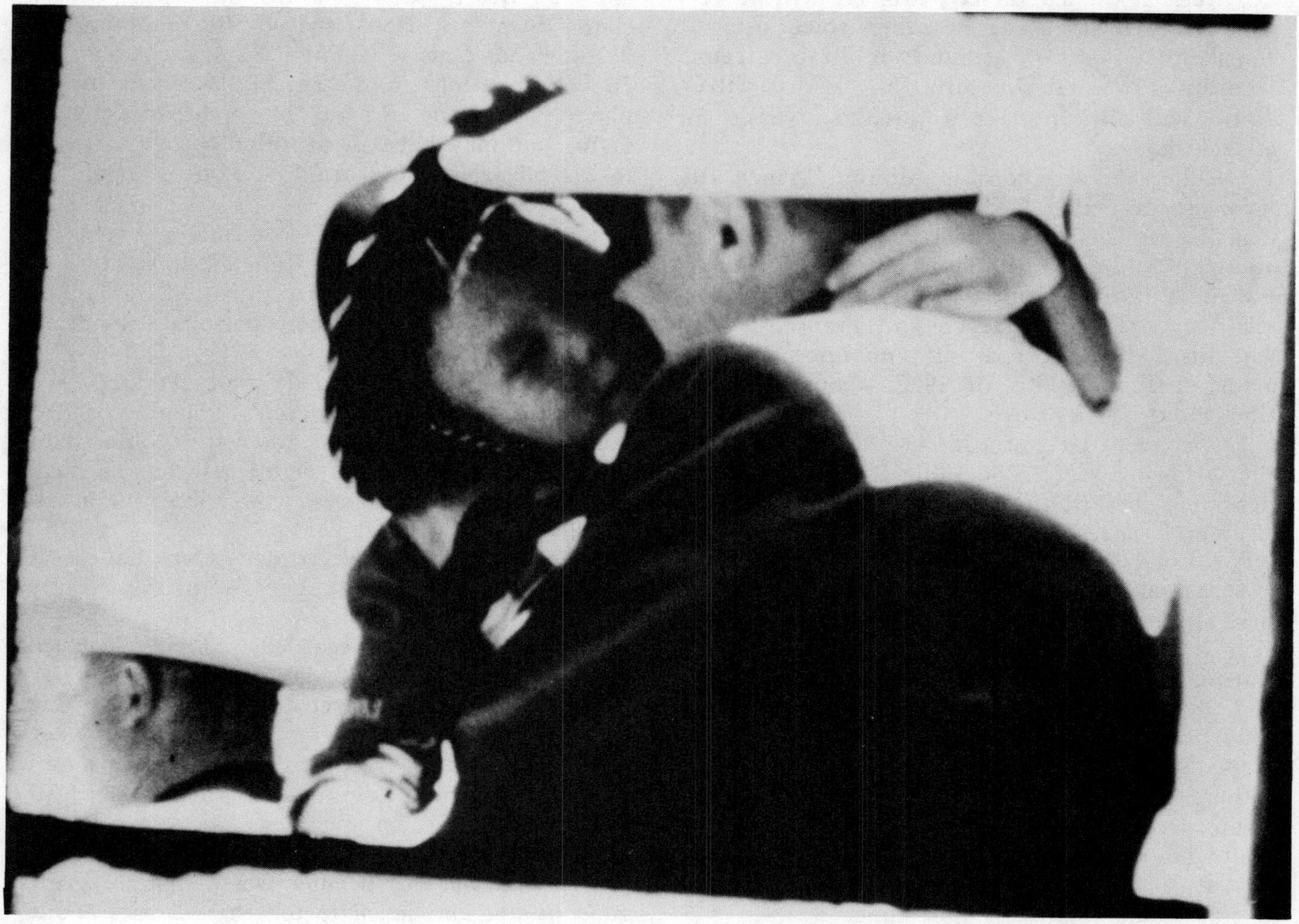

The masked man (Brace Beemer) is receiving a close-up inspection from a young fan in this candid shot. (circa 1948)

Brace Beemer, better known to all of us as the Lone Ranger. He entertained millions of us as we grew up. He was to an entire generation of people who were weaned on radio drama, the voice of honesty, justice, and law and order in the old West.

As you know, all of us were shocked and saddened when Brace Beemer died suddenly earlier this week at the age of sixty-two. He will be very much missed, and his booming voice uttering the familiar cry of—(sound of Brace Beemer recording of "Hi-Yo, Silver")—"Hi-yo, Silver, away" will always strike a nostalgic twinge for all of us.

Mr. Beemer was born in Mount Carmel, Illinois, on December 9, 1903. At the age of fourteen he enlisted in the Army to become the youngest soldier in the American Expeditionary Forces in World War I. He then served 111 consecutive days in the trenches in France. He began his radio career as an announcer and an actor in Indianapolis in 1922, about the same time radio had its birth.

He came to Detroit with WXYZ in 1932, and the following year "The Lone Ranger" made its debut on the air. In a recent interview with Mr. Beemer I asked him how long he had been with "The Lone Ranger."

BRACE BEEMER: (recorded) Well, I made the first appearance on the horse in 1933, the same year it started, and the pictures were all of me during the entire run of the show.

J. P. MC CARTHY: He was, however, not the only Lone Ranger.

BRACE BEEMER: (recorded) We had three [other] Lone Rangers. I think the first one's name was Deeds, if I'm not mistaken. Now I could be, but I'm pretty sure I'm not.

J. P. MC CARTHY: (recorded) He was the Lone Ranger for a relatively short time.

BRACE BEEMER: (recorded) Then George Seaton, as you know. Then Earle Graser, who was killed. I'm not sure of the year I went back in—1938, I think. I played the last seventeen years.

[Author's note: Mr. Beemer's memory was inaccurate on his dates and years. He actually took over when Earle Graser died on April 8, 1941, and continued until September 3, 1954, when the program ceased live network broadcasting.

By this time the reader is undoubtedly aware of the conflicting memories concerning the sequence of actors who played the Lone Ranger on radio. The three actors who have a just claim to playing the role are George Seaton, Earle Graser, and Brace Beemer. Jack Deeds, if he really did play the role in an on-the-air broadcast, only did it a few times. Jim Jewell, the first director, apparently played the part once or twice in an emergency. There is even some confusion concerning whether Brace Beemer may have played the role in 1933, between Seaton and Graser. *Time* magazine, in a 1941 obituary of Graser, says that he did. Jim Jewell claims that Jack Deeds played the role between Seaton and Graser; George Seaton claims that Jim Jewell told him that Jack Deeds never played the Lone Ranger on a broadcast program, but may have in a "pilot" program prior to the official starting of "The Lone Ranger" in 1933.]

J. P. MC CARTHY: The second most important character on "The Lone Ranger" was Tonto—Tonto, his faithful Indian companion, played by John Todd. Were they close personal friends in real life?

BRACE BEEMER: (recorded) Not very, no. We were friends, but we weren't friends socially. John had his group. John was a little older than I was; John was in his eighties when he died. He had his drama classes, which I wasn't at all interested in.

J. P. MC CARTHY: (recorded) So that great camaraderie, that classic friendship was strictly confined to the show.

BRACE BEEMER: (recorded) That's correct. "Tai, kemo sabe." (both laugh)

J. P. MC CARTHY: (recorded) Listen, Brace, what does "kemo sabe" really mean?

BRACE BEEMER: (recorded) "Tai" means hail in Potawatomi. "Kemo sabe" means faithful friend. So put them together "tai, kemo sabe," hail, faithful friend.

J. P. MC CARTHY: Beemer was a man of great good humor and loved to tell these stories about the man who played Tonto.

BRACE BEEMER: (recorded) John Todd loved to double parts and he had several voices. He liked to double an Englishman's part. So one time he was doubling this Englishman in this same show, and he's riding on a stagecoach. A jack rabbit is supposed to run out along side the stagecoach. John is supposed to say (affecting an English accent), "I think I'll chance a shot, you know." He's making a motion with his hands to give the appearance, like I'm doing, now, of riding, you see, and he's supposed to shoot. His next line is, "Ah, a hit!" Instead of that, when the director threw him the cue after the shot,

This candid shot of Brace Beemer was taken at the time he was studio manager for WXYZ and narrator for "The Lone Ranger." (circa 1933)

he said, "Ah, a cue!" (both laugh) There was another funny one—Tonto and I were up in the hotel room searching these outlaws' luggage, baggage, so forth and so on. At the end I'm supposed to say, "All right, Tonto, there's nothing here. Let's get back to camp." John says, "Ah, kemo sabe. Gettum up, Scout." (both laugh) We're in the second floor of the hotel.

J. P. MC CARTHY: Another voice familiar to millions of "Lone Ranger" fans was the voice of the narrator, Fred Foy. Fred Foy is now with ABC in New York and we contacted him by phone yesterday and asked him about Brace Beemer.

FRED FOY: (recorded) Well, I can say, number one, he was a good friend and to me a wonderful person because he carried over the character of the Lone Ranger into his personal life. In fact, to me he was the Lone Ranger, whether on the microphone or off. He brought this character to life to a great deal of youngsters both on the air and off the air. I know it was one of his prime purposes to visit children's hospitals where many youngsters, of course, idolized the Lone Ranger. This was to them a real-life hero, and there were many instances where in just going in in his full regalia as the Lone Ranger, the mask, and so on, that this would give the youngsters a tremendous lift. He was to me a very good friend and a wonderful person, and it was quite a shock to learn of his sudden passing.

J. P. MC CARTHY: The second part of Brace Beemer's career, as we all know, developed just a few weeks ago. A series of commercials were produced with his voice and some nostalgic moments from "The Lone Ranger" program itself. Well, the man whose idea it was is here with us tonight, Don Dolen of Young and Rubicam Advertising Agency here in Detroit. Don, when did the idea happen and how did it come about?

DON DOLEN: Well, about three or four months ago, which, I think, is about two months before we started to put the stuff on the air, we did a demo tape with Brace for another product. Because of his style of delivery and so forth, it just never developed. But then we were asked by our local clients here—they wanted to do something that sort of pinned down the fact that Chrysler was started here, was still built here, and so forth—so one thing led to another, and we said, "My goodness, Brace is living out in Oxford and the star of a show that originated here and made good nationally." So we just naturally tied the thing; it was Detroit's hometown car and Detroit's hometown radio show. Can I say one thing?

J. P. MC CARTHY: Sure.

DON DOLEN: The day we called up Brace and asked him to do this, there is only one thing he said to me. He said, "Sure, I'll do it, if it's in good taste." This to me sums up the whole man.

J. P. MC CARTHY: You know, the thing that amazes me, "The Lone Ranger" went off the air the last time in 1955 [actually 1954], and I can't ever recall hearing Brace Beemer's voice since then, until this period. Who discovered that Brace Beemer was in Oxford, Michigan, and how did the name pop up again? Was it your idea; did you dream it up one night?

DON DOLEN: No, the basic idea was my idea, but we were all aware of Brace being around, but we felt that, I don't know, for some reason we figured that he just wouldn't want to do it.

J. P. MC CARTHY: Well, he had been in retirement.

DON DOLEN: Yes, and we figured he wanted to just stay with his horses and not be bothered coming in from out of town to make commercials. But I think, and Brace indicated, he was having a heck of a time when he was doing these, because he was really enjoying it.

J. P. MC CARTHY: Yes, we could tell that when we talked with him.

DON DOLEN: It was a great privilege on my part to work with him because like you and like everybody else over thirty, I think, this man is an inseparable part of your childhood.

J. P. MC CARTHY: There were naturally hundreds of people connected with "The Lone Ranger" in one way or another during its first twenty-two years on the air. And we have some of them with us tonight to reminisce about Brace Beemer and the program. Many of the voices you will recognize immediately. We have the actors with us: Paul Hughes; Rolly Parker; Jay Michael; Ernie Winstanley; one of the early directors on the program, Chuck Livingstone; Fred Flowerday, one of the latter day directors and a man who has been with the show for a long time. Chuck, I think, in terms of longevity with the show, is the oldest among us, not in terms of age. When did "The Lone Ranger" start? Were you there?

CHARLES LIVINGSTONE: I wasn't there at the beginning. It started in January of 1933, and I joined the company or the cast around August of 1933.

J. P. MC CARTHY: So it was just a few months old.

CHARLES LIVINGSTONE: Brace at that time was chief announcer and studio manager of WXYZ.

J. P. MC CARTHY: What were you doing when you joined the cast?

CHARLES LIVINGSTONE: I was an actor. Probably because of my voice, I was the heavy in most of the early "Lone Ranger" programs.

J. P. MC CARTHY: You played a lot of heavies in your day, didn't you?

CHARLES LIVINGSTONE: In fact, I would say from 1933 until 1938, when I was fortunate enough to become dramatic director of "The Lone Ranger," I believe I played more heavies than any man in the United States.

J. P. MC CARTHY: Whose idea was "The Lone Ranger"?

CHARLES LIVINGSTONE: Well, the story which I believe is that George W. Trendle wanted to create a character, a Robin Hood character with a Western background. I think that was the basis for starting, and I believe then that Jim Jewell who was then director of "The Lone Ranger". . . .

J. P. MC CARTHY: Was he the first director?

CHARLES LIVINGSTONE: Yes, he was. He searched around and found this writer from Buffalo by the name of Fran Striker. Fran had been writing a play with a Western character, not based exactly the way Mr. Trendle wanted it, but from that they got together and "The Lone Ranger" was conceived.

J. P. MC CARTHY: And when it started was it on a regular three times a week basis, or how was it run?

CHARLES LIVINGSTONE: Yes, Sir. It was a 7:30 in the evening play, Monday, Wednesday, and Friday. I think it always remained that way. It developed—it was the originator of the Mutual Broadcasting System.

J. P. MC CARTHY: That's right. I understand they developed Mutual only to accommodate "The Lone Ranger."

CHARLES LIVINGSTONE: That's right. The Gordon Baking Company had purchased the show and they wanted it in the Chicago market, the Cincinnati market, the New York market, and the Detroit market.

J. P. MC CARTHY: What was Brace Beemer's affiliation with it in 1933?

CHARLES LIVINGSTONE: In 1933 Brace was the narrator, a very important part of the show.

J. P. MC CARTHY: Fred Flowerday, who now takes care of all "The Lone Ranger" tapes and guards them with his life—has them locked up in a vault—has been with the show for a long time, too. When did you start, Fred?

FRED FLOWERDAY: I started in late 1934.

J. P. MC CARTHY: What were you doing?

FRED FLOWERDAY: Well, I started doing sound effects—opening and closing doors, working with Ted Robertson, who was then the chief sound technician.

J. P. MC CARTHY: I think I should point out that at that time Fred was nothing but an acne-faced young teenage boy. Tell us about some of the sound effects. Now in those days there weren't any recorded sound effects, were there?

FRED FLOWERDAY: No, most of our sound effects were done manually. We had a large sound effects staff—I think there were four at the time I started—our gun shots were done manually, we had no recorded gun shots.

J. P. MC CARTHY: How would you do a manual gun shot?

FRED FLOWERDAY: Well, strangely enough the first gun shot was a rat trap that was fastened to a large thunder drum. On cue, when a gun shot was called for, one of us would spring this rat trap, and it would go on the thunder drum and give the effect of a gun shot.

J. P. MC CARTHY: You couldn't do any rapid firing.

FRED FLOWERDAY: Just as fast as you could work this rat trap, I presume. But then we went to an improvement over that; we had large cardboard boxes that we would hit with a stick. The famous series of gun shots—the six at the opening—were done by a sound technician as he hit this large cardboard carton.

J. P. MC CARTHY: Tell us about some of the other early sound effects—the horse's hooves.

FRED FLOWERDAY: Well, the hoof beats progressed in the same way the gun shots did. They were done manually, of course, they always have been. We did the rhythm of the horses galloping on our knees with our hands.

J. P. MC CARTHY: How would you do that? Would you slap your thighs?

FRED FLOWERDAY: We'd slap our thighs. (He does so.) That's a bad gait right there; I'm not used to doing it. (laugh) Then we'd hit our chests in the rhythm of the horses. (He does so.) From that we went to the sink plungers, the short handled sink plungers that we'd clop together in rhythm, one against the other. We were continually trying to get better sounds and we prided ourselves on our sound department. We tried hard and I think we got some good ones. We went to a box that was filled with gravel, oh, a foot and a half deep. We would vertically plunge the sink plungers into the gravel to give us the sound. . . .

J. P. MC CARTHY: Sound like a horse galloping down the trail.

FRED FLOWERDAY: Sound effects were so much a part of radio drama. As we all know, it's all imaginary; it's what the mind envisions. I can't imagine anybody listening to a "Lone Ranger" program ever thinking of a couple of plungers in a box of gravel when they heard the horses galloping. We changed the terrain, too. If we had the Lone Ranger and Tonto going into sandy soil, we'd have one part of the box reserved for that particular material. If they were going through underbrush, we would use broomcorn to get the sound of horses going through. We even went so far as to use the sound of the bridle.

J. P. MC CARTHY: How would you do that? . . .

FRED FLOWERDAY: We actually had some bits of bridle that we'd hold in our hands so when the horse was galloping, we'd have the jingle in time with the gait of the horse.

JAY MICHAEL: Tell him about when the horses would jump a chasm—one mountain side to the other—about forty feet.

J. P. MC CARTHY: How would you do that?

FRED FLOWERDAY: We'd just stop galloping, J. P.

JAY MICHAEL: Dead pause.

ROLLON PARKER: Then, Fred, when the horses went over a bridge.

FRED FLOWERDAY: Yeah. We would switch from the gravel box to a sound like a wood floor, and we'd invert the sink plungers and do the hard wood handles on the wood floor to get the sound of the horses on the bridge.

J. P. MC CARTHY: Fred, who would give the cues for all this? Now you had one director; Chuck was the director at the time you were doing most of these manual effects. (to Charles Livingstone) Would you have to cue the actors and the sound effects people all at the same time.

CHARLES LIVINGSTONE: Yes, Sir.

J. P. MC CARTHY: It took a lot of synchronization.

CHARLES LIVINGSTONE: It did.

J. P. MC CARTHY: Did you keep your fingers crossed?

CHARLES LIVINGSTONE: Well, this group, these boys, they worked show after show after show, and they became used to this method. It was different from most dramatic shows in that we had a separate studio for sound effects so that we could set a level that wouldn't drown out the voices of the actors in a different studio. This way we kept it balanced between the voice and the sound, so that it was easy to understand. We also had a problem, remember, with the music, Fred, when "The Lone Ranger" first went on the air. There were complaints that the music was too loud. Well, the engineers were carrying the music at a zero level on their volume control indicators and the music, it wasn't slopping over the zero, but it was too loud. We'd get letters of complaint and Mr. Trendle would get at us. Finally, we decided the thing to do was hold the music at a minus four and peak the voices at zero, and from that time on people did not have to touch their radio sets when the music came on.

J. P. MC CARTHY: Chuck, speaking of the music, the "William Tell Overture," for as long as any of us live, will not be the "William Tell Overture" but "The Lone Ranger" theme. Was it always "The Lone Ranger" theme?

CHARLES LIVINGSTONE: Yes. One time they did try the "Light Cavalry Overture," but this didn't carry the feeling they wanted. It [the "William Tell Overture"] was the only one used on the air.

J. P. MC CARTHY: One of the most celebrated and publicized change of voices, you'll recall, was when Bobby Breen's voice changed. Another one, equally important and equally traumatic, I'm sure to the guy involved, was the man who played the Lone Ranger's nephew, Dan Reid—Ernie Winstanley. When did you start as Dan Reid?

ERNIE WINSTANLEY: Well, in early '34 right after Chuck [started with the program]. As a matter of fact, Chuck used to pick me up out in Orchard Lake and bring me in in corduroy knickers. I played that for about three years, as I recall, two or three years and my voice changed. And then I graduated into the sound department under Fred. I had been doing a little bit of sound work before that.

J. P. MC CARTHY: How did they write you out of the script, Ernie?

ERNIE WINSTANLEY: There were, as I recall, about five or six different Dan Reids. He was not in every show, of course. He was in maybe one out of twelve. Right, Chuck?

CHARLES LIVINGSTONE: That's right.

J. P. MC CARTHY: It had to be a heartbreaking experience for you when you found your voice getting lower and lower.

CHUCK LIVINGSTONE: Oh, I think he kind of liked it because he got to play these young men,

. . . these handsome heroes.

J. P. MC CARTHY: Ernie, you actually grew up with "The Lone Ranger."

ERNIE WINSTANLEY: Oh, yes.

J. P. MC CARTHY: Tell us about the different parts you've played. Proceed from where you were Dan Reid, after your voice changed.

ERNIE WINSTANLEY: Then I played, as Chuck said, the dashing young juvenile right through until. . . .

J. P. MC CARTHY: Always the good guy?

ERNIE WINSTANLEY: Pretty much in those days, until 1941 when I went in the service. When I came back, Chuck started me playing all different types of characters, as we all did. You never knew what you were going to play until you appeared at rehearsal.

JAY MICHAEL: We all did ad-lib [parts].

J. P. MC CARTHY: That voice, ladies and gentlemen, belongs to Jay Michael. Jay has one of the most easily recognized voices, I think. You all will recognize it when you hear him speak. How long were you with "The Ranger"?

JAY MICHAEL: I hate to say it, but I arrived on the scene about twenty-nine years ago.

J. P. MC CARTHY: How many different parts do you figure you've played?

JAY MICHAEL: Just about everything. I think I played more villains than anything else, though.

J. P. MC CARTHY: You were classified as a heavy.

JAY MICHAEL: A heavy, yes, because of the heavy voice. You can't do much with it to lighten it up.

CHARLES LIVINGSTONE: Well, I know you played some old-timers.

JAY MICHAEL: (Affecting old-timer voice) Sure, I played old-timers.

FRED FLOWERDAY: . . . Chuck [Livingstone] was Black Bart originally, and then Jay became it.

J. P. MC CARTHY: (To Jay) Were you the Lone Ranger's arch rival, Black Bart? Give us the Black Bart voice. Do you recall it?

JAY MICHAEL: (Black Bart voice) I'm tellin' ya', masked man, I got ya' covered with this gun. One move and yur out of the picture, ya' understand?

J. P. MC CARTHY: Wonderful!

JAY MICHAEL: (Still Black Bart) OOOH! He shot the gun out of ma' hand. (all laugh)

J. P. MC CARTHY: Now that brings up another point. All of you who were actors on the show had to go through these tremendous sounds indicating to the audience listening that you were doing something, something physical. You were getting shot or you were in a fight. Would you do this just naturally as you were doing the script? Was it indicated in the script if you were socked by Black Bart?

JAY MICHAEL: Oh no, they didn't put "sock" in the script. There was a [sound effects] man standing in front of you with a pad and a fist and he'd go (fist sound effects) like that and you'd take an immediate reaction—"OOH!"—and you'd back up a little bit, as if you fell back.

J. P. MC CARTHY: Would you also get breathless if you'd been in a fight scene?

JAY MICHAEL: Oh, yes.

J. P. MC CARTHY: You'd just do this automatically.

JAY MICHAEL: We even had footsteps on the floor as you entered a bar. Sometimes people said, "Well, you can't hear a man walking across a bar [floor] when it's noisy," but we had them.

FRED FLOWERDAY: Well, they had spurs on, and things like that that they had sounds for.

CHARLES LIVINGSTONE: Due to this physical work they did, we always played an arm's distance from the microphone. We never crawled up close to the microphone, because you couldn't react physically if you were that close to the microphone.

J. P. MC CARTHY: Another one of the most easily recognized voices in the country is the voice that belongs to Paul Hughes. Paul, when did you join "The Ranger"?

PAUL HUGHES: Oh, I'm just one of the newer members. I didn't come in until about 1939.

J. P. MC CARTHY: I always recall you as the sheriff.

PAUL HUGHES: Yes. You never knew from day to day what you were going to do.

J. P. MC CARTHY: But most of the time you were a good guy, weren't you? Weren't you on the side of law and order most of the time?

PAUL HUGHES: I'd say about fifty percent of the time. I'd kill one day and doctor the next.

FRED FLOWERDAY: I think that one of the characters that Paul developed who was very familiar to everyone was Thunder Martin.

J. P. MC CARTHY: Tell us about Thunder Martin. Who is he; I don't recall that character.

PAUL HUGHES: Well, Thunder Martin was, ah—

CHARLES LIVINGSTONE: The Wally Beery character.

J. P. MC CARTHY: Was he a good guy or a bad guy?

PAUL HUGHES: He was a good guy—always getting into trouble. The thing that impressed me about this show was the speed. I remember my first script. I had a "well" and a "but" on the second page. (all laugh) I remember turning away from the microphone at the top of the page to clear my throat, and when I came back, they were way at the bottom of the page. I never did get my "well" and "but" in. (all laugh)

JAY MICHAEL: We never waited.

J. P. MC CARTHY: Rolly Parker is another familiar voice to all, and, Rolly, I think you were on almost every "Lone Ranger" episode I ever heard.

ROLLON PARKER: Not quite that many.

J. P. MC CARTHY: How many do you figure that you did?

ROLLON PARKER: Oh, it's hard to say. Over a period of nineteen years, maybe twice a week. (pause) What would that be? Quite a few.

JAY MICHAEL: Fifteen, sixteen, seventeen hundred, probably.

J. P. MC CARTHY: I seem to remember you as a good guy most of the time. We're trying to separate the good guys from the bad guys tonight.

ROLLON PARKER: Well, as we say when some novice asks you, "What did you do on "The Lone Ranger'?" The only answer you can give is, "good guy, bad guy, Chinese cook, Mexican, old man, young man, banker, lawyer." Chuck had us rotated so that each time we came down to rehearsal, "Oh, boy, just a short part, but it's an old man"—next time, a long part of a villain.

JAY MICHAEL: You did a lot of dialects, Rolly.

J. P. MC CARTHY: And didn't you all do many different parts in any given "Lone Ranger" episode?

ERNIE WINSTANLEY: I wish Rolly would tell the story . . . Rolly doubled Tonto a lot when John Todd was on vacation.

ROLLON PARKER: Unfortunately.

J. P. MC CARTHY: I didn't know that.

ERNIE WINSTANLEY: There's a very funny story about the woman who called after a broadcast.

ROLLON PARKER: Oh, during one vacation period, somehow or another, Mr. Livingstone, Chuck, put me in as Tonto for a couple of weeks. I was lousy. There was a phone call that Chuck told me about. I can't use the word, but the lady said, "That's an Indian!" (all laugh)

J. P. MC CARTHY: Is that the only time you played Tonto, for those two weeks?

ROLLON PARKER: Four weeks all together, and that was it.

J. P. MC CARTHY: Would you just as soon forget that period?

ROLLON PARKER: Sure would.

J. P. MC CARTHY: How would you do several parts in one show? Would you ever have one speech as one character, for example, and then run into yourself—in other words, have a conversation with yourself?

ROLLON PARKER: No. They were sometimes written that way, but the director, Chuck Livingstone, would fix it so that you'd have plenty of time to go from (old-timer voice) "Well, howdy, Mam" to something like (tough outlaw voice) "That's enough out of you, now." You wouldn't do it immediately; he'd have some other speeches in between.

J. P. MC CARTHY: Most of those "Lone Ranger" episodes were done live. [Author's note: All of the programs were done live throughout the series. Only repeats for the Midwest and West were on tape during the later years of the program.] There was no tape in those days, so they had to be perfect. There was no fluffing aloud and there were very. . . .

ROLLON PARKER: No fluffing aloud? (laugh)

J. P. MC CARTHY: There must have been some interesting, maybe some amusing experiences that you guys remember. Tell me about them.

ROLLON PARKER: I can tell you one. You might have forgotten, fellows. John Hodiak, who is not with us now, he had a line as a big hero, "I'm off to the execution." At the time he was taking voice lessons, and he said, "I'm off to the elocution!" (all laugh) Remember that one?

J. P. MC CARTHY: Now it would seem to me that that would send a nervous cast into gales of laughter.

JAY MICHAEL: It would; but when you looked at Chuck's face in the control room, you soon regained your poise. (much laughter)

J. P. MC CARTHY: Was he a little blue in the face?

JAY MICHAEL: A little bit, or he disappeared down below the counter.

J. P. MC CARTHY: How about some of the other. . . .

JAY MICHAEL: Let me tell one, if I may, that Brace told on an interview last year. Frank Russell, dear soul, who played character parts with us, was playing a sheriff one night. He and the posse had located the gang of crooks. It was at night and they had their little camp in a circle surrounded by a forest. Well, Frank deployed his men all around, and on a certain signal they were all to come in and he would say, "All right, Gents, get your guns up." So the time came and he stepped out into the clearing and said, "All right, Junts, get your gens up; Gens, get your junts up. Oh, shoot em!" (all laugh)

J. P. MC CARTHY: The script, of course, was always timed to run just a half hour, wasn't it, Chuck?

CHARLES LIVINGSTONE: That's right. We were fortunate; I don't think we ever ran over once.

J. P. MC CARTHY: Was there ever a time when you had to cut some lines?

CHARLES LIVINGSTONE: Oh, yes. Sometimes we had to cut quite a bit.

J. P. MC CARTHY: How would you do this?

FRED FLOWERDAY: Chuck, I think it would be interesting to give sort of a production schedule as to how we did the show. These actors came in with a cold script, J. P., they never had seen it before the rehearsal was called.

CHARLES LIVINGSTONE: We had three hours to do the show.

J. P. MC CARTHY: What time would the actors get there?

CHARLES LIVINGSTONE: Well, let's see, was it 3:30 we got started?

FRED FLOWERDAY: I think 3:30 P.M.

CHARLES LIVINGSTONE: We'd take a reading [rehearsal] which took approximately one hour, and then the timing [rehearsal was] one half hour, because we would have our script cut down to just about the size we needed. Then we had a break.

ROLLON PARKER: Yeah, a Casino break [card-playing break].

CHARLES LIVINGSTONE: Then we'd have the production rehearsal where we put the sound effects and everything in it. This took one hour, then a half hour for dress rehearsal.

J. P. MC CARTHY: And at the dress rehearsal you'd presumably have everything chopped down to time.

CHARLES LIVINGSTONE: Everything was timed every fifteen seconds and at the end of the scene, and the time at the beginning of the next scene. We also backed up from the closing time that we had to have [to allow for the closing theme]. We had a deadline that we had to meet, which either meant we had to speed them up at times or slow them down. We had a system of signals which they all understood. When I took my hand and brought it down palm toward them, it meant slow down, and when I turned my hand the other way and brought it up, it meant pick it up. And when you wanted them to get back to their normal tempo, it was a horizontal movement of the hand which meant go back to normal.

J. P. MC CARTHY: How was Brace Beemer to work with as an actor and as a man, Chuck?

CHARLES LIVINGSTONE: As a man Brace was one of the finest individuals I've ever had the good fortune to know and to work with. He had a heart as big as he was. He was a man's man, let's say. He was opinionated. He definitely had his own ideas on how certain things should be done, and naturally, in the stress of rehearsals we used to come to differences of ideas, but Brace's ideas were entirely set on what the Lone Ranger would say and do. He was the man physically, he was the man mentally, and he was the Lone Ranger in his heart.

J. P. MC CARTHY: He really was, wasn't he? Now, I talked to Brace Beemer just a couple of weeks ago and I asked him the same thing. Where did Brace Beemer stop and the Lone Ranger start, and vice versa. He told me that as soon as he went home he was no longer the Lone Ranger. But everybody I talked to, all of you people who worked with him say that was not so. He was the Lone Ranger, always.

CHARLES LIVINGSTONE: He was. His feelings toward people, his interest in people, and the things he did for people followed right straight through with the Lone Ranger's character.

ROLLON PARKER: He was a great humanitarian. . . .

ERNIE WINSTANLEY: He believed in the ideals of the Lone Ranger and he carried them through in his life outside of the studio.

J. P. MC CARTHY: Chuck, you were telling me before we started here, reminiscing, about an instance you recall that probably vividly and dramatically demonstrates what we are trying to say about Brace Beemer.

CHARLES LIVINGSTONE: Well, this happened at the time we had a contest and one city in the United States was picked to change its name to "Lone Ranger Frontier Town" for a day. This happened to be Cheyenne, Wyoming. Brace had to go out there to make a personal appearance. We all went out on the train. In Chicago where we changed trains, it became apparent that the news had gotten out that we were on the train. Brace got out on the platform between two of

Russ Livingstone
luck to a fine little man.
Brace Beemer
"The Lone Ranger"
1943

This publicity photograph was autographed by Brace Beemer for the son of Charles Livingstone, the director of "The Lone Ranger."

the cars and looked out the window. As we came along through the little cities, little towns, there were, oh, I would say, groups of from forty to two hundred school children who had heard about this, and as we came by they'd all wave at him and he'd wave his hand at them. I stood there watching him and, golly, the tears were just streaming down his face. It was something which I shall never forget. It definitely demonstrates the feeling that this man had. Brace never felt that it was honoring Brace Beemer. Well, it was, in a way, but this was a salute to this person, this character which he had played so well and so long.

J. P. MC CARTHY: That's a beautiful story. Paul, do you have any particular memory that you'd like to talk about tonight? An amusing incident or anything in your many years with "The Ranger"?

PAUL HUGHES: Oh, many of them, but I can't tie it down to any particular one.

J. P. MC CARTHY: How about the pay, Paul? Was it pretty good in those days?

JAY MICHAEL: Sure was. (laughter)

J. P. MC CARTHY: This might be interesting to people. Say it's 1938 and you're all gainfully employed actors on "The Lone Ranger." How much could you make?

CHARLES LIVINGSTONE: In those days it wasn't bad. Golly, when I started in 1933 it was $2.50 a show.

JAY MICHAEL: We got ten dollars for "The Ranger" and that was with two repeats. We did the show three times a night.

J. P. MC CARTHY: Once for the East Coast, once for Central, and then for the West Coast.

FRED FLOWERDAY: And glad to get it.

ERNIE WINSTANLEY: I think there were five or six actors under contract. Johnny Hodiak was one; Jay was another.

JAY MICHAEL: Al Hodge, Brace Beemer.

ERNIE WINSTANLEY: For forty-five dollars a week.

J. P. MC CARTHY: Those were high-paid fellows.

ERNIE WINSTANLEY: That was for doing nine shows.

JAY MICHAEL: I'll never forget the time John Hodiak's and my contract came up for renewal at the same time. John said, "You go up first." So I went upstairs and talked to Mr. Campbell who was then vice-president. He started pulling out the files and showing me letters he had from all over the country, people who worked cheaper than we. (all laugh) I cried a little bit and finally said, "I might as well sell insurance." I started to walk out. He said, "I'll give you forty-five dollars." I said, "Sold." John Hodiak went up and they wouldn't give him a cent more, and he went to Chicago and from there became a movie star. (all laugh)

ERNIE WINSTANLEY: I can tell you that Fred and I got $12.50 a week as. . . .

J. P. MC CARTHY: Sound effects men?

ERNIE WINSTANLEY: Uh huh. Was that your start [salary], Fred?

FRED FLOWERDAY: I think it was just about that.

ROLLON PARKER: Of course, you fellows didn't use your voices then. (laugh)

ERNIE WINSTANLEY: I doubled many times.

J. P. MC CARTHY: You were just wearing out your hands with the plungers in the box of gravel. For years now, ever since "The Lone Ranger" went off the air, Fred Flowerday and Ernie Winstanley have had every day to pass by a file drawer full of these magnificent old tapes. I'm certain that on every day you guys walked by them you must have thought, "When can we get it back on the air?" What are the prospects now? Is there any chance? I know it's running on several stations around the country.

FRED FLOWERDAY: Yes, and I have hopes that it will run on a lot more. There have been a total of about thirty-two stations that have contracted to run these "Lone Ranger" shows which are on tape. The quality is good and the interest has been excellent from stations in New Jersey, Phoenix, the South, and New York state. Every day we have inquiries from other stations wanting to know if it is available for their market. I sincerely hope that the Lone Ranger will still ride for a good many years.

J. P. MC CARTHY: He certainly will for all of us, Fred. I guess I remember more about the ending of "The Lone Ranger" shows than I do now in retrospect about everything else. . . . I recall the show would always end the same way. The evildoers, of course, had been brought to justice and, generally, the bad guy was getting arrested by the sheriff, and there was another guy there too. The bad guy would look at either the sheriff or the other fellow, and he would be very put out because he had been taken in by this masked man. He would always say, "Who was the masked man?" Could we recreate that now with Paul Hughes and Jay Michael and Rolly Parker? Rolly, you be the bad guy who's getting arrested by the sheriff, and you're put out. Paul, you be the sheriff; and Jay, you be the bystander, the town mayor. All right, Rolly.

ROLLON PARKER: (Bad guy) "Who was that masked man?"

PAUL HUGHES: (Sheriff) "The masked man? I don't know; who was he?"

JAY MICHAEL: (Mayor) "Why, that was the Lone Ranger."

(Theme music up—"William Tell Overture"—transition into "Origin of The Lone Ranger" episode followed by a complete thirty-minute "Lone Ranger" adventure.)

J. P. MC CARTHY: We wish to thank Fred Flowerday of Special Recordings for the use of "The Lone Ranger" program. The Players: Paul Hughes, Jay Michael, Rollon Parker, Elaine Alpert, Ernie Winstanley, and Frank Russell. Our Technical Advisor was Danny Dallas. Recording Engineer, Norm Henry. The program was produced by Bill Booth. This is J. P. McCarthy.

(Tribute music theme up, and then under voice:)

J. P. MC CARTHY: Part of our great American heritage has been our Western lore and the romantic and adventuresome names it produced. Names like Wyatt Earp, Billy the Kid, Bat Masterson, Wild Bill Hickok, The Daltons, The Youngers, Jessie James, and Pat Garrett. And most of the time you couldn't tell the good guys from the bad guys. Not so with the Lone Ranger. He was *the* good guy—and Brace Beemer *was* the Lone Ranger. And it is to his memory that this program has been respectfully dedicated.

(Music up and slowly out.)

6

"Even the Lone Ranger Got His Hat Dirty Occasionally"

THE MOVIE SERIALS

RIGHT from the creation of the character in 1932, George W. Trendle delighted in telling anyone who would listen how he initially developed the concept of "The Lone Ranger"; gathered his staff around him; outlined his thoughts to them on this Horatio Alger-inspired, Zorro-like character; and how, then, in the heat of this creative fire, the soon-to-be-famous "Champion of Justice" was born.

Trendle always demanded and, of course, received solo credit for creating "The Lone Ranger." He personally oversaw the writing and production of the radio series. When the television series came along in the late 1940s, he sent a "production coordinator" to Hollywood to oversee it so that the "integrity" of the character would be maintained on television. When he eventually sold the property to Jack Wrather in the mid-fifties, he felt it was appropriate that a Texan should be the purchaser.

In a statement at that time Wrather said, "The Lone Ranger is a composite of every man who stands for law and order, [he] always stresses the fact that the young people of America owe much to their ancestors. To pay this debt, they must maintain their heritage and pass it on to their own descendants. All of these things teach something. They teach patriotism, fairness, tolerance, sympathy, religion. Yet they don't preach. These lessons once learned can never be forgotten." Trendle couldn't have expressed his own feelings about the Lone Ranger any better. His comment was, "The Lone Ranger is in good hands."

Only once over the years did Trendle "goof" in his handling of "The Lone Ranger" property and that was when he dealt with the minimogul of Republic Studios, Herbert J. Yates. For a man as cautious in business and as protective of "The Lone Ranger" as George W. Trendle was, it is absolutely astounding that the two Lone Ranger movie serials, *The Lone Ranger* and *The Lone Ranger Rides Again* were ever produced. Yates or his very sharp lawyers apparently were clever enough to purchase the rights to "The Lone Ranger" without any stipulation that the plot of the movie serials must be consistent with the radio adventures listened to by millions each week. That Trendle and his lawyers would overlook this point during negotiations with Republic is, to say the least, surprising.

Regardless, the two movie serials were produced in 1938 and 1939, and the plots bore scant resemblance to the familiar radio characters and

This was the poster used to announce the arrival of the Lone Ranger to the silver screens of America. (Republic Pictures, 1938)

This three-column ad cut for newspapers pictorially lured young and old to movie theatres in 1938. Additional ad lines included: "Thrill as the Lone Ranger and his Indian friend, Tonto, crash into action in mighty protest against the ruin of the West threatened by the range underworld!" (Republic Pictures, 1938)

Chief Thunder-Cloud (Tonto) and Lee Powell (Lone Ranger), ready for action in this publicity still from the serial, The Lone Ranger. (*Republic, 1938*)

adventures. In the first serial the Lone Ranger was described as "a man of mystery"—and for good reason to those who felt they knew him through radio. As the pressbook touts it, "In 'The Lone Ranger' there are five leading men [Texas Rangers], any one of whom can be the star [Lone Ranger] of the picture. They are all the same height, weight, and with similar characteristics. They are all seen in circumstances which might prove each one is the Lone Ranger. Such a unique situation adds to the mystery and excitement of this unusual story." In case you are Sherlock Holmes enough to check for a Ranger character by the name of Reid, you will be disappointed; there is no Reid. By the end of chapter fifteen all but one of the five Rangers is dead. When he takes his mask off he is revealed to be Allen King (who?) played by Lee Powell.

This is not to say that the serial was poorly produced. Republic reportedly spent more money on *The Lone Ranger* than any serial it had produced to that date. It was, according to those who have seen it, a far above average slambang Western serial. Serial fans, young and old, flocked to see it and it made a pile of money. Probably only purists (and I'm not sure how many of those there were in 1938) objected to the divergence from the "true" story of the Lone Ranger. Among those purists, though, was George W. Trendle. When he discovered what Republic had done to his property, he raged and fumed, but to no avail; Republic had him by the fine print of the contract and there was nothing he could do.

The Lone Ranger cast included no big Western stars of that era, but there were a number of about-to-be-born minor stars and some who had seen their best days on the screen. Among them: Herman Brix, who later became well-known by the name Bruce Bennett; George Letz, later a star as George Montgomery; Hal Taliaferro, formerly a Western star known by the name Wally Wales; Lane Chandler, a star of silent pictures years before. Lee Powell, the only surviving Ranger in the serial (thus the "Lone" Ranger) was a promising young actor who worked in numerous B-Westerns after *The Lone Ranger* serial. When the war came, he joined the Marine Corps and served for two years in the Pacific before being killed in action in 1944.

Lynn Roberts, who for a while was known as Mary Hart, was the heroine of *The Lone Ranger* serial. She went on to become one of the most popular leading ladies at Republic Studios during the 1940s. (She was certainly my favorite during those years of childhood Republic Picture watching.)

Chief Thunder-Cloud, a full-blooded Cherokee Indian, was presented as a rather stolid, glum-looking Tonto. (Looking at some of the publicity stills from the serial, I have come to the conclusion that the "real" Lone Ranger would have found this faithful Indian friend a rather dull companion.)

Stanley Andrews (The Old Ranger of television's "Death Valley Days") was the villain of the serial. Farther down the cast listing other names well-known to serial and B-Western fans appeared: William Farnum (who was celebrating his fiftieth anniversary in show business), George Cleveland (a friend of Lassie's years later on television), John Merton, Tom London, and Edmund Cobb. Yakima Canutt doubled all the Lone Rangers in the action sequences and the radio Lone Ranger, Earle Graser, dubbed the "Hi-Yo, Silvers!" Oh, yes, Silver was played by a handsome steed called Silver Chief.

The Lone Ranger was directed by Republic Studio's young, hotshot team of William Witney (age twenty-one) and John English (age twenty-nine). Trendle would have appreciated Witney's Horatio Alger-like rise to fame and success. According to the pressbook, William Witney was practically raised in the motion picture studios. He had worked as a prop boy, studio janitor, guide, script clerk, electrician, assistant cameraman, and assistant director before getting his first directing job. At twenty-one years of age Witney had already directed six Republic features.

It took a writing team of five to prepare the original screenplay for the serial. Republic sent four of the writers to Detroit to confer with Fran Striker before writing the script. It is to be suspected that a lot of his advice got lost on the return trip to Hollywood. It appears that Striker had no other connection with the project and is thus probably blameless for the divergent screenplay that resulted. A 1939 *Saturday Evening Post* article incorrectly credits Striker with editing the movie serials.

Perhaps the one lasting contribution of *The Lone Ranger* movie serial was the exciting music score of Alberto Colombo that was incorporated thereafter into the radio series episodes, and eventually was used in the television series.

Republic, overjoyed with the public reception of the first Lone Ranger serial, quickly (they

Title lobby card for the first of the two Lone Ranger movie serials. Notice that George W. Trendle's name does not appear in the credits. (Republic Pictures, 1938)

A worried Lynn Roberts (also known for a time as Mary Hart) is counseled by the five Rangers while the ever-alert Tonto watches for danger. Left to right: Hal Taliaferro (earlier Wally Wales), Herman Brix (later Bruce Bennett), George Letz (later George Montgomery), Lane Chandler, and Lee Powell. (The Lone Ranger, *Republic Pictures, 1938)*

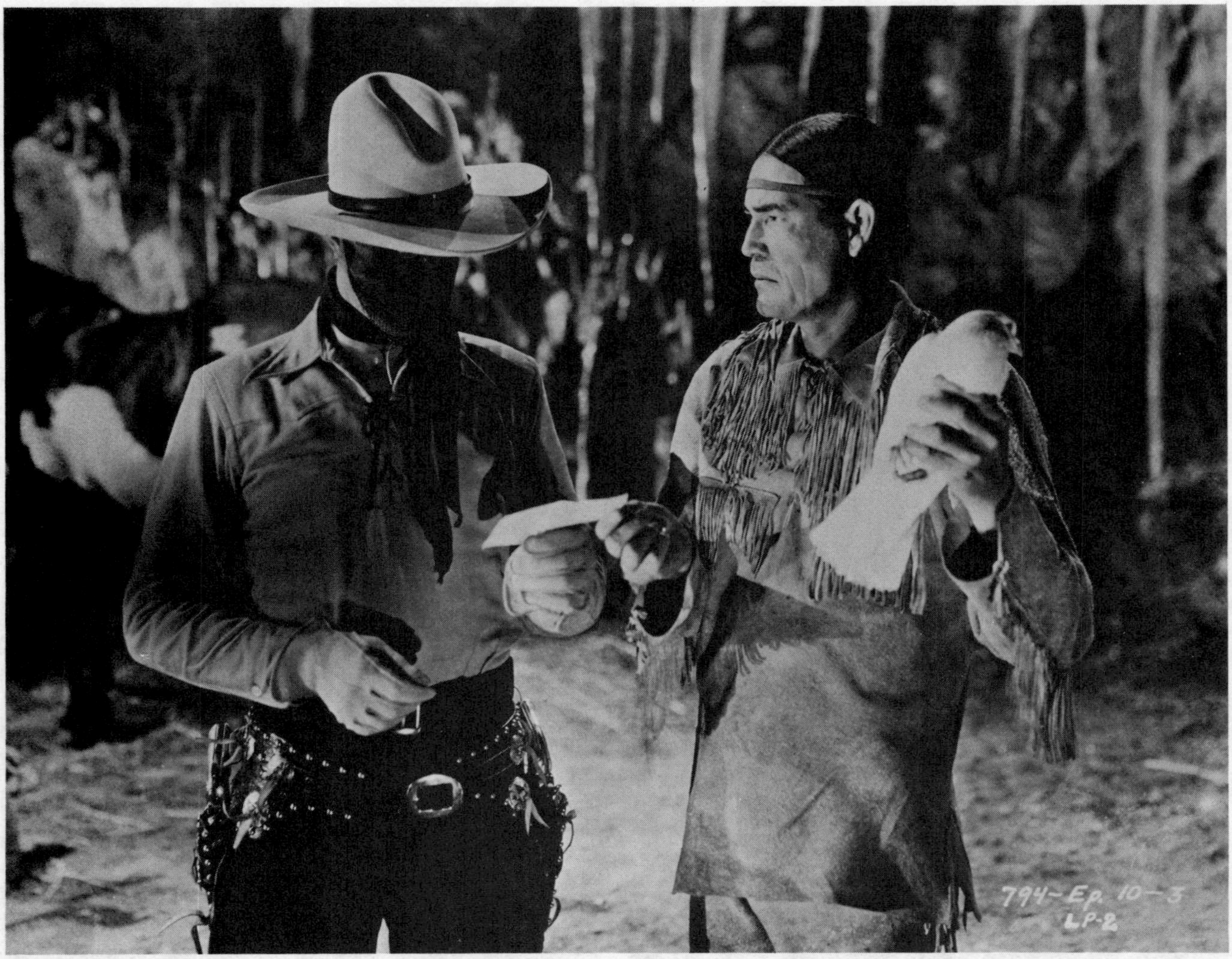

Camping in the famous Republic Pictures' "caves," the Lone Ranger (Lee Powell) and Tonto (Chief Thunder-Cloud) receive an important message. This still from The Lone Ranger *typifies the stolid, glum-demeanored Tonto of the movie serials. (1938)*

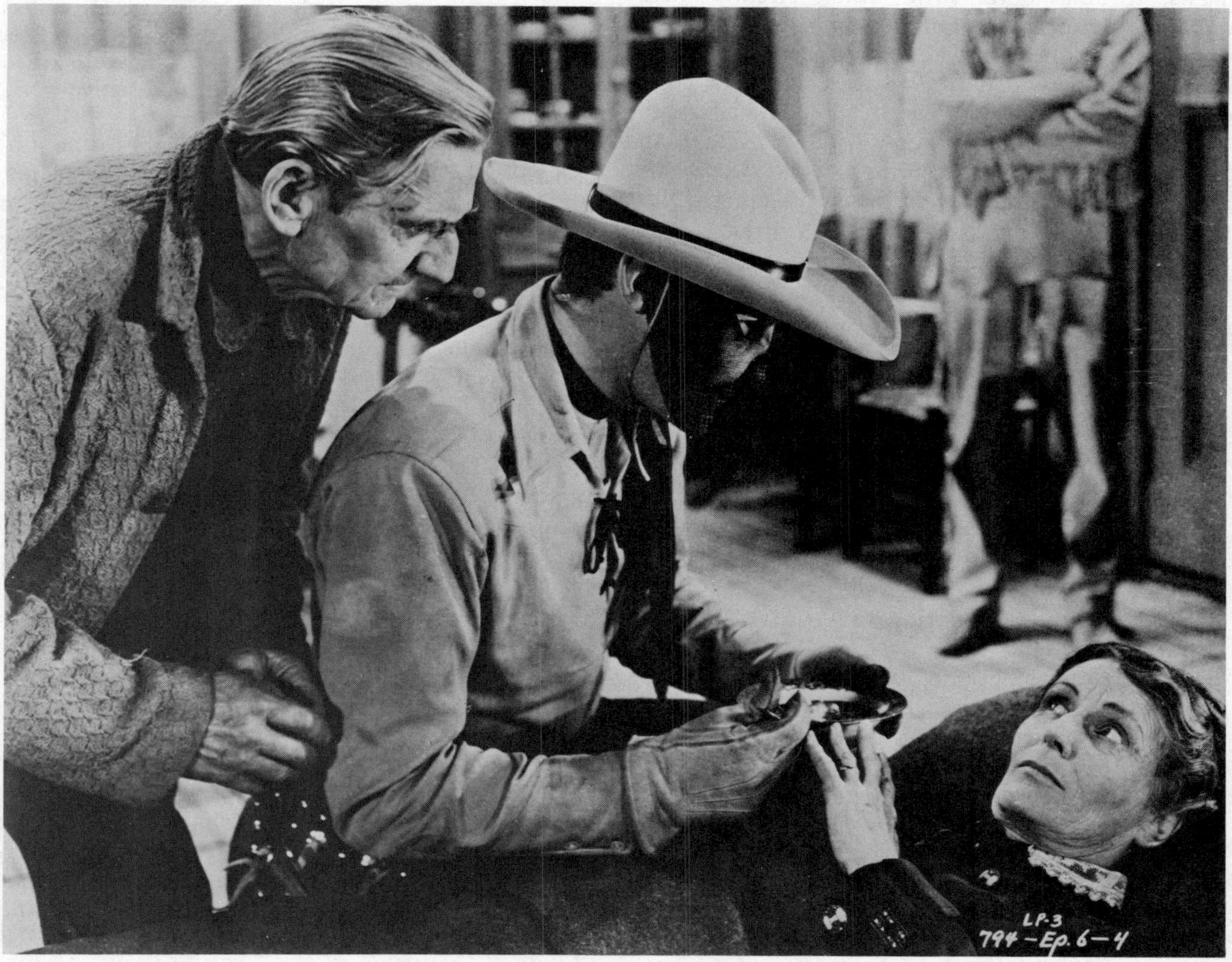

The Lone Ranger (Lee Powell) comes to the assistance of an elderly couple. Notice that in the Lone Ranger movie serials the lower portion of the famous black mask is constructed of a mesh material. (Republic Pictures, 1938)

were known for doing everything quickly) went into production on a sequel called *The Lone Ranger Rides Again.* Even though three of the four screenwriters were carryovers from the first serial, there was no plot connection between the two serials and still little resemblance to the radio series. In the first serial the surviving Ranger was named Allen King; in the sequel he became Bill Andrews.

In the acting department, only Chief Thunder-Cloud (Tonto) and Silver Chief (Silver) survived the previous fifteen chapters. Republic decided to cast its young star from the popular "Three Mesquiteers" series, Robert Livingston, in the title role.

In the sequel the Lone Ranger was Bill Andrews, troubleshooter, who, when circumstances dictated, donned the famous mask and became the Lone Ranger. It was all handled very similarly to the way Charles Starrett in later years covered his face with a black kerchief and, "presto," was "The Durango Kid." Unlike Fran Striker's original Lone Ranger who wore the mask all the time—even when sleeping—this movie Lone Ranger, alias Bill Andrews, only wore the mask when called upon to act in the name of law and order. As the pressbook stated,

> Republic Studios deliberated long before deciding to make Livingston's identity known to audiences throughout the serial. The Lone Ranger is a man of mystery. Republic kept the masked rider as such by having Livingston remain unknown to the villains, but with the audience in full knowledge of his name throughout the production. The audience knows from the second episode that the nester named Andrews is in reality the Lone Ranger.

Fast action and daring adventure are the prime ingredients in a good movie serial; the plot must never get in the way. After having tried in vain to follow the plot twists and turns in the summaries of the fifteen episodes in each of the two Lone Ranger pressbooks, I will spare the reader that mind-boggling experience. It is enough to say that in the sequel it's the cattlemen versus the nesters plot. The Lone Ranger and Tonto come to the assistance of a group of nesters trying to settle in San Ramon Valley. The cattlemen in the district, led by chief heavy Bart Dolan, seek to drive them out and are aided by a mysterious band of Black Raiders.

The Lone Ranger valiantly combats Dolan and the others with the help of Tonto, Silver, and a mexican companion, Juan Vasquez (who is hustled into the plot in the first chapter in what appears to be a contrived method to bring additional marquee strength in the form of Duncan Renaldo, later television's "Cisco Kid"). Regardless, after facing certain death for fourteen chapter weeks, the Lone Ranger brings "Frontier Justice" (the title of chapter fifteen) to the San Ramon Valley.

The pressbook summary of the events leading to Bart Dolan's demise, overflowing with classic serial plot elements, is perhaps unintentionally humorous:

> The Raiders, aware of the failure of their plot and fearing the on-coming cavalry, order a wagon-load of explosives rolled down onto the fortress walls. The Ranger, arriving in time, mounts the wagon and brings it to a stop before it crashes. He orders the settlers to the far side of the enclosure. Bart Dolan, investigating the cause of failure, is killed when the explosive finally does its destructive work.

Dolan apparently suffered from the same uncontrollable curiosity that so often, years later, foiled the "Roadrunner" coyote when the trap or bomb or "whatever" didn't work as planned. He had to go see why not!

As with the first Lone Ranger movie serial, the cast was composed of talented young performers on the way up and established character actors familiar to regular patrons of serials and B-Westerns. Robert Livingston's star was on the ascent at this point of his career. In 1936 he had created the "Stoney Brooke" character in the popular "Three Mesquiteers" series and had been given the opportunity by Republic to perform in features outside the Western mold. In 1942 Livingston contracted with Producers Releasing Corporation (PRC) to star in a B-Western series in which he played a masked man called "The Lone Rider." (Trendle must have loved that!)

Livingston, though quite handsome and possessed of a breezy, very likable screen personality, never became the star that Republic hoped for. He never came close to being in the Gene Autry, Roy Rogers, or even Johnny Mack Brown league. In the late forties he tried desperately to tie down the Lone Ranger role in the television series, but time had passed him by and the younger Clayton Moore (then "King of Republic Serials") got the role. It was rumored that Livingston, disappointed at not being cast, occasionally retreated to the nectar of the grape, and could be heard late at night crying a "Hi-Yo, Silver" into the Hollywood canyons. In the

One of the publicity posters from the movie serial sequel. (Republic Pictures, 1939)

The Republic Pictures publicity department again for the second Lone Ranger serial provided colorful, exciting lobby and newspaper "teasers" that succeeded in drawing crowds every weekend for the "next thrill-packed adventure." (1939)

The above poster is a good example of the type of publicity layouts Republic Pictures used throughout the 1930s and 1940s to promote their movies—a montage of action shots along with a generous complement of artist's drawings. (1939)

All NEW Thrills! All NEW Adventures!
WHEN YOUR FAVORITE HERO TAKES THE TRAIL IN HIS COURAGEOUS FIGHT AGAINST THE LAWLESSNESS OF THE OLD WEST!
THE LONE RANGER RIDES AGAIN
ROBERT LIVINGSTON
CHIEF THUNDER-CLOUD
SILVER CHIEF
DUNCAN RENALDO
Based on THE RADIO SERIAL "THE LONE RANGER" by FRAN STRIKER
directed by William Witney, John English
A Republic SERIAL IN 15 THRILLING CHAPTERS

Juan Vasquez (Duncan Renaldo) and the Lone Ranger (Robert Livingston) in hand-to-hand combat during chapter one when Vasquez mistakenly believes that the Lone Ranger has murdered his brother. (The Lone Ranger Rides Again, *Republic Pictures, 1939*)

The situation looks grim as Doc Grover (Ernie Adams) examines his patient. A surprisingly affectionate Lone Ranger and Tonto, and others look on. (The Lone Ranger Rides Again, *Republic Pictures, 1939)*

The Lone Ranger (Robert Livingston) and Tonto (Chief Thunder-Cloud) temporarily have the drop on villain Ralph Dunn (black vest) and his "Black Raiders." Notice that the scar-faced young outlaw next to the Lone Ranger is famous stuntman Dave Sharpe, who was unbilled in the serial. (The Lone Ranger Rides Again, *Republic Pictures, 1939*)

fifties he was to play character parts on "The Lone Ranger" television program.

Jinx Falken (later Falkenburg), not yet twenty, provided what little love interest was allowed in the movie serial. A swimming and tennis champion as well as model (she was the first Miss Rheingold), she later became a well-known radio and television personality with her husband, Tex McCrary.

Duncan Renaldo, a star of silent pictures, was most noted at the time for his starring role in *Trader Horn* (1931) and his arrest by immigration authorities on a charge of illegally entering the country. Government officials produced evidence that he was born in Romania; Renaldo claimed that he had been born in Camden, New Jersey, but was taken to Romania when he was very young. Renaldo subsequently spent eighteen months in the minimum-security prison on McNeil Island off the coast of Washington. On the day before he was to be released (January 25, 1936) President Roosevelt granted him an unconditional pardon. After his release, his old friend Herbert J. Yates, president of Republic Pictures, put him on a three hundred dollars a week salary and started him acting again. At the time of *The Lone Ranger Rides Again,* Renaldo was just beginning to get his career moving again. In the forties he became the "Cisco Kid" in a feature series for Monogram Pictures and continued the role in the famous television series until 1955.

The villainy in the second Lone Ranger serial was provided by Ralph Dunn and J. Farrell MacDonald. Others in the cast included such serial and B-Western favorites as Rex Lease, Ted Mapes, Stanley Blystone, Carlton Young, and, interestingly enough, Glenn Strange, who ten years later in 1949 would confront television's Lone Ranger (Clayton Moore) as Butch Cavendish. It was the Butch Cavendish gang, you will remember, that killed all of the Texas Rangers in Bryant's Gap, save one, who then became the Lone Ranger. Strange is most known for his portrayal of Sam the bartender on television's "Gunsmoke."

Most of the production crew from the first Lone Ranger movie serial served in similar capacities in the sequel. William Witney and John English repeated their directorial duties and would continue to direct serials and features for Republic Pictures for years to come. Their serials along with those of Spencer G. Bennett were to become appreciated by serial and B-Western buffs years later as the best of that era.

In recent years, as interest in the serials of the 1930s and 1940s has been rekindled, a cult of sorts has evolved around the Lone Ranger movie serials. This interest, perhaps, can be explained by two factors: the divergence from the character as he was known in all other media, and the fact that until recently there were no known prints of either serial in existence. As Alan G. Barbour states in his wonderful 1971 book, *The Thrill Of It All*:

> Extensive searching by numerous investigators has failed to turn up any sign of either this serial [*The Lone Ranger*] or its sequel *The Lone Ranger Rides Again.* All records of the films have completely disappeared from Republic files; no negatives or prints have been located, and the new copyright owners can offer no information of any value concerning the properties.

In November 1974, in the magazine *Films in Review,* Francis M. Nevins, Jr., writing about William Witney ("Ballet of Violence: The Films of William Witney") stated that he recently saw prints of the two serials. About *The Lone Ranger* he writes:

> The most complete existing version I know consists of scratchy and choppily re-edited segments of thirteen out of the original fifteen chapters, subtitled in Spanish, with the masked man called El Llanero Solitario and the name of his Indian companion changed to Ponto since Tonto in Spanish means fool.

Later Nevins comments on the sequel:

> Next came "The Lone Ranger Rides Again" ('39), another "lost" work. It shows the collective (Whitney and English) at its worst (I can testify as I have seen the only surviving print, a washed-out duplicate with Spanish subtitles.)

Concerning the matter of quality, Nevins seems to feel that the original was an excellent Republic serial but that the sequel had too many elements that were "simply awful, including inept fistfights, a ridiculous declamatory acting style reminiscent of riverboat melodrama, a hopeless performance by butterball Ralph Dunn as the villain, and a lame music score by [William] Lava."

Alan G. Barbour in *The Thrill Of It All* concludes:

> A detailed study of the cutting continuity (a scene-for-scene breakdown of the entire film) shows it to be merely a routine Western adventure containing

Lobby card for the second Lone Ranger serial. Uncharacteristically, George W. Trendle is not billed as the "creator of 'The Lone Ranger.'"

only the usual Republic chases, fights, etc. (not that that was bad, by any means, but audiences expected more considering the excellent quality of the first serial).

An interesting little sidelight to the two movie serials is to be found in the way in which the two serials differ in their credit references to the origin of the property. *The Lone Ranger* publicity states:

> Based on the radio serial "The Lone Ranger" created by Station WXYZ Detroit, and written by Fran Striker.

Publicity for *The Lone Ranger Rides Again* states:

> Based on the radio serial "The Lone Ranger" by Fran Striker.

These two excerpts from the publicity are, perhaps, interesting for at least two reasons: (1) neither mentions George W. Trendle by name, and (2) Striker gets solo billing on the second serial. (Maybe Trendle knew when to take credit and when not to take credit.)

And finally this—Billy Bletcher, voice imitator and animator, in *The Real Tinsel* by Rosenburg and Silverstein, writes that he was hired to dub the voice of the Lone Ranger in the first movie serial after the film was in the can. He states that it was felt the voice of the actor in the mask (presumably Lee Powell) didn't sound anything like the voice of the radio Lone Ranger (Earle Graser at that time) that children and adults were used to hearing.

Bletcher goes on to write that he dubbed the Lone Ranger voice in the second serial, too. It seems slightly dismaying and a little hard to accept that Republic had Billy Bletcher dub its well-known Western star Robert Livingston, but, of course, Hollywood has been known to do dismaying things.

George W. Trendle apparently learned his lesson. The Lone Ranger was not allowed near a movie camera for the next ten years. When the television version was about to be filmed, Trendle retained all artistic control over the series and made sure that his designated production coordinator kept a close eye on what was happening to the masked rider of the plains.

7

"Hi-Yo, Silver Lining"

OTHER WAYS TO MAKE A BUCK WITH A WINNER

THE 24,905 requests for the Lone Ranger popgun during the first few months of the radio program in 1933 convinced George W. Trendle that there was money to be made with each Lone Ranger shout of "Hi-Yo, Silver." The first task was to find a sponsor for his masked rider and by November of 1933 he had done just that.

The first sponsor, Silvercup Bread (the brand name was just a coincidence), turned out to be a long and loyal one. During the years that Silvercup sponsored "The Lone Ranger," the number of radio stations carrying the program rose with the regularity of the sponsor's bread. When Silvercup first sponsored the program there were only eight stations in its line-up. By the end of its sponsorship in 1939, there were 140 stations riding with the Ranger. Bond Bread took over regional sponsorship on twenty-two of the 140 radio stations; there were other sponsors on eighty-eight of the stations and the program was sustaining on thirty stations. The other sponsors and the sustaining stations received the 10:30 P.M. broadcast of the program. The commercial breaks during that broadcast were filled with a musical interlude. If the program was sponsored, the station would fade the music for its sponsor's message; if sustaining, the station would just fill the time with the music.

Throughout the years baking companies have had an affinity for "The Lone Ranger" program. By 1941 the program was sponsored in various regions across the country by as many as sixteen different bakeries. One baking company on the West Coast was selling a product called Gingham Bread. They had the audacity to ask if (for the West Coast broadcast of the program) the horse's name could be changed from Silver to Gingham. George W. Trendle's response was unprintable.

During the years that Silvercup Bread sponsored the program, an ingenious promotional campaign was begun for the program and the sponsor—The Lone Ranger Safety Club. It began in 1935 and continued on the program for years. The club worked this way: The young listener was told to go to his local grocer and get the Safety Club application card that was only available there. The card contained a series of ten promises that the prospective member was asked to make—promises that were sure to delight his mother and father—promises such as not to play in the streets, to always tell the truth, not to cross the street anywhere but at a crossing, etc. The youngster was to read the card carefully, sign it himself, and have one of his parents sign it, too. The card was then to be sent to the Lone Ranger.

In return, the Lone Ranger would send a membership card, a secret code for the messages,

The first sponsor of "The Lone Ranger" radio program, Silvercup Bread, sent this Safety Scout Badge to new members of the Lone Ranger Safety Club.

Sehl Advertising Agency, Inc.

360 NORTH MICHIGAN AVENUE
CHICAGO, ILL.

January 3, 1935

RECEIVED
JAN 4 1935
KUNSKY-TRENDLE
BROADCASTING
CORP.

Mr. James Jewell,
Kunsky-Trendle Broadcasting Corp.,
3d Floor - Madison Theatre Bldg.,
Detroit, Michigan.

Dear Mr. Jewell:

Mr. Wilsher submits a suggestion, as follows:

"When you are eating bread, think of SILVERCUP" and "When you are eating SILVERCUP, remember the Lone Ranger thinks of you".

Mr. Wilsher's thought is that we might build around a statement of this kind as a signature for the play each night - have the announcer work in something on this order, with a little background of music.

Perhaps you can give us a suggestion for a better wording.

The thought is that we always want them to think of SILVERCUP, and then we want all of the youngsters to believe that when they are eating it, the Lone Ranger thinks of them.

I would like the benefit of your suggestions, please.

With kindest regards, I am

Sincerely yours,

SEHL ADVERTISING AGENCY, INC.

H W Sehl

HWS-S

This letter from the Sehl Advertising Agency to Jim Jewell reveals the close Lone Ranger-sponsor identification that Silvercup Bread was striving for.

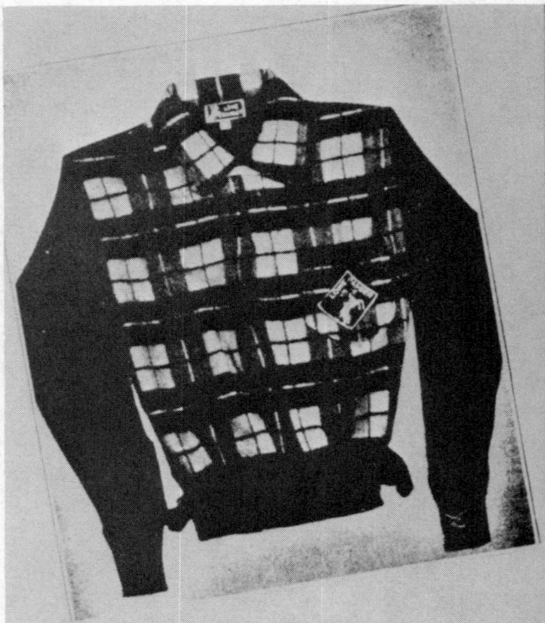

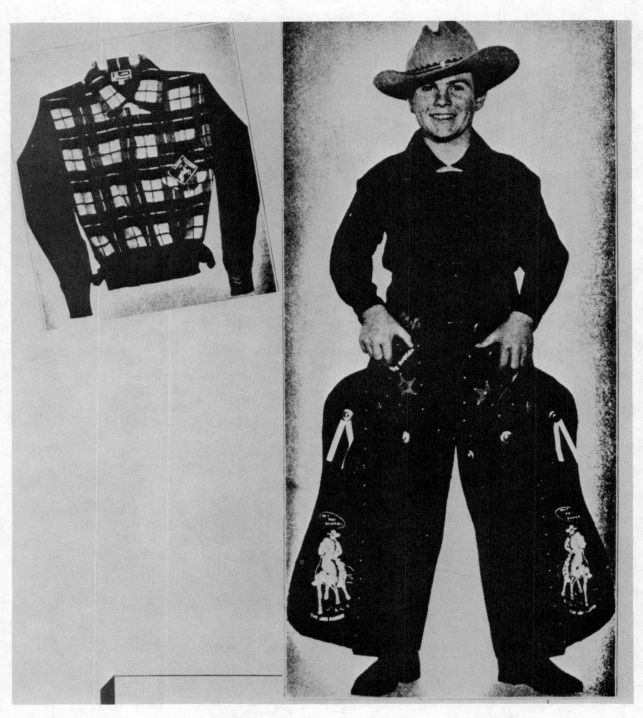

Lone Ranger cowboy outfits and "genuine leather" holsters and guns have been popular merchandising items throughout most of the years the character has been in existence. The above Lone Ranger clothes are from the late 1930s.

Starting in April of 1951 and continuing throughout most of the years since, specially recorded Lone Ranger adventures have been distributed through music and department stores. By the late 1950s it was claimed that more than a million of these records had been sold. The above 1951 album cover bears the additional art work of young Russell Livingstone, the son of the director.

This later Safety Club Badge and autograph were sent to new members when the program was sponsored regionally by Cobakco Bread.

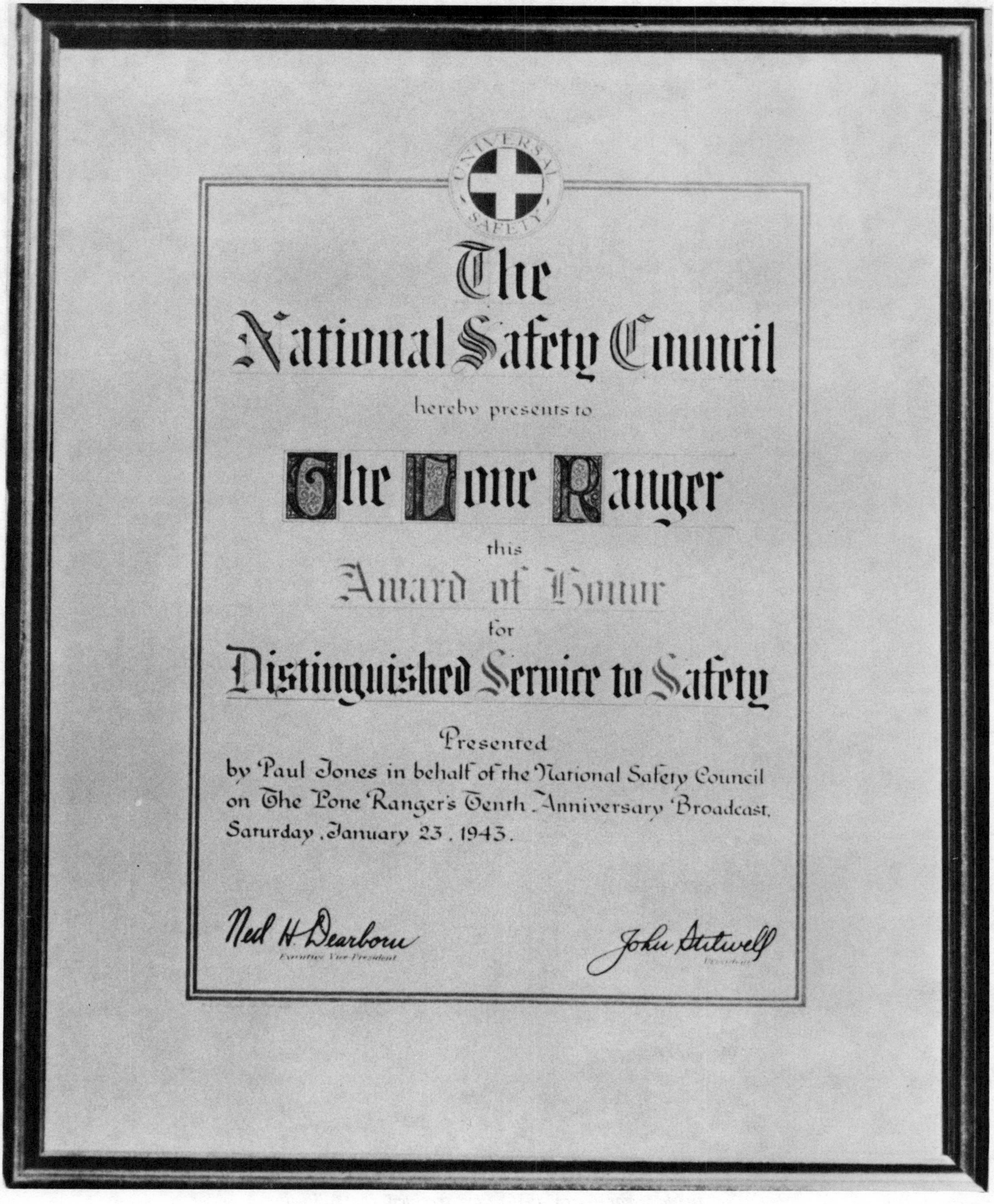

UNIVERSAL SAFETY
The National Safety Council
hereby presents to
The Lone Ranger
this
Award of Honour
for
Distinguished Service to Safety
Presented
by Paul Jones in behalf of the National Safety Council
on The Lone Ranger's Tenth Anniversary Broadcast,
Saturday, January 23, 1943.
Ned H. Dearborn
John Stilwell

"The Lone Ranger" radio program was the recipient of this "Award of Honor" from the National Safety Council in 1943 in recognition of the program's emphasis on safety as exemplified by The Lone Ranger Safety Club. The program received similar awards in 1936 and 1940 from other organizations.

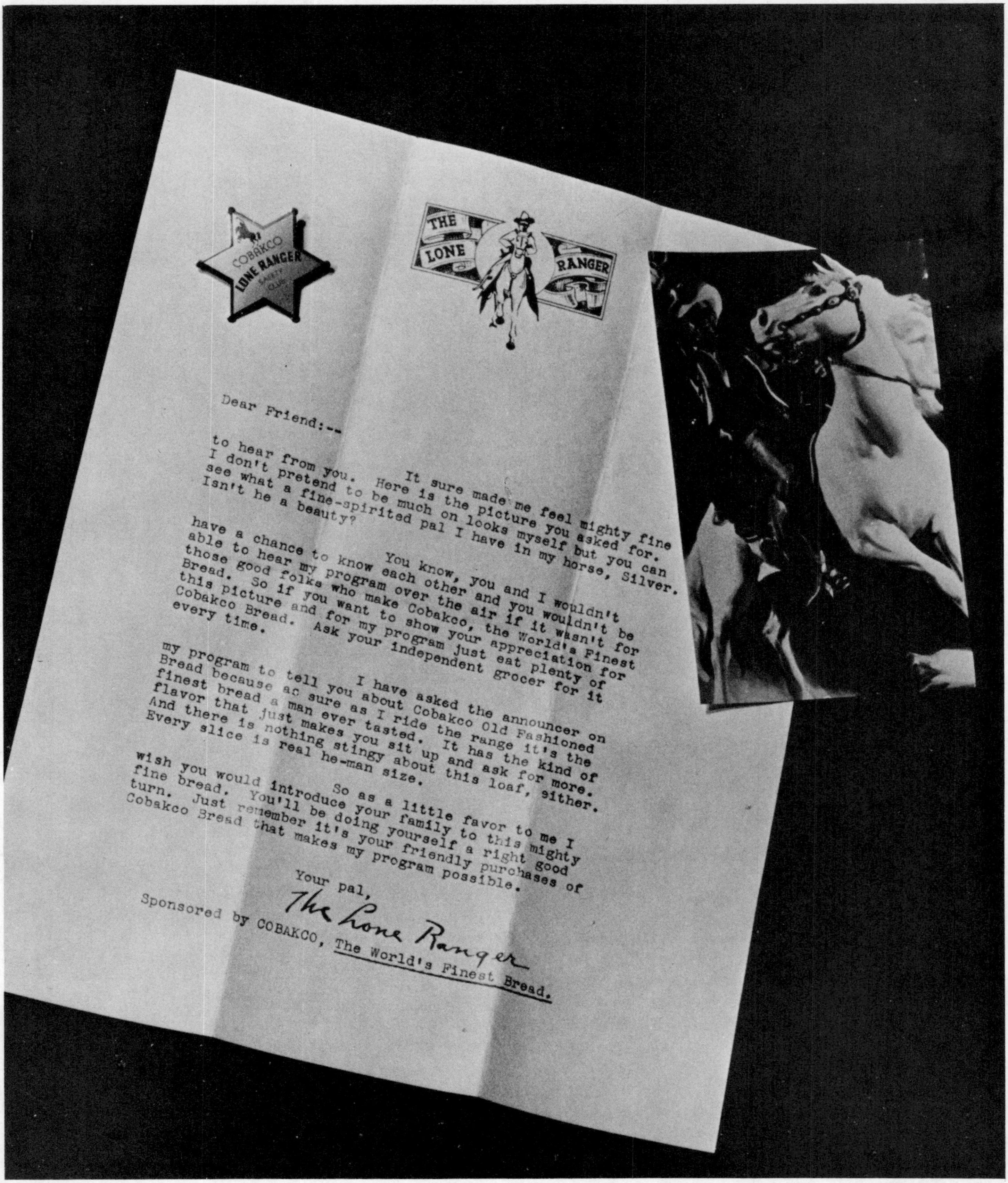

Dear Friend:--

It sure made me feel mighty fine to hear from you. Here is the picture you asked for. I don't pretend to be much on looks myself but you can see what a fine-spirited pal I have in my horse, Silver. Isn't he a beauty?

You know, you and I wouldn't have a chance to know each other and you wouldn't be able to hear my program over the air if it wasn't for those good folks who make Cobakco, the World's Finest Bread. So if you want to show your appreciation for this picture and for my program just eat plenty of Cobakco Bread. Ask your independent grocer for it every time.

I have asked the announcer on my program to tell you about Cobakco Old Fashioned Bread because as sure as I ride the range it's the finest bread a man ever tasted. It has the kind of flavor that just makes you sit up and ask for more. And there is nothing stingy about this loaf, either. Every slice is real he-man size.

So as a little favor to me I wish you would introduce your family to this mighty fine bread. You'll be doing yourself a right good turn. Just remember it's your friendly purchases of Cobakco Bread that makes my program possible.

Your pal,

The Lone Ranger

Sponsored by COBAKCO, The World's Finest Bread.

For joining The Lone Ranger Safety Club this particular year (circa 1938) you received the following items: the Safety Club Badge, a picture of the Lone Ranger, and a friendly letter from "your pal, The Lone Ranger."

and (if the prospective member had gotten three neighbor kids who did not then use the sponsor's product to promise to buy it the next time they were at the grocery store) a Lone Ranger Safety Club Badge. Over the years the items a new Safety Club member received varied. At times Lone Ranger masks were the lure; from time to time photographs of a highly stylized oil painting of the Lone Ranger were also popular.

The club was first announced on "The Lone Ranger" in October of 1935. Within six weeks almost half a million Safety Club Badges had been sent to signed-up members. By 1938 the exhibitors for the new movie serial, *The Lone Ranger,* were told by the Republic Pictures publicity department that "The Lone Ranger Safety Clubs boasting over one and one-half million members means money in the box office—and assures exhibitors of child patronage." The publicity department for the movie serial went on to say:

> One of the largest juvenile clubs ever organized for publicity purposes backs "The Lone Ranger" radio program. There are over one and one-half million members in this nation-wide organization. Every member is an enthusiastic "Lone Ranger" serial fan. These clubs were organized by and are under the supervision of the sponsors of the radio program. Contact the sponsors listed on the facing page and cash in on the great publicity angles offered by getting the club sponsors to notify club members of the coming of Republic's *The Lone Ranger.*

Although the Lone Ranger Safety Club was begun by Silvercup Bread, other sponsors around the country were able to get on the promotional bandwagon as time passed. Ultimately over half a million Lone Ranger masks and two million photographs were sent to club members. Before the Safety Club was allowed to disband, there were over two million staunch members working diligently for the sponsors around the country. It is to be suspected that today the FTC and the FCC might look askance at the slightly questionable motives of the people responsible for the Lone Ranger Safety Club, but there is no questioning that it was a beautiful promotional campaign that made young Rangers aware of safety and also moved bread off the shelves.

During World War II General Mills became the coast to coast radio sponsor of "The Lone Ranger" and generally plugged two of its cereal products—Kix and Cheerios. "The Lone Ranger" had a long and happy relationship with General Mills both on radio and television.

During the 1940s many radio premiums were offered to "Lone Ranger" listeners. If you are fortunate enough now to be able to get your hands on these premiums of the 1940s, you quickly realize that they possess unusual craftsmanship and detail. These "Lone Ranger" radio premiums were a bargain back in the 1940s. Generally all you needed was a top from a box of Kix or Cheerios (depending on which product happened to be the in-season cereal) and ten cents for the "fantastic, never to be repeated offer." As the 1950s began to loom nearer, postwar inflation hit the premium market and the price rose to fifteen and then finally twenty-five cents. But the premium was still worth the extra cost.

What you got for your box top and coin was many parted. First, there was the excitement of hearing about the marvelous ring, badge, bullet, or "whatever" that was described on each broadcast. You couldn't see it; you only heard the excited voice of the program narrator describing all the characteristics, telling you what a great time you would have with it, telling you how shiny or big or colorful or exciting it was. The narrator quickly convinced you that you *must* be the first "fellow or gal" on the block to get your premium. He never called them premiums, though. They were usually described as exciting "offers."

The second part of what you received for your box top and coin was the fun of going with your mom to the grocery store, buying the box of the Lone Ranger's cereal, writing out the order for the premium, and personally giving the letter to the mailman when he came around the next day.

Next you had about a ten-day wait for the premium to arrive. Each breakfast bowl of Kix was a reminder (as if you really needed it!) that one more day had passed—the time of arrival was growing nearer. By the seventh day of waiting you could always convince yourself that it might arrive earlier than the previous premium and that today might be the day. If for some reason you were feeling in a negative, pessimistic mood, you could convince yourself that the letter had gotten lost in the mail and that the offer would be cancelled before you could reorder. Waiting for a radio premium to arrive was one of the most exquisite anxieties I ever experienced as a child. I suspect I am not the only child of the 1930s and 1940s who experienced those feelings.

Finally the premium arrived (the next part of the premium adventure) in its small brown box.

Your name was on the label and the return address was usually General Mills, Minneapolis, Minn. (For a time some of my small neighbor friends and I thought that General Mills was a military man who owned Kix and Cheerios.)

After carefully examining the outside of the box, you opened it to find the premium you had been hearing and thinking about for several weeks. I cannot ever remember being disappointed upon opening a radio premium box. Many times the highly touted "gifts" inside cereal packages were a gyp; later television premiums were made of cheap plastic, and, besides, there was no suspense because you had seen on television exactly what you were going to get; and Cracker Jack prizes were quite often a disappointment in later years, too; but never a radio premium—there you got your money's worth.

And now, finally, the last part of the premium adventure: You and your friends got to play with your new possession and include it in your daily cowboy and Indian adventures. You could think of a hundred important (tiny) things to store in the secret compartment. The built-in trick mirror allowed you to look around corners so that you didn't blunder into the path of the wicked dry-gulcher who was out gunning for you. The fact that it glowed in the dark made it possible to send flashing signals across dark rooms. The small, attached magnifying glass could be used to examine suspicious looking fingerprints. The secret decoder gave you the chance to slip messages to your endangered amigos that the dirty, sidewinding owlhoots could never decipher (unless they, too, had sent to General Mills).

I guess no one premium contained all of those marvelous features, but eventually you had a chance to possess them all. To coin a phrase—a radio premium was a many-splendored thing!

Even though the Lone Ranger "lived" in "those thrilling days of yesteryear," this did not stop him from acknowledging the existence of the World War during the 1940s and offering radio premiums that were designed to stir a feeling of patriotism in young minds. One such premium was a ring embossed with the emblems of each branch of the armed services. When you slid the emblem out of its slot, you discovered a tiny picture of the Lone Ranger inside. Still sustaining the patriotic motif, the Lone Ranger later offered a film strip ring that depicted scenes of the landing at Iwo Jima.

The ending of the War inspired the Lone Ranger Atomic Bomb Ring. On first look, an unsuspecting person might mistake the "atomic bomb" on the ring for a silver bullet. Close inspection, however, revealed that it was, in fact, a miniature atomic bomb.

This ring, I suppose, came the closest to being a disappointment for me of all the radio premiums I ever received. The prime feature of the ring was the "flashes from disintegrating atoms" you were supposed to see upon removing the rear red tail fins and looking into the glass-covered inner part of the bomb. We were told that the flashes were more visible in a darkened area. I have the distinct impression that I spent about a week of my childhood entombed in an upstairs closet squinting vainly into the silver end of the Atomic Bomb Ring. I never saw the atomic flashes and finally settled for just wearing the ring. And it was a handsome ring. The "gold" band that held the bomb in place was embossed with what appeared to be pilot's wings. The main band on each side was embossed with a thunderbolt.

All through the years of "The Lone Ranger" radio program the popular premiums kept coming at a regular rate. Another much sought after Lone Ranger ring was the one that had a six-shooter mounted on its base. The six-shooter was even designed to shoot sparks when you fanned its cigarette lighter-like flint wheel.

Although rings were probably the most popular, there were other types of radio premiums that eager listeners sent for. For example, there were the Lone Ranger Deputy Badges and the famous silver bullets. In the second half of the 1940s, the Official Lone Ranger Pedometer was offered to all the junior Rangers. Looking at this extremely well-constructed metal pedometer today, one can be impressed with the value provided for the box top and quarter—even by the comparatively lower post-World War II cost standards.

Most youngsters of the 1930s and '40s played with their Lone Ranger ring, badge, mask, pin, or pedometer for a few days or weeks and then —in the mysterious way things vanish—it was gone. But over the years some of the premiums survived (as mine did), not because of some incredible insight that told us these things would one day—years in the future—have special meaning or value but mostly by sheer accident.

In my own case I never really realized I was saving these childhood relics. As a youngster, I

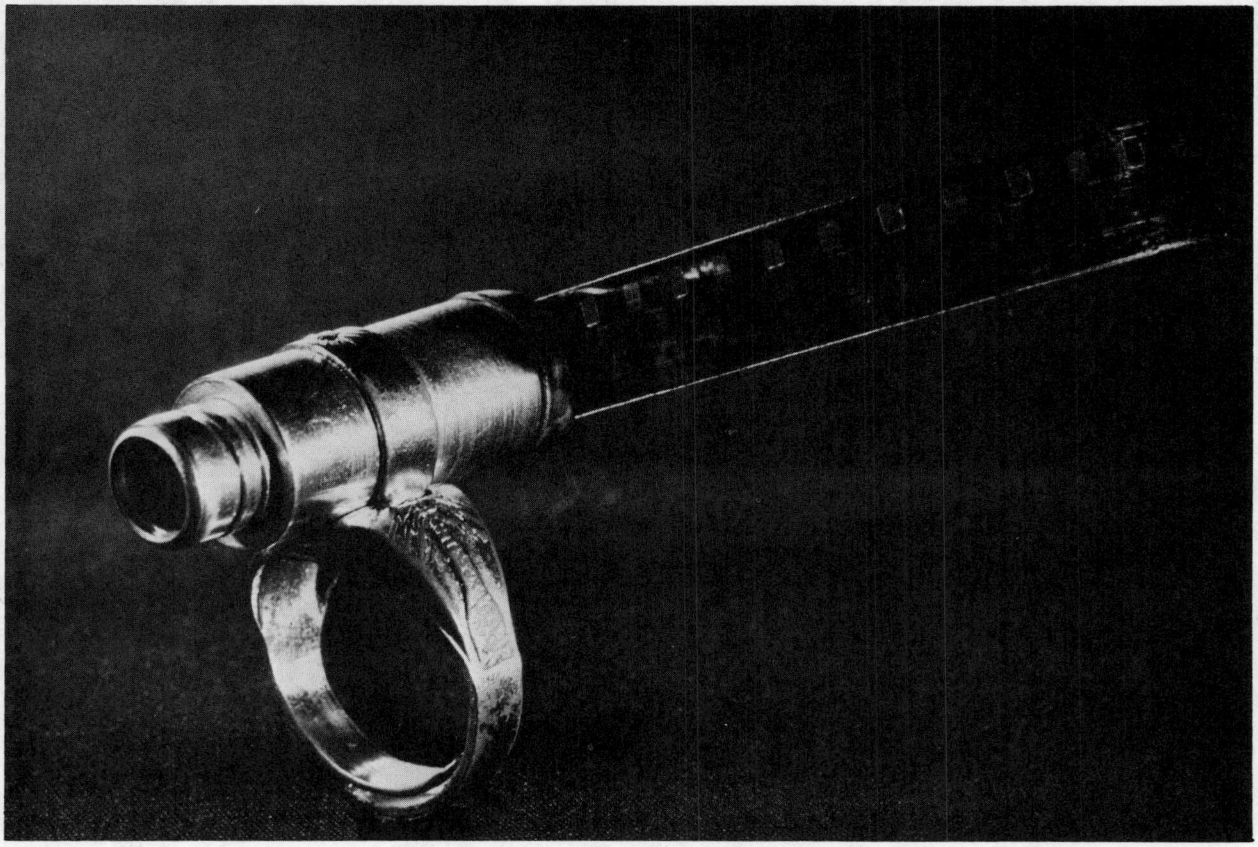

The Lone Ranger Film Strip Ring has a radio tower embossed upon the "gold" band. The tubelike viewer has a retractable focus mechanism. The color film of war scenes moves through a slot on the front of the viewer.

The famous Lone Ranger Atomic Bomb Ring.

The Lone Ranger Weather Ring

WARNING!

ALWAYS TAKE THIS RING OFF YOUR FINGER BEFORE WASHING YOUR HAND. The reason for this is because the special indicator material in the ring is very sensitive! But . . . if you do get it wet, replace the indicator material in the ring with some of the extra material which we enclose in this package.

To replace the indicator material in your Weather Ring, simply use the point of a pin to pull out the old indicator . . . being careful not to raise the plastic setting. Then trim a piece of the extra indicator material to proper size and carefully slide it into position.

REMEMBER . . .

Don't expect this ring to change with the weather while you are inside the house! For most satisfactory results, always notice the color of the ring after you have been outside for thirty minutes. When your ring turns from blue to pink that is an indication that it may rain or snow. When it turns from pink to blue that is an indication that it may clear.

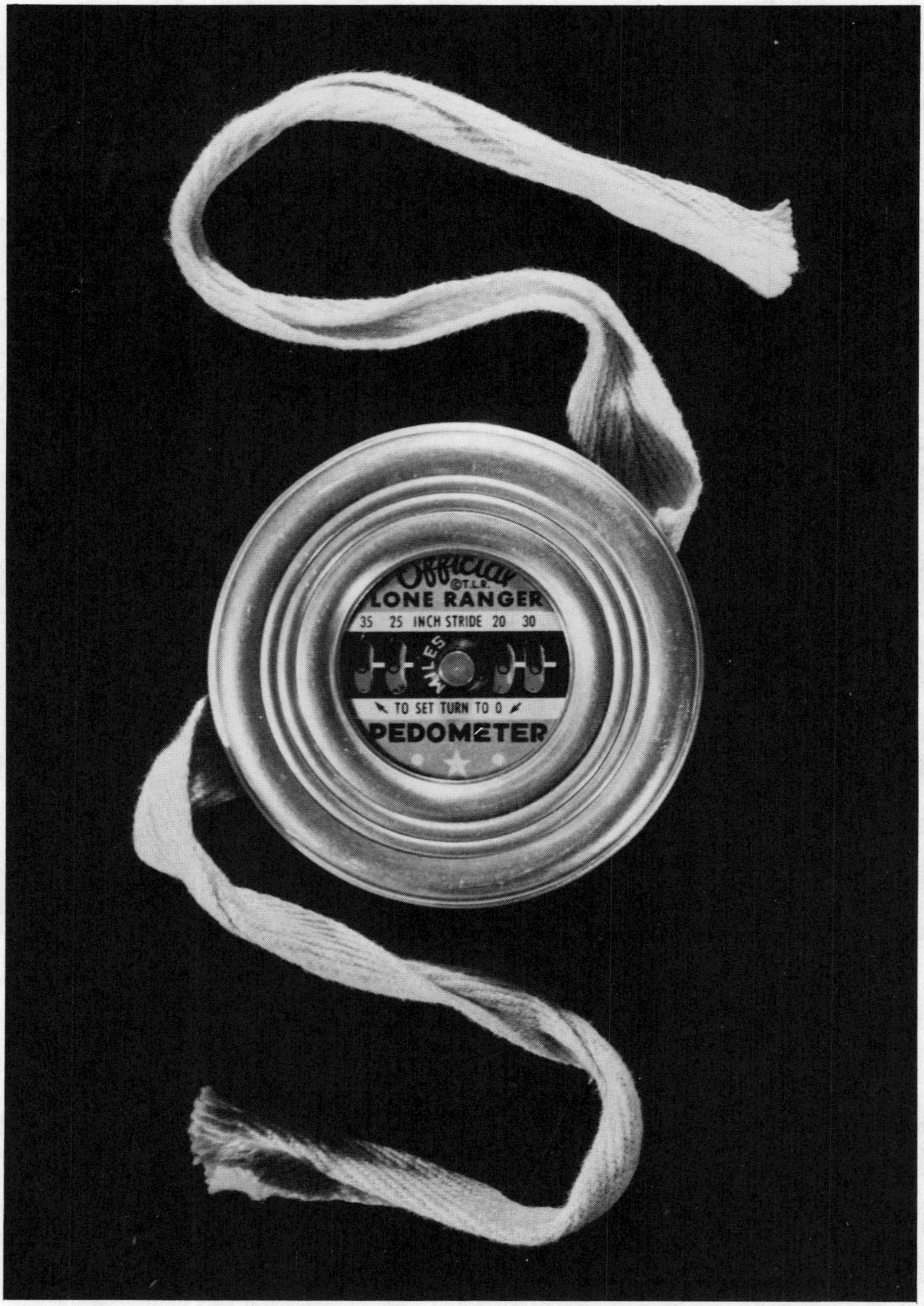

The Official Lone Ranger Pedometer. You could tie it around your leg or fasten it on your belt. Assuming you set the dial at zero prior to your walk, you could later look at the slot that corresponded with the length of your stride and determine how far you had walked.

The very rare 1942 Lone Ranger Victory Corps lapel pin is currently valued at twenty dollars or more.

put them in a cardboard men's jewel box that somehow found its way into my dresser drawer. There the "jewels" remained until after I came back from college. Sometime after I married, the jewel box joined me again. For years it remained in the back of desk drawers almost forgotten.

In the early 1970s I suddenly discovered that I possessed a small treasure in that now dilapidated box. Thousands of people in their middle years and others who were too young to remember radio premiums suddenly became interested in these remnants from an earlier time. These trinkets that were handled so casually years before were now delicately fondled as a precious treasure, and, perhaps, they are, because an era —a childhood—is there to be remembered in each of those pieces of yesterday.

In case you didn't save the premiums you collected so long ago, many of them are still available at times from dealers who specialize in memorabilia—whether it be radio premiums, old movie posters, rare comic books, pulp magazines, or Dixie Cup lids. But remember, yesterday's throwaway toy is today's collector's item. The goodies are no longer available for a box top and a dime—or even a quarter. Inflation has hit the nostalgia market, too.

The following is a list of "Lone Ranger" memorabilia available from four dealers I contacted recently. The prices vary according to supply and demand, of course, but the prices indicated are fairly typical as of this time. There is no indication that the items will not go up in value with the passing of more time.

- The Lone Ranger Secret Code Pen (blue) —$5.00
- The Lone Ranger Game (illustrated board, two spinners, instructions, six small metal figures, complete from 1938) —$20.00
- The Lone Ranger Blackout Kit (1943) in the original mailing envelope—$50.00
- Kix Tattoo Transfers (1944) The Lone Ranger, etc. in original envelope—$30.00
- The Lone Ranger Paint Book (1940, very few pictures painted in) —$12.00 (Author's note: You can get the 1975 Lone Ranger Paint Book with no pictures painted in for 39¢.)
- The Lone Ranger Flashlight Ring—$25.00
- The Lone Ranger Flashlight (no battery) —$20.00
- The Lone Ranger Wallet—$5.00
- The Lone Ranger Film Strip Ring—$30.00
- The Lone Ranger Weather Ring (in the original box with instructions)—$40.00
- The Lone Ranger Atomic Bomb Ring—$35.00
- The Official Lone Ranger First Aid Kit (1938, still has most of the contents, illustrated box a little rusty) —$45.00
- Lone Ranger Cobakco Safety Club Badge, letter, and picture—all for $40.00
- The Lone Ranger Golden Star Bond Bread Safety Club Badge—$7.00
- The Lone Ranger Deputy Badge—$18.00
- The Lone Ranger Victory Pin (1942) —$20.00
- Lone Ranger photographs (stills from movie serials and television series) —$1.50 to $3.00 each
- Lone Ranger Comic Books— (depending on condition and year) —$1.50 to $16.00 (The $16.00 comic book is #118, 1946)
- The Lone Ranger novels by Fran Striker—$3.00 to $7.00, depending on copyright date and condition (originally $1.00)
- The movie exhibitor Press books for the Lone Ranger movie serials—$5.00 to $15.00, each, depending on dealer

The Lone Ranger movie serials are a good example of the type of excellent promotion and merchandising that was employed to "make an additional buck out of an already winner." As mentioned earlier, there was the tie-up with the countrywide Lone Ranger Safety Clubs. That was just the start! Movie exhibitors were advised by the Republic Pictures' Publicity Department to contact five-and-ten chain stores to set up counter and window displays of serial photographs along with the store's Lone Ranger "Big Little Books" published by the Whitman Publishing Company. In addition, the publicity department also had "special tie-up material" for bookstores that carried the Lone Ranger novels by Fran Striker.

Another movie serial promotional gimmick was the "Lone Ranger Quiz Contest." Movie exhibitors were advised to do the following:

> To promote a sure-fire interest in the Lone Ranger serial, institute the "Lone Ranger Quiz Contest" in your theatre. Available are Quiz booklets containing illustrations of each episode, accompanied by two questions pertaining to that episode. The questions must be answered in full, and the booklet retained by the contestant until the end of the serial (15 weeks), and all questions are answered. The booklet

The LONE RANGER RIDES AGAIN
Republic SERIAL IN 15 EPISODES
BANG GUN
One of the most popular Lone Ranger novelties is the cardboard bang gun. When the gun is swung down rapidly, a paper insert snaps, making a sharp, shot-like noise. The gun can be used over and over, and is a tricky and attractive "teaser" in getting children to attend the serial's opening episode. Space on one side of the gun carries theatre imprint and playdate, while the back is left blank for local tie-up ad. Prices, including theatre imprint and playdate: $6.00 per 250; $10.00 per 500; $18.00 per thousand; $17.00 per thousand over 3000 and $16.00 per thousand over 5000. Order from Economy Novelty & Printing Co., 225 W. 39th Street, New York City.

The Lone Ranger Bang Gun was another promotional item suggested as a "teaser" to get youngsters to attend the serial sequel. When the gun was swung down rapidly, a paper insert snapped, making a sharp, shot-like noise.

The above is actually a 3¾″ x 8″ blotter that was designed as "an attractive advertising entry into schools, libraries and homes" to promote The Lone Ranger Rides Again.

is then turned in to the theatre manager, and prizes awarded for the most accurate and neatest booklet. These Quiz booklets are made of sturdy buff colored ledger paper, in four pages, size 5½ x 8½. Space is left at the top of the front page for theatre imprint. Three-quarters of the back page is open for listing of prizes and local instructions (prizes can be promoted through local merchant carrying Lone Ranger items.) A set of correct answers is sent with each order of Quiz booklets, which are priced at $2.00 for 500.

There were also music tie-ins to the movie serials. Sheet music and records of "Hi-Yo, Silver" and "The Lone Ranger's Song Book: A Collection of His 50 Favorite Songs" were distributed to music stores across the country. Such big names as Roy Rogers (Vocalian 04190) and Kay Kyser and His Orchestra (Brunswick 8165) recorded the now-forgotten (I suspect) "Hi-Yo, Silver" song. The publicity department told exhibitors that "the records will prove especially effective for use on a p.a. sound truck, a lobby phonograph or for an exit march."

Ya' say yur not satisfied; Ya' say ya' want more? Tell ya' what I'm goin' to do:

Here is an item that will outlast many other novelties—a genuine nickle-plated horse shoe nail which the children can shape into a ring. Instructions for making the rings accompany each nail. A splendid advance stunt would be to start the horse shoe nail fad among the children of your community several weeks before the serial opens, or form a Lone Ranger Club among the children, with the nail rings as membership emblems. The nails fit into slits on instruction cards, which are imprinted with theatre and playdate. Prices including imprinting: $4.50 per 500.

And there were others, but you get the idea.

Starting shortly after the mid-1930s, the Lone Ranger newspaper comic strips and comic books were an immediate popular success and a money maker for "The Lone Ranger, Incorporated." (George W. Trendle incorporated the program in January of 1935 to protect his WXYZ radio station from possible infringement suits.) The daily newspaper cartoon strip for King Features was appearing in a total of one hundred daily and/or Sunday newspapers by 1939, and it was reported that the cartoon strip, alone, brought in approximately one hundred thousand dollars a year.

The monthly Lone Ranger comic books published by Dell were equally popular and closely followed the format established in "The Lone Ranger" radio adventures. The appearance of the Lone Ranger changed gradually over the early years to conform more with the then current cowboy hero image; gone was the rather rustic

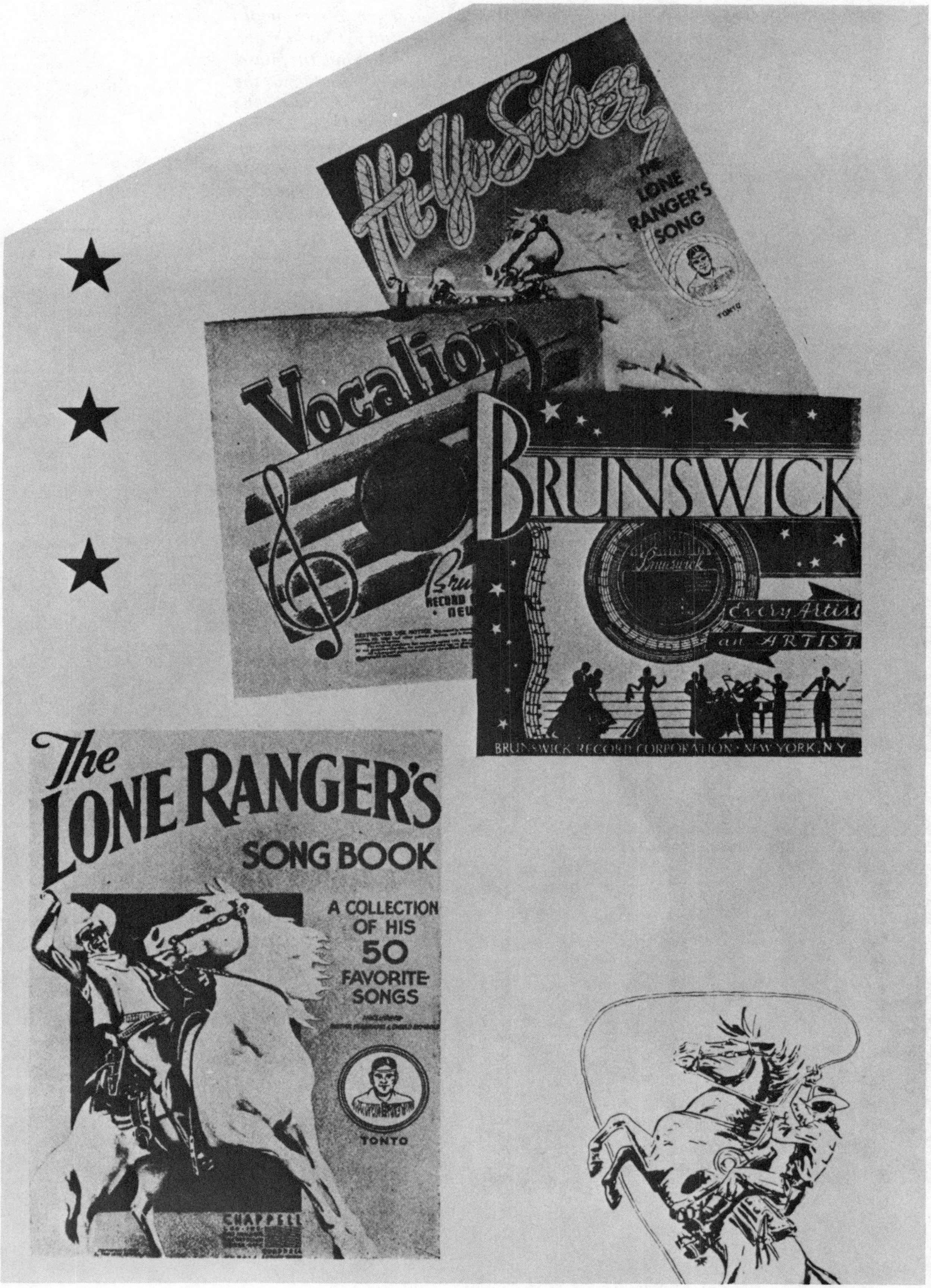
Hi-Yo Silver
THE LONE RANGER'S SONG
TONTO
Vocalion
BRUNSWICK
Every Artist
an ARTIST
BRUNSWICK RECORD CORPORATION • NEW YORK, N.Y.
The LONE RANGER'S
SONG BOOK
A COLLECTION OF HIS 50 FAVORITE SONGS
TONTO
CHAPPELL

These panels from the Lone Ranger comic books reveal the greatest challenge the cartoonist faced when drawing the title character—the eyes behind the mask. In most instances the eyes were eliminated and the masked rider of the plains faced the world with the same eyeball-less expression as Little Orphan Annie. If eyes were to be shown in a close-up panel, the immediately preceding and following panels would generally be long views or over-the-shoulder shots so that the sudden appearance of eyes would be less jarring.

KEEP FIRING THOSE THINGS AS FAST AS YOU CAN!
FIRE FOUNTAIN ALL FIX NOW.
ALL RIGHT, TONTO. LIGHT THE FUSES AND I'LL RIDE OUT TO MEET THOSE INDIANS.
WITH THE FUSES OF FIREWORKS BURNING, THE LONE RANGER ADVANCES TOWARD THE SAVAGES.
HEAR WHAT I SAY, OH, RED MEN!
GO BACK, RED MEN! GO BACK TO YOUR VILLAGES! THE FIRE GOD IS ANGRY WHEN YOU ATTACK WHITE MEN!
THE INDIANS ARE PANIC-STRICKEN.
I SAID – GO!!
LONE RANGER SCHEME CHASE ALL REDSKIN!
BY JUNIPER IT WORKED! IT WORKED! THE REDSKINS'LL NEVER TRY ANOTHER ATTACK! THE LONE RANGER'S MAGIC HAS LICKED 'EM!

These buttons were printed by the Greenduck Company in Chicago during the time the comic strip was running in the Sunday Herald *and* Examiner. *(circa late 1930s)*

The following three illustrations are examples of the Indian lore that could be found on the inside covers of Lone Ranger comic books.

OLD INDIAN CUSTOMS
EAGLES AND OSPREYS, CAUGHT AS FLEDGLINGS AND TRAINED MUCH LIKE FALCONS, OFTEN HELPED THE INDIAN WITH HIS FISHING AND SMALL GAME HUNTING.
TO COOK WILD FOWL, THE BIRD WAS FIRST CLEANED BUT NOT PLUCKED. THE FEATHERS WERE COATED WITH MUD, AND THE FOWL PLACED IN A PREHEATED HOLE, THEN COVERED WITH HOT STONES. WHEN COOKED, THE FEATHERS CAME OFF EASILY WITH THE HARD CLAY.
THE FAVORITE FOOD AMONG THE BUFFALO HUNTERS OF THE GREAT PLAINS WAS RAW KIDNEYS AND BRAINS FROM A FRESHLY KILLED BUFFALO.

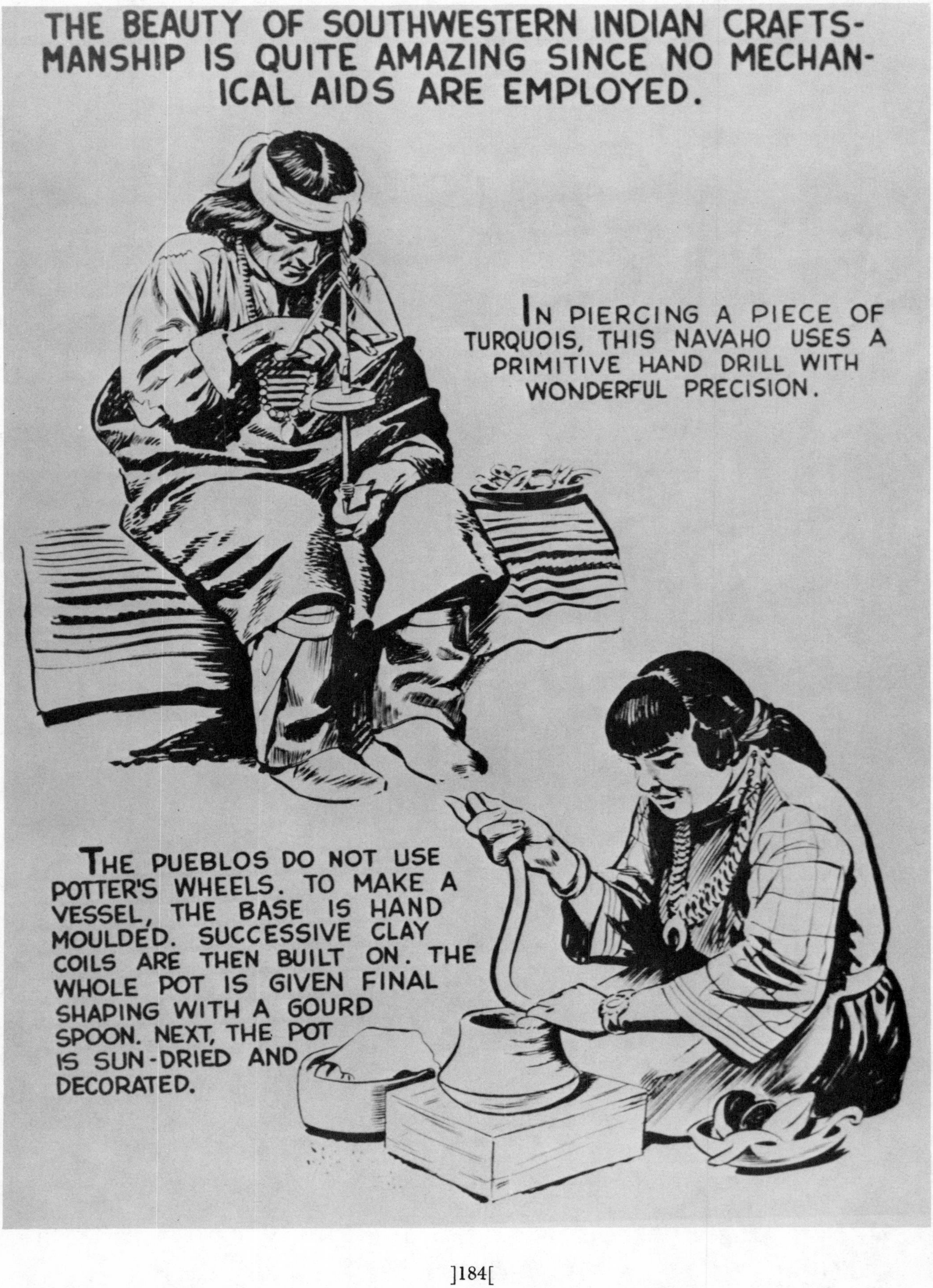
THE BEAUTY OF SOUTHWESTERN INDIAN CRAFTSMANSHIP IS QUITE AMAZING SINCE NO MECHANICAL AIDS ARE EMPLOYED.
IN PIERCING A PIECE OF TURQUOIS, THIS NAVAHO USES A PRIMITIVE HAND DRILL WITH WONDERFUL PRECISION.
THE PUEBLOS DO NOT USE POTTER'S WHEELS. TO MAKE A VESSEL, THE BASE IS HAND MOULDED. SUCCESSIVE CLAY COILS ARE THEN BUILT ON. THE WHOLE POT IS GIVEN FINAL SHAPING WITH A GOURD SPOON. NEXT, THE POT IS SUN-DRIED AND DECORATED.

This drawing of Chief David Bearspaw, Stoney Tribe, Calgary, Canada, is typical of the back cover art work to be found on the Lone Ranger comic books during the late 1940s.

The following three examples of cover art work for the Lone Ranger comic books are taken from the late 1940's, when comic book interest among youngsters reached its peak. Lone Ranger comic books are still being published today although not on a monthly basis as in the past.

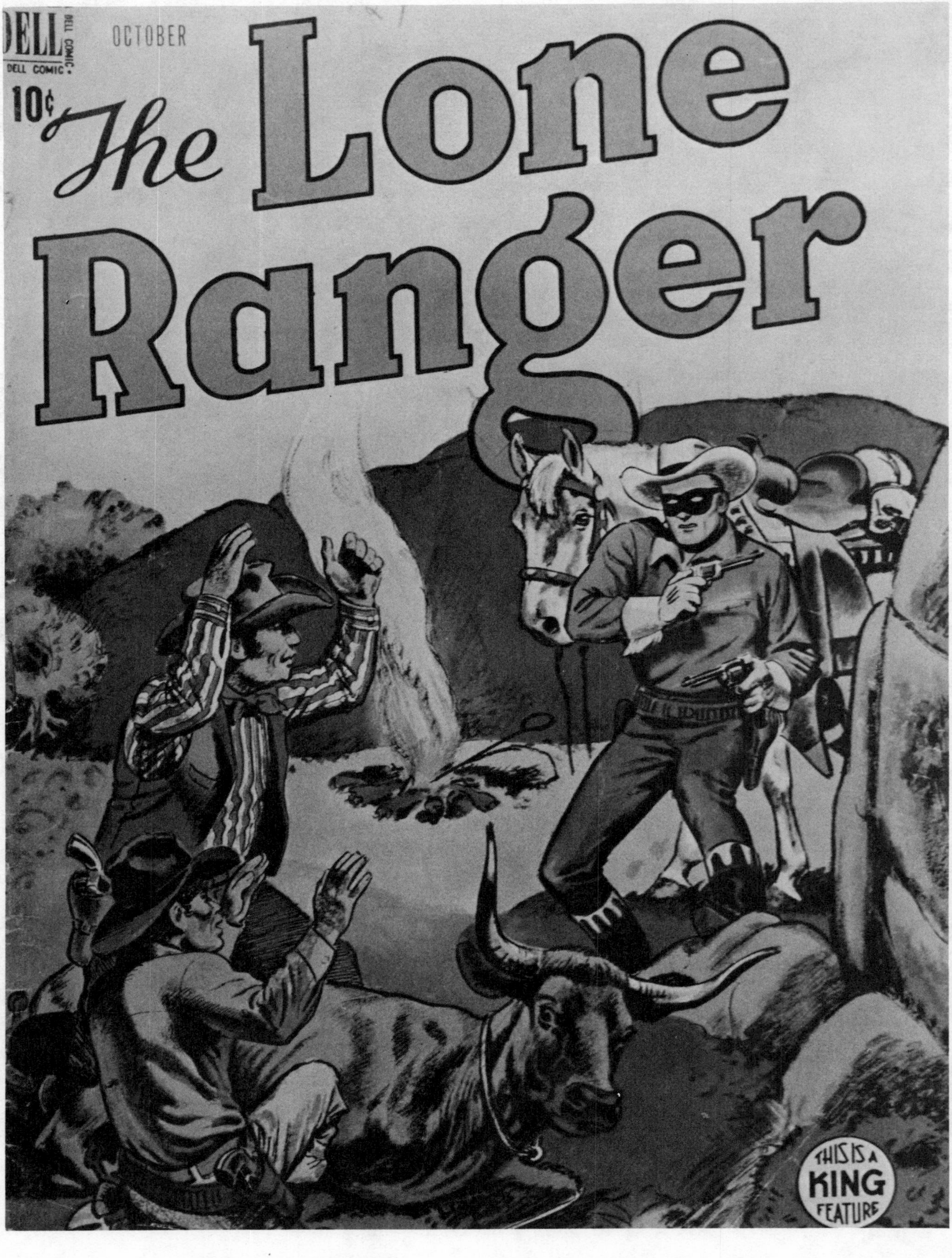

DELL
DELL COMIC
A DELL COMIC
JUNE
10¢
The Lone Ranger
THIS IS A KING FEATURE

DELL
A DELL COMIC
NOVEMBER
10¢
The Lone Ranger
52 pages
ALL COMICS!
THIS IS A
KING
FEATURE

The LONE RANGER
The LONE RANGER AND THE MYSTERY RANCH
The LONE RANGER and the GOLD ROBBERY

This familiar photograph of the Lone Ranger and Tonto (Clayton Moore and Jay Silverheels) is seen on a series of greeting cards.

appearance that was evident in the 1930s paintings that were sent to listeners. (It is perhaps interesting to note the costuming of the Lone Ranger over the years. The radio Lone Ranger in publicity stills almost always wore an all black outfit; the movie serial Lone Ranger wore a gray shirt and black pants; the television Lone Ranger wore an all gray outfit that was carefully tailored to be body fitting—the shirt had zippers on each side under the arms. The comic book Lone Ranger wore a red shirt, blue pants and, like all of the others, a white hat.) The Lone Ranger comic books were typical of other Western hero comic books except for the considerable amount of Indian lore that was featured each month for years. Each issue contained the detailed drawing of an Indian chief or warrior on the back cover. Many of the chiefs pictured were real Indians such as Chief Keokuk, Head Chief of Fox-Sacs (June, 1949) and Chief David Bearspaw, Stoney Tribe, Calgary, Canada (November, 1949). Either the front or back inside cover featured items about Indian customs ("The favorite food among the [Indian] buffalo hunters of the great plains was raw kidney and brains from a freshly killed buffalo.") or customs of particular tribes ("Since Navahos believe it was the spider woman who brought them the art of weaving, they always weave a tiny hole in every blanket in tribute to her.").

Each comic book usually contained two adventures of the Lone Ranger and Tonto; a three page narrative story with three large half-page cartoon pictures; and a final, shorter cartoon story featuring an Indian boy named Young Hawk. Fifty-two pages, all comics! all in color! and all for a dime! It was well worth it.

Considering the massive amount of scriptwriting Fran Striker had to do to keep up with the three "Lone Ranger" and two "Green Hornet" adventures each week (not to mention the other radio programs that came along), it is amazing that he would also undertake writing a series of "Lone Ranger" novels. Starting in 1936 and continuing until 1957, he proceeded to write eighteen novels based on the character. They were all originally published by Grosset & Dunlap, but the copyrights are now held by Lone Ranger Television, Inc., a subsidiary of Wrather Corporation. The novels have been out of print for some years;* however, they appear to be very much around since, after I paid five dollars for one through a nostalgia dealer, my twelve-year-old daughter proceeded to locate three others in classroom libraries and in friends' homes. This is not to say that they are commonplace or not sought after by collectors.

While recently doing some research at the University of South Florida, I visited their library of childrens' books. I found that it had two of the Striker "Lone Ranger" books in the special collection room where they could not be removed from the library. I checked with a librarian and found that the books are considered rare and irreplaceable, and, therefore, are not allowed to be checked out. They, along with the other books in the special collection room, are "bugged" undetectably so that if someone attempts to walk out with them an alarm is set off.

The "Lone Ranger" novels are surprisingly well-written with plots that are fast-moving, colorful, and in the traditional mold of the radio "Lone Ranger" adventures for the most part. The novels, perhaps, present the Lone Ranger aficionado with the most complete view of the character. On radio you had the voice of the actor as he spoke the words of the Lone Ranger, and the narrator's description of what was happening; in the novels you still have the Ranger's own words and the third person writer-narrator, but now they are not limited by the constraints of the thirty-minute time limit. Now the characters and the plot can be fully-developed to their greatest potential.

Except for possibly the first two, the novels were written primarily for youngsters in their teen years, but it is surprising how well the books hold up for an adult reader. A few of them certainly can be compared favorably with some of the novels of Jack London or with Zane Grey's romantic and quite-often plodding novels of the early West. As a collection the "Lone Ranger" novels probably lose distinction because of the self-imposed restrictions of Fran Striker and George W. Trendle on what was acceptable subject matter for the character. As a result, the novels became formula products with stock characters and situations of the Western genre. Still and all, the novels were popular and sold well at the bookstores.

For the record, the Fran Striker "Lone Ranger" novels are the following:

The Lone Ranger (1936)

The Lone Ranger and the Mystery Ranch (1938)

* Lone Ranger Television, Inc. has recently licensed a soft-cover reissue of the novels.

The Lone Ranger and the Gold Robbery (1939)
The Lone Ranger and the Outlaw Stronghold (1939)
The Lone Ranger and Tonto (1940)
The Lone Ranger at the Haunted Gulch (1941)
The Lone Ranger Traps the Smugglers (1942)
The Lone Ranger Rides Again (1943)
The Lone Ranger Rides North (1946)
The Lone Ranger and the Silver Bullet (1947)
The Lone Ranger on Powderhorn Trail (1949)
The Lone Ranger in Wild Horse Canyon (1950)
The Lone Ranger West of Maverick Pass (1951)
The Lone Ranger on Gunsight Mesa (1953)
The Lone Ranger and the Bitter Spring Feud (1954)
The Lone Ranger and the Trouble on the Santa Fe (1955)
The Lone Ranger on Red Butte Trail (1956)
The Lone Ranger and the Code of the West (1957)

The Lone Ranger was one of the best and most merchandised characters ever. During the peak years there were as many as seventy-one companies licensed for different Lone Ranger articles. As someone once said, "The character's name is on everything from lollipops to pencils."

Some elements of the program have become American clichés that are in constant use even today. A recent television program script contained a reference to a close friend as being a "Tonto." The response from the character referred to included the words "kemo sabe," which are still household words for friend or companion.

One evening while working on this manuscript, I had the FM stereo radio playing softly in the background. Suddenly my attention was jarred by the rousing strains of the "William Tell Overture," the hoofbeats of Silver and Scout, and the voices of Tonto (Jay Silverheels) and the Lone Ranger (someone who sounded like a combination of Brace Beemer and Clayton Moore, but was really neither). As the one-minute adventure commenced, the Lone Ranger and Tonto came upon a burning campfire left by a negligent camper. After dousing the fire, the Lone Ranger and Tonto cautioned me not to be a careless camper, and then rode off in a cloud of dust and a hearty "Hi-Yo, Silver, away!"

As I wandered through a department store one day, I came across the current version of "The Lone Ranger" coloring book, still published by Whitman. In the childrens' clothing department I discovered the Lone Ranger name and masked face embossed upon a cowboy hat. In the greeting cards section of the store the Lone Ranger, Tonto, Silver, and Scout wished me a "Happy Birthday, Kimosabi." A few minutes later I passed a display of super-hero put-together plastic models. There—with Superman, Batman, and Spiderman—was the Lone Ranger astride the great horse Silver. The Lone Ranger continues to ride!

8

The Television Years

The Lone Ranger should be seen as well as heard.
—George W. Trendle

AROUND 1947 a transformation began to take place in America which in a few short years would change the life style of a majority of the population. The first signs of this metamorphosis were revealed in strange human behavior: suddenly groups of ordinary-looking people could be discovered standing for many minutes (sometimes hours) in front of store display windows, seemingly transfixed by some object within; evening visitors would discover their friends' homes dark even though the hour was early and the car was in the drive. No quarantine sign was to be found on the doors of the darkened homes for the people inside possessed no communicable disease; they did, however, possess a mania that was symbolized by a peculiar-looking skeletal apparatus that could be seen with ever-increasing frequency on housetops throughout the country—the television mania had begun and, like most blessings, it was a mixed one.

Most forms of commercial entertainment were forced to adjust to this new upstart. The golden glow of the radio station indicator was illuminated less often as millions gradually defected to television and the ghost-ringed images of Ted Mack and "The Original Amateur Hour," Arthur Godfrey and his "Talent Scouts," "Martin Kane, Private Eye," and especially Milton Berle and his "Texaco Star Theatre."

The movie industry felt the impact of this entertainment interloper and at first tried to pretend that it either wasn't there or that it would eventually go away. Finally, when neither of these things happened, the movies rediscovered wide screens and 3-D. Concurrently they stopped production on the now unprofitable B-movies and sold them to the enemy, television. The result: B-movies became very popular on television and more movie theatre seats were empty.

Broadway, "The Fabulous Invalid," had a relapse and began a decline that was to continue for over twenty-five years. Some viewed the "Invalid" as a "terminal case."

During the first few years television screens were, of course, very small (eight- and ten-inch screens were standard) and quite expensive. Finally an eccentric millionaire used-car dealer named "Madman" Muntz started manufacturing a television set that cost ten dollars a screen inch —$170 for a seventeen-inch screen—measured diagonally, of course. Regardless, the television set was now within reach of most people's pocketbooks and, pretty soon, the weather vane on the roof acquired a companion—the television antenna.

George W. Trendle, naturally, was well aware of the sprouting television antennas and translated them into dollar signs. He observed the

Clayton Moore and Jay Silverheels as the Lone Ranger and Tonto.

shrewd business dealings of William "Hopalong Cassidy" Boyd during the earliest days of commercial television. Boyd, sensing the financial possibilities of the new medium, sold his ranch and borrowed every penny he could to buy all of the rights to "Hopalong Cassidy," including the dozens of motion pictures he had starred in as the title character. Boyd's sales and merchandising of the character during the late 1940s through the late 1950s (seventy million dollars was grossed in the peak year of 1952) started a whole new career for "Hoppy" and William Boyd.

George W. Trendle felt he could do as well on television with his character, the Lone Ranger, but this time (unlike the movie serial debacle) he would keep control of the property and would see that the "integrity" of the character was maintained. Trendle went to his long-time sponsor of the radio series, General Mills, and proposed that they sponsor a thirty-minute weekly television version of the masked man's adventures. He informed General Mills that he would only accept a deal like the radio one—General Mills would stand the cost of production, but the actual production would be the responsibility of The Lone Ranger Incorporated (Trendle). General Mills would have nothing to say about casting, writing, directing, or filming. Surprisingly, General Mills accepted the proposal (probably because of the excellent track record of "The Lone Ranger" over the years) and Trendle began pre-production plans on the television series.

George W. Trendle selected Jack Chertok as his television producer. Chertok was Trendle's kind of man. He had started his career as a script clerk at MGM. Over time he had worked his way up to assistant cameraman, to assistant director, to head of the music department, to producer of short subjects, and then, finally, to producer of feature pictures. From 1939 until 1942 Chertok produced such MGM features as *The Penalty; Joe Smith, American; Kid Glove Killer; The Omaha Trail;* and *Eyes in the Night.* In 1942 he left MGM and went to Warner Brothers where he continued to produce until 1944. It was through his own newly formed production company, Apex Film Corporation (he was president), that he started to produce "The Lone Ranger" television series for George W. Trendle.

Young director George B. Seitz, Jr. (age thirty-three) was brought in by Chertok as screenwriter and one of the three directors of the original series. Seitz had first gotten to know Jack Chertok while they were both at MGM. Seitz had been assistant to another MGM producer and later a writer of MGM short subjects. Prior to "The Lone Ranger" television series, Chertok had used Seitz as director for some technicolor feature documentaries filmed in Alaska. The documentaries had been produced by Chertok's production company for the United States Air Force.

Because Trendle wanted no tampering with the program characters and format, George Seitz was instructed to work closely with Fran Striker, the head radio script writer. Ultimately, many of the television scripts were adapted from Striker's "Lone Ranger" radio scripts. (Striker got a lot of mileage out of some of the old radio scripts—using them first for a "Lone Ranger" radio episode, then refurbishing them slightly for a "Challenge of the Yukon" radio stanza or maybe even a "Green Hornet" radio adventure, then translating some of them into "Lone Ranger" television programs.)

George Seitz and producer Jack Chertok worked together closely on the testing of the many actors who wished to audition for the Lone Ranger and Tonto roles in the television series. Finally the choices were submitted to George W. Trendle for approval: Clayton Moore and Jay Silverheels were selected to become the visual personifications of the masked rider and his Indian companion. Interestingly, Brace Beemer, the radio Lone Ranger, wanted very badly to play the role in the television series. He was (as mentioned earlier) an accomplished horseman, marksman, and master of the bull whip and felt that he could do the part justice on television. Despite his valiant efforts to slim down physically for the part and the fact that his voice had for so many years symbolized the Lone Ranger to millions of radio listeners, there is no evidence that anyone considered him very seriously for the television role. This can probably be attributed to the fact that he had no experience as a film actor. Beemer stayed with "The Lone Ranger" radio program until it reached the end of the trail in September of 1954. Then, surprisingly, he took on the title role of Sergeant Preston during the last year of the "Sergeant Preston of the Yukon" (formerly "Challenge of the Yukon") radio series.* (There must have

* Copyright ownership to "Sergeant Preston of the Yukon" is also held by Lone Ranger Television, Inc.

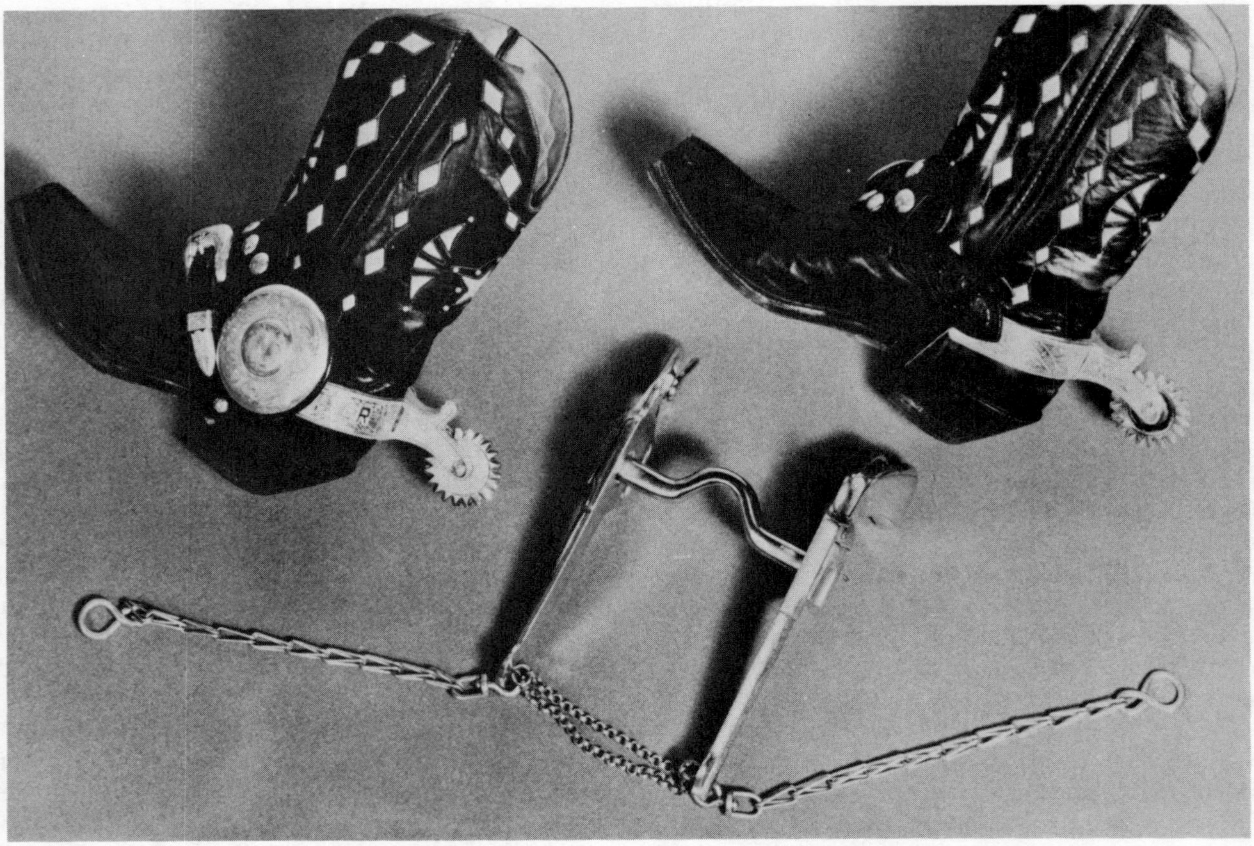

The Lone Ranger's spurs and Silver's bridle bit. The "six gun" bit appears to be almost identical to the famous one used on the bridle of Champion, Gene Autry's horse.

been some confused listeners when the Lone Ranger's voice began to speak from the mouth of Sergeant Preston.)

Just about everyone agreed that Clayton Moore was an excellent choice for the Lone Ranger. Not quite thirty-five years old when he was assigned the role, Moore was in excellent physical condition and was well-known in the film business for his ability as a stuntman, horseman, and expert gun twirler. Born in Chicago on September 14, 1914, he had spent his youth as a trapeze artist with a circus; later (1935–38) he had been a model for John Robert Powers. This had led to motion pictures in 1939. He had floated from Warner Brothers to MGM to Edward Small Productions between 1939 and 1941. During the time he was with Edward Small he had played a small part in *Kit Carson* (UA, 1940), which, coincidentally, was directed by George B. Seitz, Jr.'s father. Prior to serving in the Air Force from 1943 to 1945, Moore had played the male lead in what was his first of many Republic Pictures' serials, *Perils of Nyoka.* (Interestingly enough, the cast of this serial contained two other actors who would seven years later in 1949 play important characters in the three-part television version of the Lone Ranger origin story. Tristram Coffin would play the part of Captain Reid, the Lone Ranger's doomed brother, and George Lewis would be the traitorous guide, Collins, who led the six Texas Rangers into Butch Cavendish's ambush in Bryant's Gap.)

After the war, Moore had returned to films at the B-picture studios—Monogram, Columbia, and Republic—where he worked steadily in serial leads from 1947 until 1949. He became known as "King of the Serials" at Republic Pictures starring in *Jesse James Rides Again* (1947), *The Adventures of Frank and Jesse James* (1948), *G-Men Never Forget* (1948), and *Ghost of Zorro* (1949) just prior to becoming the Lone Ranger. (It would be interesting to know if George W. Trendle knew that Moore had just played Zorro, a character that allegedly had such a strong influence on Trendle at the time of the creation of "The Lone Ranger" back in 193[illegible] and if so, if that had anything to do wit[illegible]ore's casting.)

[illegible] playing starring roles in serials during [illegible] war years, Moore had been cast by [illegible] in only secondary roles in their B-fea[illegible]etimes being listed far down in the [illegible] in Allan "Rocky" Lane's *Sheriff of* [illegible] (Republic Pictures, January, 1949), when he was listed fifth in the cast. This had been just a few months prior to going into production as the star of "The Lone Ranger" television series. It would appear that Moore did not possess an ego problem since he apparently was amenable to accepting any role, large or small, that was proffered to him during most of his career.

After Clayton Moore had appeared in the first "Lone Ranger" television series made in 1949 and 1950, he balked at returning to the series without a substantial salary increase. (He reportedly was receiving somewhere around five hundred dollars per episode as star of the series.) When George W. Trendle refused to submit to his demands, Moore left the series and the role was taken over by John Hart. During this hiatus from "The Lone Ranger" series, Moore returned to the B-studios and resumed where he had left off, playing whatever roles were offered to him and seemingly gaining little for having been the star of a successful television series. (Perhaps because his face was covered by a mask in the television series, he and the producers felt that he could go unrecognized in other roles.) Regardless, during the period Moore was out of "The Lone Ranger" series, he played the main villain's henchman (listed fifth in the credits) in *Radar Men From the Moon* (Republic serial, 1952); starred in *Son of Geronimo* (Columbia serial, 1953); *Jungle Drums of Africa* (Republic serial, 1953); Alan G. Barbour in *Days of Thrills and Adventure* says, ". . . almost everyone agrees, [*Jungle Drums*] was the weakest of the sixty-six serials turned out by Republic"); and received second billing in his last serial, *Gunfighters of the Northwest* (Columbia serial, 1954). His only starring feature up to this time was an extremely low budget, poorly produced Western entitled *Buffalo Bill in Tomahawk Territory* (United Artists, 1952). I saw the film in 1952 and was saddened to see Clayton Moore, an actor whom I had enjoyed and admired as the Lone Ranger and as a serial star of previous years, involved in such a dismal production. During this same period of time while he was out of "The Lone Ranger" series, he also accepted secondary roles in B-Western features and other Western television series (examples: eighth billing in Rex Allen's *Down Laredo Way* feature (Republic, 1953); the heavy on one of Bill Boyd's "Hopalong Cassidy" thirty-minute television series episodes produced during the early 1950s).

Perhaps Moore, tired of free-lancing in serials

The Lone Ranger (Clayton Moore) in a contemplative mood. Moore's natural athletic ability, handsome physique, and sensitivity to the aura of the character made him the ideal choice to portray the Lone Ranger on television.

The Lone Ranger (Clayton Moore) and Tonto (Jay Silverheels) are on the trail of another outlaw in this publicity still from the television series.

and B-features, began to long for a return to "The Lone Ranger" series, or perhaps George W. Trendle, distressed at the inadequacy of John Hart as the Lone Ranger, began to feel that Moore might be the key to continued success for the television series; regardless, when the third "Lone Ranger" series went before the cameras in 1954, Moore was there and remained there until the series ended first-run production in 1957. It proved a long and happy relationship for all involved, most especially the viewers.

Jay Silverheels was certainly an excellent choice for the role of Tonto on the television series and played the part throughout the many years of the series. Silverheels, born in Ontario, Canada, in 1920, was a full-blooded Mohawk and the son of a Mohawk chief. Silverheels had been raised on the Six Nations Indian Reservation in Ontario and as a youth had displayed outstanding abilities in athletics. He had become something of a sports hero playing lacrosse and in 1936 he had become a professional player (lacrosse is the Canadian national game) and won recognition as one of the best players in his country.

Joe E. Brown had observed the handsome Silverheels playing in a lacrosse game and encouraged him to think about acting for a career after he was through with professional sports. By 1938 Silverheels had come to the United States and established himself in another sport, boxing, and qualified as a Golden Gloves contender, finishing the competition as a runner-up to the winner.

Postwar Hollywood was a bustling place and Jay Silverheels had found work at most of the studios in both A and B productions. With Hollywood grinding out a record number of Westerns, a *real* Indian who was good-looking and talented couldn't miss—and Jay Silverheels fit the requirements.

Captain From Castile (Twentieth Century-Fox, 1947) was his first film; others included *Yellow Sky* (Twentieth Century-Fox, 1948), *The Cowboy and the Indians* (Columbia, 1949) (it is an interesting coincidence that both Clayton Moore and Silverheels had appeared in this Gene Autry Western in secondary roles just a few short months before taking on the leading roles in "The Lone Ranger"), *Broken Arrow* (Twentieth Century-Fox, 1950), *The Black Dakotas* (Columbia, 1954), and many others during the years that he played Tonto on the "Lone Ranger" television series.

Jay Silverheels became closely identified with the Tonto role, but it would be unfair, I believe, to say that he became hopelessly typed in the part as some have suggested. Throughout "The Lone Ranger" television years Silverheels found additional work playing large and small roles. It's true, of course, that he was typed as an Indian and that he found movie and television work harder to find after "The Lone Ranger" series expired in the late 1950s. This was because there was a general lessening of interest in the genre and fewer and fewer Westerns were being made. Unfortunately, this is still true today.

The other television Lone Ranger was a lesser-known actor by the name of John Hart who, as mentioned earlier, replaced Clayton Moore for the second series of "Lone Ranger" television films. Hart, whose qualifications for the role were his ability as a horseman and physical good looks, lacked personality and demonstrated little acting talent. The relative naturalness and gracefulness of Clayton Moore were almost totally lacking in Hart and, try as he might, he just couldn't be convincing in the role.

A great part of John Hart's problem was lack of experience. He had only played one lead role previous to taking on the Lone Ranger role—the title character in the Columbia Pictures' serial *Jack Armstrong* (1947). The only lead motion picture role he played after his single "Lone Ranger" series was in the serial *Adventures of Captain Africa* (Columbia, 1955), one of the last five serials ever produced in Hollywood. In 1956 he starred with Lon Chaney, Jr., in the low-budget syndicated television series entitled "Hawkeye and the Last of the Mohicans." Thirty-nine half-hour programs were produced in the series. John Hart hasn't done much acting in recent years. He lives in Van Nuys, California, and sells raw-stock film to various studios.

In July of 1949 Jack Chertok started production on the television series that was scheduled to premiere September 15, with General Mills sponsoring. George B. Seitz, Jr. was charged with directing the first thirteen episodes and writing the first three. Ultimately, Seitz directed approximately forty-five of the first ninety films and wrote about half a dozen of them. Interior filming was accomplished at the General Services Studio in Hollywood with location work done at Iverson's Ranch or Corriganville where most of the television Westerns were shot. (Corriganville was developed by cowboy star Ray "Crash" Corrigan into a movie studio ranch with a western street and rugged terrain suitable for just about any western movie situation.)

Jack Chertok was contracted by Trendle to produce the series for an agreed upon total amount of money. Broken into individual programs the budget was approximately fifteen thousand dollars per episode, which was about average for half-hour television programs at that time, but certainly contained no fat and resulted in a program series with the look and sound of a low-budget production. Considering the complexities of filming a period Western series requiring location shooting, costuming, horses, wagons, and all of the other production necessities plus the always present budget limitations, it is amazing that the series had the production values it did have. And it should be stated production deficiencies were not limited to just this television series; this was true of many, perhaps even most, of the television series of that era—especially those catering primarily to youthful audiences. It is interesting, perhaps, that by 1954 the cost per episode had risen to only eighteen thousand dollars. George W. Trendle was keeping a tight rein on the purse strings as had been his custom over the years.

One could carp that the plots for "The Lone Ranger" television series were cliché-ridden with stereotyped characters. As with most of the early television Westerns it was a "black hat-white hat" plot situation. All of these things and more can be said in criticism of the television series, but despite its faults, "The Lone Ranger" series worked! It, perhaps, never had the impact of the radio series, but the long-nurtured mystique of the radio Lone Ranger and Tonto characters carried into the television series nonetheless. The established integrity of the radio characterizations was sustained for the television series; the actors selected for the visual medium personified magnificently the mental images of the millions of radio listeners, and the carefully designed and tailored costuming completed the image to perfection.

Perhaps the discriminating viewer could find some fault with the plots or production values, but the heroes—the Lone Ranger and Tonto—were all that anyone could ask for. They stood for and did all of the things heroes were supposed to do in those simpler times when right and wrong, good and evil seemed easier to define.

Each "Lone Ranger" adventure dealt with one small, clear-cut example of good and evil much in the manner of a parable. At the end of each episode "good" triumphed over "evil." The television series, like its predecessor on radio, was and still is a favorite of parents who, without qualms, could allow their children to view each new episode with the knowledge that such values as honesty, integrity, helpfulness, sympathy, love, and dependability were being modeled by the Lone Ranger and Tonto in everything they said and did.

It's Americana; it's American heritage.
—Charles D. Livingstone

DAVID ROTHEL: You were with "The Lone Ranger" television series in Hollywood for a period of a couple of years, weren't you?

CHARLES LIVINGSTONE: I went with the television show in 1954 as television coordinator. During the shooting Jay Silverheels had a heart attack and we had to lay off for eight weeks, so we didn't finish the series until early into 1955.

DAVID ROTHEL: What specifically did Trendle have you do as television coordinator for the program?

CHARLES LIVINGSTONE: I would work with the story editor and his writers to make sure they didn't have the Lone Ranger doing things he shouldn't do. I also okayed the payments to the producer as the episodes were finished. A lot of the responsibilities were the same as I had had as director of the radio series. I was getting into the business part of it, but at the same time, I was watching the director to see how these motion pictures were put together.

DAVID ROTHEL: How did you gradually work your way into directing?

CHARLES LIVINGSTONE: While I was out there as television coordinator, I used to spend a lot of time on the set watching the crew work. In my spare time I'd be with Jack Chertok's production head, Harry Poppe, Sr. When we'd get the okayed scripts, I would sit with Harry and help him time them. This, of course, was something I knew about; I'd had close to twenty years of doing this for the radio program. Eventually, Harry just gave the scripts to me and let me time them for him. I'd go through the entire script to figure how closely the dialogue and action equalled the program time so that adjustments could be made where necessary and the

THE LONE RANGER WATCHES

The two publicity shots pictured here are quite rare in that they show John Hart playing the role of the Lone Ranger.

THE LONE RANGER ON GUARD

While the John Hart "Lone Ranger" series is, according to Lone Ranger Television, Inc., still in syndication in a few areas, the Clayton Moore series is still the one most viewers are familiar with.

LONE RANGER SERIES
7TH GROUP
PROD. #87

JACK CHERTOK PRODUCTIONS, INC.

CALL SHEET

PICTURE "DELAYED ACTION" DATE FRIDAY, AUGUST 1, 1952

LOCATION GEN. SERVICE STAGE #4 DIRECTOR JOHN H. MORSE

COMPANY CALL 8:30AM SHOOTING CREW CALL SEE BELOW

SETS: EXT. BANK & STREET (D) - Sc. 4 to 11
EXT. JAIL CELL WINDOW (D) - Sc. 88-92-94
INT. CABIN (D) - Sc. 66-67-72-74
EXT. HILLY TERRAIN (D) - Sc. 18 to 21
EXT. MOUNTAIN TRAIL, ROCKS (D) - Sc. 27 to 39
EXT. CABIN (D) - Sc. 65-69-70-71-73-75

CAST	CHARACTER	MAKEUP	READY ON SET
James Griffith	"Flint"	8:00AM	8:30AM
Ben Welden	"Pete"	7:45AM	8:30AM
Sailor Vincent	"Jim"	8:00AM	8:30AM
Franklyn Farnum	"Teller"	7:30AM	8:30AM
Jay Silverheels	"Tonto"	8:30AM	9:00AM
John Hart	"Ranger"	11:00AM	11:30AM
2 Standins		Thru Gate	8:00AM
4 Townspeople		Thru Gate	8:00AM

LIVESTOCK -- 8:00AM

Scout
3 Saddle Horses

TRANSPORTATION

Truck to pick up 4 horses at Hudkins Barn at 7:00AM

STAFF & CREW CALL

John Morse, Director	
L. Guthrie, 1st Asst. Dir.	
D. Bremerkamp, 2nd Asst. Dir.	
D. Yutzi, Script	8:00AM
B. Pittack, Cameraman	8:00AM
A. Daniel, Cam. Opr.	8:00AM
H. Stengel, Cam. Asst.	7:45AM
E. Petzoldt, Gaffer	8:00AM
C. Henningson, Best Boy	8:00AM
Electricians	8:00AM
G. Widrig, 1st Prop	7:30AM
R. Zambel, 2nd Prop	7:30AM
G. Fenaja, 1st Grip	8:00AM
R. Gibson, 2nd Grip	8:00AM
J. Vengelisto, Laborer	7:30AM
E. Snyder, Mixer	8:00AM
R. Post, Recorder	7:45AM
W. Brady, Boom	8:00AM
T. Coodley, Makeup	7:30AM
H. Dunn, Wardrobe	7:45AM
C. Holzman, Greens	8:00AM
C. Archer, Wrangler	6:00AM
, 2nd Wrangler	6:00AM

ASSISTANT DIRECTOR LESTER GUTHRIE

Pictured above is a copy of a daily call sheet from the 1952 "Lone Ranger" television series.

David Rothel and Charles D. Livingstone discuss the television years of "The Lone Ranger" series as they walk along the beach near Livingstone's home.

shooting schedule could be planned. There were six minutes taken out of a thirty-minute program for commercials and opening and closing segments; actually, the amount of time in the script was twenty-three minutes and thirty seconds. You had to leave thirty seconds for the station break. All during this time I would ask questions about things on the set. I had to learn a great deal because, of course, this was entirely different from radio. Finally, Jack Chertok, the producer, gave me the chance to direct. It was a story about the Lone Ranger and Tonto looking for a treasure that had been hidden somewhere in the mountains. Let me tell you, at the end of the first day's shooting I was exhausted. Honest to God, if it hadn't been for my assistant director who pushed me around and told me where to be, I never would have made it through that first day. So much depended on one man even though he had people to help him. The director has to make all of the decisions. All of these people were standing there waiting for me to tell them what to do. They were used to this work from so many years of experience; I had to learn it all. I once did a show with a terrific cameraman where he had the camera constantly moving. I shot for five minutes; I thought it was beautiful. If the actor walked over there, I'd pan with him and dolly back as he walked toward the camera. When Chertok saw this, he raised Cain with me. "Oh, God no, Chuck. You've got to go in for close-ups. The television sets are so small; you've got to have close-ups."

DAVID ROTHEL: How long did it take to shoot a program in the series?

CHARLES LIVINGSTONE: We did the exteriors for three shows one week and the interiors at the studio the next.

DAVID ROTHEL: Were you involved in shooting the location footage or did they have a second unit director?

CHARLES LIVINGSTONE: Oh, no, I was right there. The regular director would shoot it all. The cameraman, his assistant, and the assistant director would pick me up each morning at the

Charles D. Livingstone and his wife Harriet are seen here with Silver and his handler. In the background is General Service Studios where "The Lone Ranger" series was filmed.

corner of Sepulveda and Ventura with the limousine that would take us to Iverson's Ranch for the location shooting. During this time another Western series began and their people were picked up at the same place I waited each morning. The star of this new Western series was a young actor by the name of Jim Arness.

DAVID ROTHEL: I wonder what ever became of him!

CHARLES LIVINGSTONE: I got to know those fellows as we stood waiting to be picked up each morning.

DAVID ROTHEL: Were they shooting at Iverson's Ranch, too?

CHARLES LIVINGSTONE: They were shooting either at Corrigan's or Iverson's. When we had Iverson's they were probably shooting at Corrigan's. These were the two ranches in the San Fernando Valley where Westerns were shot.

DAVID ROTHEL: What kind of planning did you have to do before location shooting?

CHARLES LIVINGSTONE: My assistant director and I would go out to the location site prior to the week of shooting and plan scene by scene for each day. We set our schedule so that the sun would always be to our backs as we shot each scene during the day. Another thing we had to plan was the transition from location scenes to the accompanying interior scene which would contain the dialogue. You see, we hardly ever shot dialogue on location; it was always shot on the green set in the studio. The green set had fake trees, brush and boulders. Generally a location scene would end with the actors riding their horses out of sight behind a boulder or pulling to a stop from a gallop. Then we would cut to a similar shot on the green set with them riding out from behind some rocks and trees, stopping, and delivering their dialogue.

DAVID ROTHEL: Even as a kid I was concerned with the production end of motion picture making, and one of the disturbing things on "The Lone Ranger" (and most of the other Western series for that matter) was the acoustical difference between actual outdoor location sounds and the interior sound of the green set. You could tell that the actors were in an enclosed building instead of outdoors. The Dodge City set on "Gunsmoke" was another example where the acoustics immediately told the program audience that the actors weren't really out on a Western street, they were on a sound stage. Perhaps I'm nit picking, but it always bothered me. Tell me about location work on "The Lone Ranger" program.

CHARLES LIVINGSTONE: You know, when we were shooting on location we would sometimes save a lot of time by shooting the Lone Ranger and Tonto riding left to right on the screen with one type of background; then we'd take the camera to the other side of the road and shoot them riding again left to right with a different background. These scenes could then be edited together with insert shots and in the final print they seemed to be going in the same direction, only with different backgrounds, as if they were further down the trail. You never could shoot on location until the water wagon had gone over the road. You had to settle the dust or when the horses came to a stop, you would lose your picture in the dust that would be kicked up and you could never match it in the studio for dialogue scenes because you couldn't duplicate the dust on the green set. It seemed as if we were always held up waiting for that damned water wagon to go through.

DAVID ROTHEL: The opening scene on the television series had the Lone Ranger coming up a little rise and over to a huge rock where Silver would rear up.

CHARLES LIVINGSTONE: Yes. That was the place where all the screen tests were made when we were looking for a replacement for John Hart as the Lone Ranger.

DAVID ROTHEL: Well, that particular place became a fascination for me because I used to see so many Western movies as a kid, and I kept seeing that rock appear on the screen. Movie cowboys were constantly riding past that place and I would say, "There's the Lone Ranger rock again!"

CHARLES LIVINGSTONE: Yes, it's out at Iverson's Ranch. In the years following my directing of these programs, I would see movies and television programs and say to my wife Harriet, "Do you recognize that setting or that location?" You get so you know them despite the camera angle that is being used. They're old friends that sneak into the backgrounds of new stories on television and in the movies. Remember, David, that these "Lone Ranger" shows were "quickies." There wasn't time or money to go to new locations that would be totally unfamiliar to the audiences.

DAVID ROTHEL: How many studio sets did you have?

CHARLES LIVINGSTONE: Well, there was the Western street with stores and a sheriff's office that was open on the sides so that you could shoot inside the office as well as out. There was a farmer's house and, of course, the green set

The director and his crew watch as the Lone Ranger (Clayton Moore or his double) brings an outlaw to justice.

that we've talked about. Other sets would be built as needed, but these were the stock sets. All of these sets were in one big studio.

DAVID ROTHEL: Did you ever work with a stock company of actors on the television series as you did on radio?

CHARLES LIVINGSTONE: No, no. At casting sessions when I first got out there, I would go to the big books from Central Casting. I was just a beginner in casting for motion pictures, so I went with whoever Harry Poppe and Ruth Burch, who was casting director, would suggest. They felt that in casting the parts, other than the Lone Ranger and Tonto, we should cast against type—take a person who looked like a villain and cast him in a hero's role. This off-casting made the stories just that much more interesting, though this rule was not followed on all episodes.

DAVID ROTHEL: But you didn't hold over actors for three or four programs, or you didn't contract with an actor to do three programs, say, in the series?

CHARLES LIVINGSTONE: If they were continuing characters we did, but otherwise, no.

DAVID ROTHEL: Did you "edit in the camera" or were you able to do extra takes and/or cover shots?

CHARLES LIVINGSTONE: Well, I shot extra film. In later years when I got to doing industrial films, I would shoot extra film, also, David. You know, I thought when I got with The Ford Motor Company it was going to be so great because they had lots of money, and I wouldn't have to worry about budget. They were worse than the guys out in Hollywood!

DAVID ROTHEL: How many minutes of footage did you figure you had to shoot a day on "The Lone Ranger"?

CHARLES LIVINGSTONE: I had to shoot approximately fifteen minutes a day to keep up with the schedule.

DAVID ROTHEL: In a major motion picture they'll shoot four or five minutes a day and feel they are doing well.

CHARLES LIVINGSTONE: Yes, I know it. And a page of script varies greatly as to how many minutes of shooting it takes. Sometimes it's all action and sometimes it's just dialogue. You see, in the breakdown of scenes my assistant director and I had to plan for each scene we were going to shoot that day.

DAVID ROTHEL: And, of course, you didn't shoot in sequence.

CHARLES LIVINGSTONE: No, never. This is one of the reasons why the director is so much more important in motion pictures than he is in radio or on the stage. He knows the continuity—how the scenes progress from one to another. The director alone sees the picture as a whole and his taste must serve as the representative of all the audiences who will ever see the film. He must create the picture in his mind with interesting camera movements, close-ups, over-the-shoulder shots, dollies, and pans. At the same time he must make sure the actor stays in character in spite of the confusion of the different camera angles and set-ups and repeated takes. Therefore, he must keep the whole story straight in his head and be able to properly prepare the actors before each scene. It would certainly be wonderful to have that luxury of shooting in sequence, but it just can't be done.

You have to shoot out of story sequence for economy, of course—economy of shooting and economy of number of actors needed for each day. My assistant director and I would have to work all of this out well in advance. Twenty-four hours a day just weren't enough.

DAVID ROTHEL: Did you have much rehearsal time while shooting the television series?

CHARLES LIVINGSTONE: The actors were all professional and, of course, knew their lines when they reported to the set. They would run through the scene once or twice for the cameraman and then we would shoot it.

DAVID ROTHEL: After a while did you get comfortable directing television programs?

CHARLES LIVINGSTONE: As I directed my second, third, and fourth shows, I felt much better about it. I began to learn the tricks of the trade; I learned that you had to decide which scenes were most important and to shoot the hell out of them—the close-ups and over-the-shoulder shots—and give the editors just as much as possible in those particular scenes. The rest of the scenes you did quickly—just "walk away from them," as someone once said to me. I had to learn to do this—get enough so that it would play, but then forget it and go on. I quickly learned to use the full-head close-up so that on those little television sets you could see what the actors looked like.

DAVID ROTHEL: Did you work at all with the film editor?

CHARLES LIVINGSTONE: No, I didn't. During the morning of shooting, film strips would be delivered of the stuff that had been shot just an

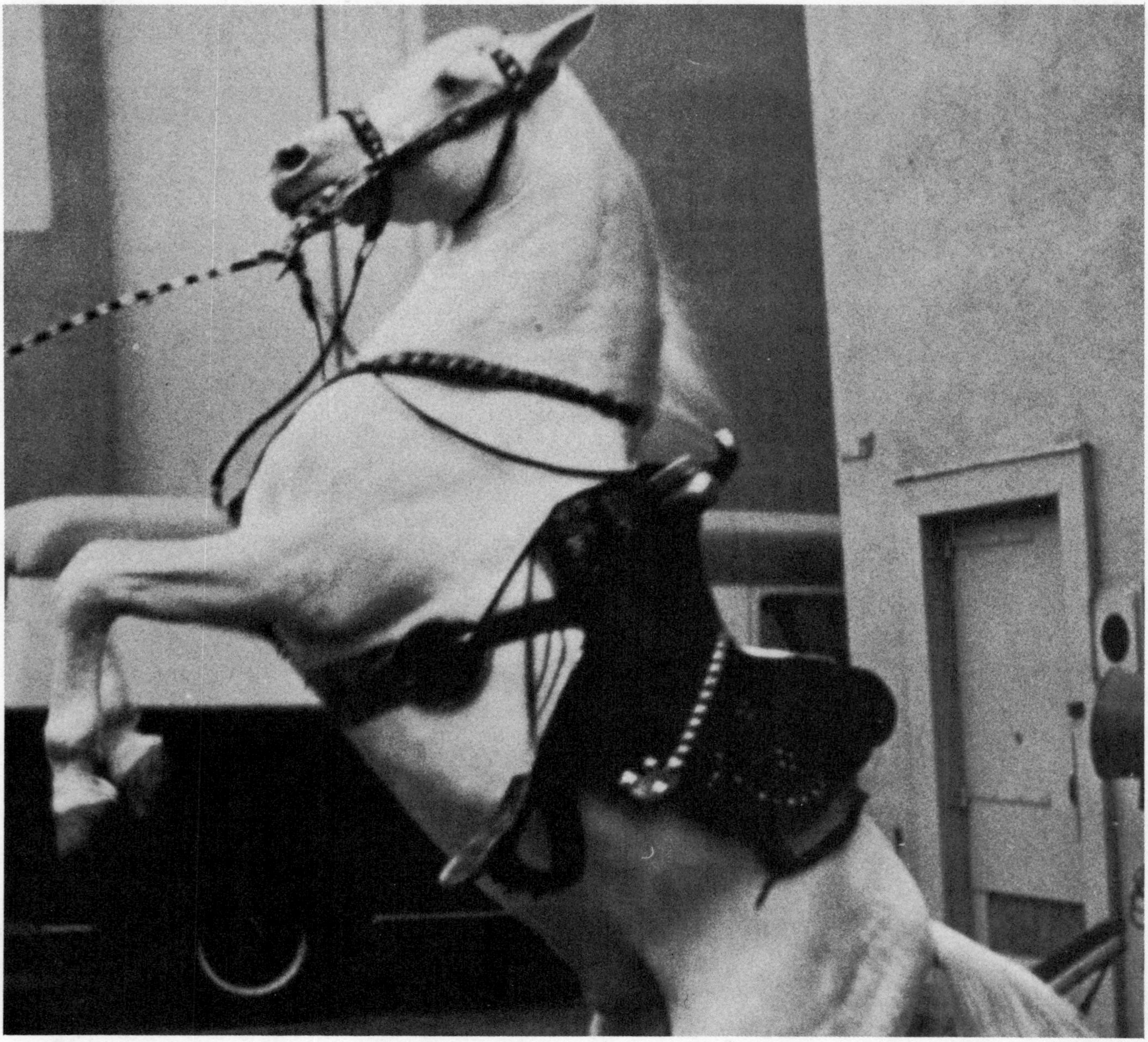

The great horse Silver is seen here performing for Charles D. Livingstone's personal camera. The picture was taken at the end of a day of shooting "The Lone Ranger" at the General Service Studios.

Now retired, Charles Livingstone enjoys acting in community theaters and speaking to theater and civic groups about his early days in radio, television, and the theater.

hour or so before. The cameraman would look at them and check the exposure to be sure that everything was all right. Then at noon we saw the rushes of the day before. If I were ever to get ulcers, this was the time, because everything looked so much better behind the camera than it looked on film. A director feels so alone at this time. Nothing really looks or sounds right when you see the rushes; you really have to have a good imagination when looking at them and a lot of faith in the film editor and the sound department. The sound levels are, of course, not set correctly until the dubbing re-recording when the dialogue, narration, music, and sound effect tracks are interlocked and run against the picture. The mix is very important to the success of any motion picture.

DAVID ROTHEL: John Hart was gone as the Lone Ranger before you really got involved with the television series.

CHARLES LIVINGSTONE: Yes, but I met him when Mr. Trendle sent me out to the coast in 1952.

DAVID ROTHEL: Did you ever really know him?

CHARLES LIVINGSTONE: Yes. I was quite thrilled at meeting Hart; here was the guy who was playing the Lone Ranger—a well-known actor.

DAVID ROTHEL: I first saw John Hart in a movie serial called *Jack Armstrong* back about 1947. I had a mental image from the radio series of the way Jack Armstrong should look and act, and I felt that Hart left a great deal to be desired in the part. As an actor he was almost totally expressionless. Around 1949, I saw Clayton Moore on television as the Lone Ranger and immediately recognized him as the actor I'd seen and enjoyed for a number of years in Republic Pictures' serials. Then when John Hart came in and took over for Clay, I was rather dismayed.

CHARLES LIVINGSTONE: I don't know who sold Mr. Trendle on him or how that came about.

DAVID ROTHEL: Did you have anything to do with Clayton Moore returning as the Lone Ranger?

CHARLES LIVINGSTONE: Right after I arrived in Hollywood in 1954 we started auditioning for a new Lone Ranger. I saw everybody who auditioned or did tests for the part. Then Mr. Trendle came out and finally agreed to go back to Clay. I think that was merely a money thing. Clay, I believe, wanted more money after the first series and Trendle wouldn't pay it. It wasn't that Clay wasn't doing a good job as the Lone Ranger.

DAVID ROTHEL: Did you get to know Clayton Moore very well?

CHARLES LIVINGSTONE: Oh yes, we were at his home in Sherman Oaks a number of times. His wife was a very nice person, too.

DAVID ROTHEL: Did they have any children?

CHARLES LIVINGSTONE: I think so, but I'm not sure.

DAVID ROTHEL: There were three "Lone Ranger" series shot while Trendle owned the property weren't there?

CHARLES LIVINGSTONE: That's right. You see, there were about seventy-five "Lone Ranger" programs in the first series starting in 1949 starring Clayton Moore. At that time, of course, I wasn't out there.

DAVID ROTHEL: And then John Hart took over as the Lone Ranger and made. . . .

CHARLES LIVINGSTONE: Fifty-two episodes. And then there was a third series of fifty-two with Clay. Those three series were made by Trendle before he sold the rights to Wrather Corporation.

DAVID ROTHEL: What kind of personality did Clay Moore have?

CHARLES LIVINGSTONE: Pleasant, not temperamental. He was a self-confident, very down-to-earth person, and a good athlete, too. Clay could take those running leaps onto Silver. You know, he was a stuntman before he became an actor. He sometimes had trouble with lines though—saying them so that they had just the right inflection. I'd go over his lines with him at times. Clay could play character parts very well, but playing a straight lead was more difficult for him. You know, motion pictures just aren't like the theater; you can't take time for lengthy rehearsals. Time costs money. You can't take time for the actors to work out a characterization on their own. Even with "The Lone Ranger" on radio I didn't take time to let the actors work it out themselves; I gave them readings when necessary. There was another thing with Clay that I had to learn about. (laugh) When he was doing something close to the camera, I couldn't yell, "Action!" It would completely unnerve him. I had to learn to say it softly and use a gentle hand gesture. (laugh) You find these funny little peculiarities with actors, as you well know, David. Clay was a great guy though. He knew what I was going through on those first few shows and was very helpful. He and Jay [Silver-

After a hard day of location shooting, Clayton Moore paused long enough for this shot taken by Charles Livingstone.

heels] would come over and pat me on the back after a particularly rough day and give me encouragement.

[*Author's note*: It was my wish to interview Clayton Moore for this book. Chuck Livingstone very graciously agreed to call him on the phone to introduce me and to assure him that my intentions were honorable. Chuck had lost contact with Moore over the years, but I was able to track him down through Harry Poppe, Jack Chertok's production assistant during the Lone Ranger television years. Mr. Poppe wished me good fortune with the book and gave me Moore's address in Incline Village, Nevada. When Chuck finally got Moore on the phone, he found him to be as warm and friendly as he had been twenty years before when they had last seen each other.

Despite Chuck's overtures on my behalf, however, Moore was firm in his refusal to submit to an interview. He said he has requests every week and has had to call a halt to it. "Besides," he said, "we're working on a book about my life—my early years in the circus, the features and serials at Republic, and the later years as the Lone Ranger. As a matter of fact, my biographer just happens to be here now working with me." He told Chuck that he still occasionally makes appearances as the Lone Ranger for Lone Ranger Television, Inc. (He apparently has maintained his excellent physique despite his sixty years. It's hard to believe that *all* of the Lone Rangers are either dead or in their fifties or sixties. George Seaton and Moore are in their sixties; John Hart must be in his late fifties; the rest are dead.) Moore's final comment to Chuck was, "They [writers] can get and use any information they want, but they won't get it from the horse's mouth." I don't suppose he was referring to Silver.]

DAVID ROTHEL: Jay Silverheels—what's he like?

CHARLES LIVINGSTONE: A wonderful person. One of the warmest, nicest fellows I ever met. He's very quiet, but has a great sense of humor. He's a college graduate, married with a family. He and his family lived in the valley, too. We visited them. They lived just as comfortably as Clay Moore. Jay had played leads in many features before "The Lone Ranger" series. He was a handsome guy.

DAVID ROTHEL: When did Trendle sell "The Lone Ranger"?

CHARLES LIVINGSTONE: During 1954. Trendle wanted me to stay with him after he sold it, working with the "Sergeant Preston of the Yukon" television series, but I didn't feel I wanted to. He said he had plans for a television version of "The Green Hornet," too. My saying no, of course, made him sore because I had told him that I would stay with him through thick and thin, but suddenly he had sold "The Lone Ranger." For all I knew he might sell out "The Green Hornet" or "Sergeant Preston of the Yukon" the same way, and here I was with the opportunity to direct television programs with the Jack Chertok Company. So, Chertok hired me to direct the "Steve Donovan, Western Marshall" series during the spring and summer of 1955. I directed most of the twenty-six programs in that series and some of the "Sergeant Preston of the Yukon" television programs. That carried me into 1956. I thought maybe I could find myself as a television director on the Coast, but it didn't work out that way. At least I got the experience I needed in film directing to go successfully into industrial film directing for the Ford Motor Company and Jam Handy.

DAVID ROTHEL: Do you think the Lone Ranger can continue to remain popular as a character on radio or television, or is the world changing too much for him to continue to be accepted and believed?

CHARLES LIVINGSTONE: No, I think he can. It's Americana; it's American heritage. This is something this country needs right now, I think, to pull it together. I don't know the exact percentage, David, but "The Lone Ranger" audience was pretty close between children and adults. [Author's note: In 1941 surveys indicated that at least sixty-three percent of the radio audience was composed of adults. In 1953 it was figured that fifty-two percent of the combined radio and television audience was adult.] The older folks—grandparents—definitely loved the show just as much as the youngsters because it brought back memories to them of days gone by. I don't think the radio program would work in an evening hour because of television. My thought, and I've had this for a few years, is that it could go on at 7:30 A.M. in the morning when the children are eating breakfast and getting ready for school.

DAVID ROTHEL: Do you feel that the Lone Ranger is a relevant hero for today's youth—one that they will accept?

CHARLES LIVINGSTONE: Oh, maybe not. He may be, ah . . . what's the term the kids use now? Not being cool. . . .

DAVID ROTHEL: Square?

CHARLES LIVINGSTONE: Square. He'd be square,

Tonto and Scout. Jay Silverheels played the role of Tonto throughout the television series and in two feature movies.

This painting was given to Charles Livingstone at the time of his retirement.

When asked which of the days of his active career he considers the most important, most exciting, Livingstone likes to quote George W. Trendle's response to the same question, "Tomorrow!"

The Lone Ranger (Clayton Moore) and Silver in a publicity still from the television series.

maybe. I'm not sure they'd accept the fact that he'd just shoot the gun out of the hand of the bad guy—never shoot to kill and things like that. The Lone Ranger came at just the right time in our history—the 1930s through the early 1960s—and we hadn't yet become so cynical. Now we have all this antihero stuff, the James Bonds, the Clint Eastwood and Charles Bronson movies with their brand of values and morality. Remember at the end of each "Lone Ranger" program that justice triumphed and the villain was captured and had to pay—retribution always came through. My wife Harriet calls it corn.

DAVID ROTHEL: But blue-ribbon, Chuck. It was blue-ribbon corn.

The Lone Ranger is a composite of every man who stands for justice. . . .

—Jack Wrather

In early August of 1954 it was announced that: " 'The Lone Ranger,' a twenty-two year old show, was sold by the George W. Trendle interests of Detroit on August 3, for three million dollars (believed a record price in radio-TV) to Texas oil and TV operator Jack Wrather of Dallas and his associates."

A story that is quite often told of the negotiations that took place between Trendle and Wrather states that the two parties had come to within twenty-five thousand dollars of each other when Trendle turned to H. Allen Campbell, his business associate, and asked if he had a fifty cent piece. Then with the coin in his hand, Trendle is quoted to have said to Wrather, "I don't want to drop a deal of this size for the sake of twenty-five thousand dollars. If you're game, I'll flip this coin to decide whether you pay the difference or not." Wrather supposedly laughed and said, "You, Mr. Trendle—everyone knows that you don't gamble." Wrather then spoke privately with his associates. During these tense moments Campbell reportedly said quietly to his long-time friend and business associate, "I'll eat my hat if he takes this one."

After a few moments Wrather turned to Trendle and said, "Mr. Trendle, I know you don't usually gamble and I suggest that now gambling would have no point. Suppose we just split the difference." Trendle agreed; the deal was concluded, and Trendle said to H. Allen Campbell, ". . . you said you'd eat your hat if we got a higher price. Now, let's see you take a bite."

In recent correspondence between Jack Wrather and Edwin Tornberg* that was shared with me, a different rendition of the coin-flipping story is remembered. The recollection is that George W. Trendle failed to advise the Wrather people that he (Trendle) personally owned Silver, his saddle and trappings, and they were not, therefore, included in the sale. The value was twenty-five thousand dollars. Some vagueness of memory exists as to whether Silver was actually part of the twenty-five thousand dollars or whether it was just the saddle and trappings, but regardless, Trendle's announcement caused a "mini-holocaust" that was only resolved when H. Allen Campbell suggested the toss of the coin to settle the matter. The compromise of a split in the amount was then agreed upon.

As Mr. Tornberg recently commented in a letter to Jack Wrather: "The only person that ended up 'eating his hat' was George Trendle when he found out how well you did with the property."

Wrather Corporation purchased the entire "Lone Ranger" property—all of the radio programs, 182 half-hour Trendle-produced television programs, the comics, the right to all the merchandising items—the works!

The new owner brought a revitalization to the property. Thirty-nine new "Lone Ranger" adventures were produced in color—the first in color—for the 1956–57 television season. New standards for production and story were put into effect for this series. Each episode was filmed with more care, skill, and technical quality than had been displayed during the earlier television years of the series. As a press release in late summer of 1956 stated:

> The new Lone Ranger series, starting at 7:30 P.M. Thursday, September 6th (ABC-TV), will give a panorama in color of the scenic, historic southwest, photographed on location to frame the living legend of the masked rider in its natural setting.
>
> While most western adventure television pictures are photographed at near-to-Hollywood sound stages and ranches, The Lone Ranger, during the spring and summer, took its company of 70 persons thousands of miles for 10 varied locations.
>
> "The new Lone Ranger series literally will take

* Edwin Tornberg is a prominent broker in the radio and television field who originally brought the Lone Ranger deal to Jack Wrather and was involved in all the negotiations to obtain it.

Lone Ranger to Ride for New Boss

DETROIT, Aug. 3 (AP)—Hi-Ho Silver, but the Lone Ranger went for gold. For $3,000,000 in cash, the Detroit-originated radio-television show was sold to a Los Angeles-Dallas-New York group.

Tonto, Silver and all rights to assorted Lone Ranger enterprises went in the deal. The sale price was reported to be the highest ever paid for a radio-television property.

The Lone Ranger show is carried on 50 television stations and 249 radio stations a week. In addition, the masked ranger and his Indian pal Tonto and horse Silver help capture stagecoach robbers in comic strips appearing in 300 daily newspapers and in comic books selling 2,000,000 copies a month.

The sale raised the question whether the shows would continue. The new owners said: The Lone Ranger will ride again.

The Lone Ranger says
Join
The Peace Patrol

In 1958 the Lone Ranger Peace Patrol was created to encourage boys and girls to buy United States Savings Stamps at their school or post office and become members of the Peace Patrol.

Secretary of the Treasury, Robert B. Anderson (left) is shown here meeting with the Lone Ranger and sponsors of "The Lone Ranger" program to outline the nationwide plans of the United States Savings Bonds Peace Patrol. Shown left to right are J. T. Callier, Advertising Manager for American Bakeries; James F. Stiles, Jr., Assistant to the Secretary and National Director, U. S. Savings Bonds Division; Mrs. Ivy Baker Priest, The Treasurer of the United States; the Lone Ranger; Jack Wrather, President, The Lone Ranger, Inc.; Under Secretary of the Treasury, Julian B. Baird; and Harry Bullis, Chairman of the Board, General Mills, Inc. In the foreground, left to right, are Bill McDonald, Assistant National Director, U. S. Savings Bonds Division; William Shay, The Lone Ranger, Inc. (1958)

The Lone Ranger and The Treasurer of the United States, Mrs. Ivy Baker Priest, pose with this giant-sized copy of the Peace Patrol Membership Card.

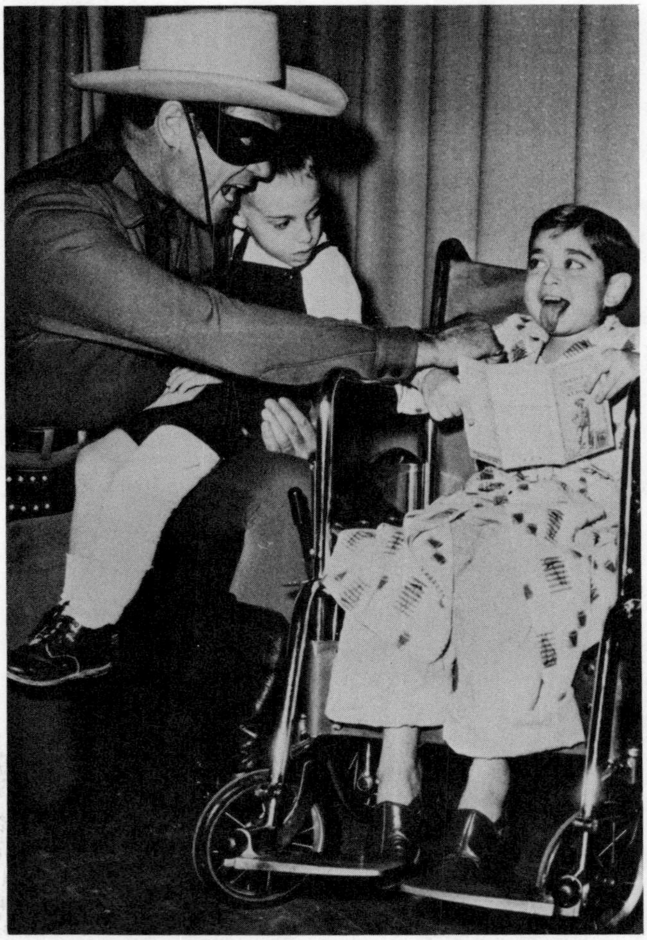

One of the first stops on the Lone Ranger's itinerary while in Washington, D. C. was a visit to the crippled children at the National Institute of Health in Bethesda, Maryland. While there he signed up two Peace Patrol members, one of whom is ready and waiting to lick his savings bond stamps.

While in Washington, D. C., the Lone Ranger met with the then Vice President Nixon and presented him with silver bullets for his two daughters.

America on a tour of its most picturesque country from Utah through the varied scenery of northern, central and southern California," said Jack Wrather, President, Lone Ranger, Inc.

"We chose to put the new series in color for the first time to enhance the quality of entertainment The Lone Ranger has been affording for nearly 24 years. We believe Americans are as proud of the beauties of their country as they are of the heritage for which The Lone Ranger fights: justice, enlightenment and clean living."

Lone Pine, California, 300 miles north of Los Angeles, was the first outdoor location selected. It affords bright, blue skies, snow-capped Sierra Nevada mountains, clear mountain streams and richly-hued flora. The company made the trip by plane.

Kanab, Utah, near the famous Utah National Parks—"land of varied smokes—" contributed its majestic beauty for other Lone Ranger stories.

Sonora, California, in the verdant north, lent its beauties to the color cameras for some Lone Ranger pictures, with other northern scenery photographed at Dardanelles and Murphy's. Dardanelles is above the timberline. Kernville contributed the central California flavoring, while farther south near Los Angeles the World's Most Famous Movie Ranch at Corriganville provided location headquarters while Melody Ranch and Iverson's Ranch, near Hollywood, were used for additional scenes. Desert scenery was filmed at Apple Valley.

Tons of equipment, cameras, sound trucks, costumes, props, makeup and all the minutiae of make-believe were flown or trucked to the ten locations. "Native" Indians were hired as actors from the Utah tribes.

And in Hollywood, for the new series, studio work for The Lone Ranger was done at Carthe Sound Stages, the film city's newest and most complete independent television plant. The new stages were opened for The Lone Ranger production.

A follow-up press release proclaimed:

> Not only is production of The Lone Ranger programs of top quality, but the writing and content also maintain a consistent excellence. Twelve top motion picture and television writers, including three distinguished American novelists, scripted the new series, retaining The Lone Ranger precepts and teachings, but adding new scope and action to the thrill-packed films.

Nothing, of course, is ever quite as grand as a press release would like you to believe, but there is no question that the quality of the Wrather series was head and shoulders above its predecessor's.

During that 1956–57 television season it was estimated that fifty million people watched "The Lone Ranger" each week. The first-run series was running on the ABC television network on Thursday evenings, while reruns could be seen on Saturdays over CBS television stations. In Canada another million viewers watched the programs over Canadian Broadcasting Corporation stations.

In early December of 1956 it was announced that "The Lone Ranger" television program would go international on Christmas Day when the series would be launched in Great Britain over the British Broadcasting Corporation. It marked the first time that the program had been televised on an overseas network.

With the start of the 1957–58 television season, "The Lone Ranger" went into reruns on national and eventually regional television networks, and continued in this fashion until 1961. From that time to the present, the program has continued successfully in syndication in cities throughout the United States and also in many foreign countries.

Wrather Corporation introduced "The Lone Ranger" property in yet another medium—feature motion pictures—which George W. Trendle had never entered even during the lucrative B-movie series years of the 1940s. (It seems incredible that Trendle would not have been tempted by the success of such B-Western feature series as "Hopalong Cassidy," "The Cisco Kid," or the Charles Starrett series, "The Durango Kid." One can only speculate that, perhaps, the bad experiences with the Republic serials in the 1930s soured Trendle on Hollywood until television came along.)

In August of 1955 production was begun on *The Lone Ranger* color feature film at Warner Brothers Studios. Clayton Moore, Jay Silverheels, Bonita Granville (Mrs. Jack Wrather), Lyle Bettger, and Robert Wilke were the leading performers in the feature, which was produced by Jack Wrather and directed by Stuart Heisler.

The film was shot on location in southern Utah, around the little town of Kanab. One of the highlights of the film was a specially prepared, rousing arrangement of the "William Tell Overture" which was used behind the opening credits.

Money was not scrimped on the production and the resultant box-office gross in the United States alone justified the investment. In *Variety*'s end of the year listing of top-money pic-

Sometimes in this modern world the Lone Ranger needs a different type of "horsepower" to take him to visit fans nearby and in distant places.

The Lone Ranger and the sheriff of Frontier Land meet by the river boat in Disneyland.

At the Washington Monument.

Exchanging autographs?

Preparing to make an appearance, the Lone Ranger encounters a curious ringmaster in his makeup room —Jerry Colonna.

On the streets of the old West—Western Europe.

Paying a friendly visit to the Palace. (One can only speculate what must be on the mind of the unflinching Royal Guard.)

At Warner Brothers Studio the Lone Ranger and Tonto (Clayton Moore and Jay Silverheels) pose with the new owner of "The Lone Ranger," Jack Wrather (nearest to Tonto and Scout below and on following page), and other executives at the start of production on the first Lone Ranger movie feature. (1956)

At Warner Brothers Studio.

In 1956 Warner Brothers sent the Lone Ranger (Clayton Moore) on a nationwide, thirty-three-city, personal appearance tour to tout the first full-length feature film production based on the character.

tures during 1956 (the year the feature was released), *The Lone Ranger* ranked 65 out of 109 features released during the year and had a U.S. gross of $1,550,000.

The Lone Ranger (Clayton Moore) was sent on a nationwide, thirty-three city, personal appearance tour to coincide with the release of the movie. It was the first time that the masked lawman had made such an extended countrywide sweep in his twenty-three year ride.

Bosley Crowther (no less) of the *New York Times* in reviewing the feature on February 10, 1956, said,

> You would think that, after all these years of championing law and order on the screen and radio, not to mention television, the Lone Ranger would be pooped. At least you would think the people assigned to keeping him going would be tired—tired of all those endless cattle rustles, slashing fist-fights and Western clichés.
>
> But apparently a new team at Warners has taken over the job of reviving the famous masked hero in all his glory in color and Cinemascope and has had at the task with the vigor of zealots inspired with a fresh idea. And "The Lone Ranger," which opened yesterday at the Mayfair, has the unwearied spirit of a noisy kid.

In June of 1958 a second feature was released through United Artists, *The Lone Ranger and The Lost City of Gold*. The leads for this feature were the same as before, but a new director was brought on board—veteran film maker Lesley Selander, who had been directing Westerns and other action pictures since 1936, as well as hundreds of television films. Supporting cast members included Douglas Kennedy, Charles Watts, Noreen Nash, Ralph Moody, John Miljan, and Lane Bradford.

The plot was standard Western-action fare, but still contained a few nice touches. As stated in the pressbook,

> The Lone Ranger (Clayton Moore) and Tonto (Jay Silverheels) learn that some hooded riders have been murdering Indians near the town of San Doria.
>
> The leader of the raiders, Ross Brady (Douglas Kennedy) and his girl friend, Frances Henderson (Noreen Nash), see a threat to their plot to steal

Following are two of the publicity posters used to promote the second feature movie based upon "The Lone Ranger." (1958)

five medallions which when put together reveal the location of an Indian lost city of gold.

Chief Tomache (John Miljan) has given five pieces of the medallion to five of his friends and relatives, three of whom have now been killed. The Lone Ranger takes it upon himself to save the two survivors, a grandson and a nephew. He is too late to save the nephew who is killed by one of Brady's henchmen.

As a result of the Lone Ranger's getting hot on their heels, Brady and Frances have a falling out, and she kills her boyfriend as the Lone Ranger and Tonto come upon them. They take Frances into custody, and the lost city of gold remains with its rightful owners—the Indians.

The film was shot in Eastman color on location in Tucson, Arizona. The entire company was transported by chartered plane to Tucson for the three weeks of location shooting. A new song entitled, "Hi-Yo Silver" (not to be confused with the "Hi-Yo, Silver" song from the 1938 Lone Ranger movie serial) was written by Les Baxter and Lenny Adelson and was featured on the sound track during the opening credits. A recording by Bob Carroll was released on United Artists Records.

As with the first feature movie, there were numerous promotional tie-in's with television sponsors; comic book, comic strip, and novel publishers; record album manufacturers and distributors; toy manufacturers; and other Lone Ranger merchandisers.

In 1958 as part of the twenty-fifth anniversary celebration for "The Lone Ranger" as well as for promotion of *The Lone Ranger and The Lost City of Gold* and the television series, the publicists became fascinated with statistics concerning the property. For example:

- More than two and a half million feet of film have been used during the television career of the Lone Ranger.
- A total of 21,734 "bad men" have been brought to justice by the Lone Ranger dur-

GENERAL MILLS GIGANTIC POINT-OF-SALE PROMOTION!

61,000,000 People Watch "The Lone Ranger" every week on 82 ABC-TV Network Stations (sponsored by General Mills, Inc.) and on 76 CBS-TV Network Stations sponsored by General Mills, Inc.-Nestles. Also 4 CBC Stations in Canada.

90,000,000 Consumers reached through store displays carrying General Mills products and thru newspaper and magazine ads.

50,000,000 Cereal boxes of Wheaties, Cheerios and other General Mills cereals have carried Lone Ranger promotions consisting of cutouts on the outside of the package plus mail-in offers of Lone Ranger plastic figurines.

This photo shows how supermarkets and grocery stores help exploit THE LONE RANGER.

More than 6000 supermarkets and grocery stores in 40 states display the giant Lone Ranger spectacular standees, window cards, insert cards and other promotional material.

1000 General Mills fieldmen are out working on the 25th Lone Ranger Silver Anniversary with which this picture is identified. They will work with you.

Live shots of The Lone Ranger and Tonto are featured on the Cheerios and Wheaties commercials.

This is a reduced reproduction of a typical cereal box-front and back showing the direct tie-in with "The Lone Ranger."

HERE'S WHAT YOU CAN DO:

- Make earliest possible contact with nearest General Mills representative (see list below) . . . and set up cooperative arrangements for your picture campaign. Every one of the more than 1000 General Mills fieldmen is ready to work with you on cooperative theatre-store tieups.
- Work with local TV and Radio stations carrying "The Lone Ranger" show for tie-ins with your play-date. Adapt the day-to-day stunts described on page 6 to tie-ins with local stores.

SPECIAL NOTE FOR CANADIAN EXHIBITORS

General Mills, Ltd. (CANADA) is alerted ... *you in the same manner as the United*

This photograph from the pressbook for The Lone Ranger and The Lost City of Gold *demonstrates how the promotion for the movie feature, the television series, and the sponsor's product are intertwined for maximum effect.*

ing his twenty-five years on radio and television.

- The masked lawman, who has never killed anyone with silver bullets, has used a staggering total of 12,684 silver bullets.
- A record number of five million pieces of fan mail has been received by the Lone Ranger during his twenty-five years on radio and television.
- If all the Lone Ranger newspaper comics ever printed were placed on a continuous sheet, they would make a comic strip 48,447,007 miles long—one that would reach from here to the moon and back over twenty-two times.
- If all the original scripts and manuscripts concerning this legendary American hero were brought together in one pile, they would make a stack approximately 1,170 feet high. That's about twice the height of the Washington Monument.

(Author's note: No, I did not check out any of the above statistics for accuracy.)

While very successful, *The Lone Ranger and The Lost City of Gold* did not have the impact of the first feature. With the completion of the second feature movie, "The Lone Ranger" motion picture and television series ceased production and no more live-action adventures were ever made.

In what has been described as "an amicable

Television animators used models like these shown for drawing "The Lone Ranger" cartoon series.

The four panels pictured above are examples of "The Lone Ranger" cartoon series as it appeared to Saturday morning television viewers.

working relationship" with Lone Ranger Television, Inc. and Wrather Corporation, Clayton Moore and Jay Silverheels have from time to time over the years continued to portray the Lone Ranger and Tonto for various personal appearances and for occasional commercials that have utilized the characters.

In 1965, with the Saturday morning television cartoon ghetto for children serving as a seemingly perpetual money tree for television networks, Wrather Corporation entered into agreements with three animation houses for the production of seventy-eight, six and a half minute "Lone Ranger" television cartoons. From the fall of 1966 until 1969 the cartoon series ran on the CBS Television Network Saturday mornings. The cartoon series was no better or worse than most other television cartoon fare, but it did very little to promote the quality and integrity of the property. George W. Trendle said of the cartoon series in 1969, ". . . those animated cartoons they run of 'The Lone Ranger' are downright ridiculous." Despite what Trendle may have thought, the cartoon series proved to be very popular with youthful viewers who kept coming back for more—once again proving the enduring popularity of the character.

Michael Rye provided the voice for the Lone

Ranger in the cartoon series. Michael Rye earlier in his career had played "Jack Armstrong, The All-American Boy" on radio. John Hart, the television Lone Ranger for one season, was Jack Armstrong in the movie serial. James Jewell, the original director of "The Lone Ranger" on radio, later was the director of "Jack Armstrong" on radio. As Jim Harmon and Donald F. Glut suggest in *The Great Movie Serials,* ". . . the Lone Ranger is really only Jack Armstrong grown up."

Over the years "The Lone Ranger" television and radio programs have received more awards for distinguished accomplishment than any other entertainment series on the air. During its forty-plus years it has been presented with over 154 scrolls, plaques, and other symbols of recognition from major organizations and groups throughout the United States.

Outstanding among these have been four awards from the American Legion Auxiliary, the "Golden Mike" award given for "The Best Program for Youth on Radio." Such groups as the Boy Scouts of America, the National Federation of Women's Clubs, the National Safety Council, and the Parent-Teacher Association have seen fit to recognize "The Lone Ranger" for "excellence." Commendations for the program have appeared three times in the *Congressional Record.*

Stanley Stunell, Assistant Vice President and Assistant Treasurer for Wrather Corporation, currently has the responsibility of overseeing the "Lone Ranger" property. He recently commented, "I'm fond of saying, 'The Lone Ranger' is bigger than all of us, and he'll live longer than all of us. Just as I'm the, so to speak, current 'caretaker,' I imagine when I'm long-gone there'll still be somebody performing this function."

Epilogue

And so the Lone Ranger rides on—perhaps not to *new* adventures, but certainly to new generations of audiences that will appreciate the excitement, the fascination, and the intoxication of "those thrilling days of yesteryear." For those of us who have already shared many adventures with the Lone Ranger, the novels, comics, radio programs, television and movie films, and all of the memorabilia hold an era frozen in time. Through them we can relive the era—our youth —if only for a few minutes or hours.

My favorite closing to a Lone Ranger adventure is not from the radio or television series; it is from Fran Striker's novel, *The Lone Ranger in Wild Horse Canyon.** As usual, the Lone Ranger has rounded up all of the outlaws and the sheriff has them in tow. It is night in Wild Horse Canyon as the Lone Ranger says his good-bye to the heroine.

"Good-bye, Betty, and good luck," he had said, touching his hat with his left hand in salute. "There's still a lot of work to be done in this great West of ours, Betty, and trails seldom cross again once they're behind us."

Then he was gone. She could hear the sound of shale under Silver's sure-footed hoofs. She heard the splash as he entered the stream. Then, suddenly, from up the canyon came the crack and thud of many hoofs, the snorting and shrill nickerings of a stampeding band of wild horses. Betty's heart had leaped to her throat for fear that the masked man might be caught in that charge of the wild horse herd.

As she strained her eyes in the deepening dusk, she caught sight of a blur of white. There, on a low shelf of rock above the canyon floor a level ray of the disappearing sun illuminated for an instant the tableau of a great white stallion and his gallant rider. A moment later the canyon was in darkness and the sound of wild hoofs was dying away in the distance. Suddenly a clear voice rang out above all the other sounds of the night: "Hi-Yo, Silver—away!"

* © Lone Ranger Television, Inc.

Appendix: The First "Lone Ranger" Radio Script

During the final day of my visit with Jim Jewell in Chicago, he handed me a copy of an early radio script from "The Lone Ranger" series and told me I could keep it. After I returned to my hotel room later that evening, I showered and settled sleepily into bed with the old script. Within moments I was very much awake with the dawning knowledge that I didn't have just an early script in my hands. I had what appeared to be the *original* script from "The Lone Ranger"—Jim's own annotated copy that he had used to direct the program.

The next morning before catching my plane back to Florida, I called Jim to verify my belief. In the process of questioning him about the script, I read aloud the announcer's opening speech containing the "hearty laugh" line that was cut from the first program just prior to air time because of George Seaton's inability to laugh in character, thus bringing about the creation of the "Hi-Yo, Silver" shout.

I mentioned to Jim the other "laugh" lines included in the script that George W. Trendle was acknowledged to have criticized. Also, I pointed out that the script contained no mention of Tonto who reportedly did not appear until the tenth script—the Lone Ranger was really alone in this adventure.

After I had finished presenting the "evidence" to prove my case that the script in my hands was the original, Jim acknowledged that in fact it probably was one of the very earliest—"Oh, and by the way, David, after you have had a chance to make a Xerox copy, would you please return it as soon as possible?" I lacked the courage to remind Jim that the day before he had told me I could keep the script. I couldn't fault him, though; he hadn't realized what he was giving away.

When I got home, I made a Xerox and returned the original. It wasn't until a couple of months later that I reread the script and remembered a question that I had forgotten during that phone call just before my homeward flight from Chicago. I was curious that at no time in the original script is there mention of a black mask. It is obvious that the Lone Ranger is not wearing one and no mention is made of a disguise. I wanted to ask Jim if it might be possible that the mask was a feature of the character that came some time after the first episode.

Before I had occasion to contact Jim again, I received a telephone call from New York from the vacationing Chuck Livingstone who informed me that he had just heard on the radio that Jim Jewell was dead. The emphysema that had made talking so difficult for Jim during my visit had taken its final toll.

And so my question about the mask has gone unanswered. No one remembers any longer.

Here is that first "Lone Ranger" radio script—perhaps a little primitive by later program standards. There is even the feeling of a "pilot" program about the script—creators feeling their way along with an unfamiliar character that is still under development; an announcer telling us more about the Lone Ranger than will be necessary later when the character becomes known to his audience.

I have transcribed the radio script as I found it with most of the oddities of spelling and punctuation left intact. The bracketed notes represent the scribbled crayon notes (those that were decipherable) of director Jim Jewell.

THE LONE RANGER*

FANFARE: (HOOFS & SHOTS) ["William Tell" finale]

ANNOUNCER: (CUE FROM JEWELL) A fiery horse, with a speed of light—a cloud of dust, a hearty laugh.

RANGER: (LAUGHS)

ANNOUNCER: The Lone Ranger!

MUSIC: [Music background]

ANNOUNCER: The Lone Ranger is perhaps the most attractive figure ever to come out of the West. Through his daring, his riding and his shooting, this mystery rider won the respect of the entire Golden Coast—the West of the old days, where every man carried his heart on his sleeve and only the fittest remained to make history. Many are the stories that are told by the lights of the Western campfire concerning this romantic figure. Some thought he was on the side of the outlaw, but many knew that he was a lone rider, dealing out justice to the law abiding citizenry. Though the Lone Ranger was known in seven states, he earned his greatest reputation in Texas. None knew where he came from and none knew where he went. [Cut Music]

*********** (STORM EFFECT BACKGROUND FOR SPEECH)

ANNOUNCER: Old Jeb Langworth lived alone in his small shack just outside the wide open community of Red Rock. One evening as he was watching the coffee boil and the bacon sizzle in the pan, and thinking of how snug his cabin was, with the storm raging outside, there came a knock on the door.

(b) STORM BACKGROUND

(c) RAP ON DOOR

JEB: Now who in tunket c'n be out of a night sech as this bee . . . (RAISE VOICE) HULOO. . . ? COME ON IN STRANGER.

(d) *Door opens, storm increases and door closes with storm softened again.*

RANGER: Rather wet out doors tonight. (APPROACH) I saw the light of your cabin.

JEB: An' right welcome yew be too, stranger, haul over to the fire here an' take the chill outen your hide.

RANGER: Thanks.

JEB: I'm jest a ficin' up some chow. I reckon' I better lay on a few more slabs o' bacon eh?

RANGER: I could eat without any trouble.

JEB: Jest make yerself right toh hum. Whar'd yew come from?

RANGER: No Place in particular.

JEB: Prospectin'?

RANGER: Nope.

JEB: I 'low a man's business is his own affair, an' if yew don't callate tew talk, I ain't the one tew be askin' questions. Lay off yer boots an' gun an' make yourself right tu hum. Ole Jeb Langworth ain't never turned a man out yet.

RANGER: Thanks. I'll keep my gun on though. Never know when I'll need it.

JEB: That's yore own business too.

(b) *Extra burst of storm*

JEB: GEEEEMINIY. Ain't that storm a buster though?

RANGER: Wild night alright. You are Jeb Langworth?

JEB: Yep, that's me. Deppity Sheriff is my callin'.

RANGER: So I see by your badge. Who is the Sheriff at Red Rock?

* © Lone Ranger Television, Inc.

JEB: Name is Obie Cuyler, an' he's as square a man as yew'd find in a long ride. Me an' Cal Steward is his Deppities, and 'tween the three of us, they hain't much goes on that ain't right an' in the law.

RANGER: I see you've a poster, advertising a reward for the Lone Ranger.

JEB: Yep. I reckon' they hain't a Sheriff in this part o' the country that haint a lookin' fer that feller.

RANGER: What has he done?

JEB: Now yew don't say yew haint heard tell o' him? Why they say that he's the most dangerous feller that's ever been out in these parts.

RANGER: Indeed?

JEB: Speaks like a gentleman from one of them Eastern collidges, an' shoots so fast thet his six gun is back in his holster afore a man c'n see his draw.

RANGER: But why is there such a big reward for him? What has he done?

JEB: Danged if I knows what he's done. I know one thing though . . .

RANGER: What's that?

JEB: My brother . . . he was ailin' an' ready fer tuh die, with some injuns brandin' him, and burnin' him one.

RANGER: Your brother?

JEB: Yep, an' this here Ranger, he comes in about that time an' gits my brother sot free, and he didn't have tuh fire a single shot for tuh do it.

RANGER: How did he do it?

JEB: Wal, he seems tuh hev spoke to the injuns, in their own crazy way of talkin', an' by golly in less'n a minute they was all bendin' down an' cow towin' tuh him like he was some sort of a god. Then they loosed the ropes that was tyin' my brother, an' they brought roots an' grease an' things, an' fixed him all up as good as new, an' let him go.

RANGER: And still you would capture this Lone Ranger if you could find him eh?

JEB: By gosh, I don't know whether I would 'er not.

RANGER: And you DO know that he saved the life of your brother, and you DON'T know what he's done that's so terrible.

JEB: Wal, they say that he killed a lot of fellers . . .

RANGER: Perhaps they needed killing.

JEB: Mebbe so, mebbe so . . . say I reckon this Ranger must talk a lot like you do . . . you talk might well eddicated yerself Stranger.

RANGER: Have you ever seen bullets . . . like THESE?

JEB: HUH? WHY . . . BY GOSH . . . THEY . . . THEY BE SILVER . . . AN' THEY SAY THIS RANGER . . . USES SILVER BULLETS . . . BY GUM YORE THE LONE RANGER!

RANGER: (LAUGH)

JEB: AN' THAT LAUGH . . . THAT'S ANOTHER THING . . . YORE HIM AIN'T YAH?

RANGER: You have my gun, Jeb. What are you going to do with it?

JEB: Here, take it back, Ranger . . . put er whar she belongs. I aint the man tuh turn in a feller like yo'. No Sir. Haul yer chair over now an' see how yuh like my cookin'. I allus said that sometime I'd git a chance tuh show how much I 'preciated what yo' done fer my brother.

RANGER: Thanks. Where is he now?

JEB: Oh he's dead these two years.

RANGER: A bit late for you to be eating your supper isn't it?

JEB: Yep, I was busy over tuh Red Rock till after eight. I reckon' it must be close on't nine o'clock haint it?

RANGER: Yes, just about.

JEB: You better spend the night here Ranger, yore right welcome. Whar's yer hoss tied?

RANGER: He isn't tied. That horse will go into the trees and hide until I whistle for him, I . . .

(d) *RAP ON DOOR*

JEB: GOSH . . . WHO'SE THAT?

RANGER: I'll step back of the curtain here. Don't tell anyone that I'm here.

JEB: Al . . . Allright.

RANGER: Call, and see who is there.

JEB: (CALL) WHO IS IT?
CAL: (DISTANT MUFFLED) It's me Jeb, Cal Steward. Lemme in!
RANGER: I locked the door behind me, is that the Deputy?
JEB: Yep, an' I reckon' yo' better hide Ranger, Cal aint the kind tuh see yuh git away if he c'n git his hands on yuh. I'll let him in an' see what he wants.
RANGER: Go ahead.
JEB: (CALL) Jest a secunt Cal . . . (FADE BACK)

(d) DOOR OPENS
Storm increases and door closes

CAL: (APPROACHING) Golly what a night this is, Jeb.
JEB: Aint it now? What brings yo' out of a night like this, Cal?
CAL: The p'int is this, I come to borry somthin' from yuh, Jeb.
JEB: Sure, anything yuh wants.
CAL: It aint much that I wants, it's just a bucket of oil, the lamps in my shack is runnin' low an' I got some records tuh go over. I thought if yew c'd lemme take some oil till mornin. . . ?
JEB: Sure . . . I'll git it right off. I keeps it back in the woodshed. I'll git yuh some right away Cal. (FADE BACK)
CAL: That's mighty accommodatin' of yuh Jeb. You been out tonight?
JEB: Who . . . me?
CAL: They's wet tracks . . .
JEB: Oh . . . Oh yeah, I jest got in a few minutes ago. Them's my tracks.
CAL: I see.
JEB: I . . . I'll get that oil. (FADE OUT)

1. INTERLUDE . . . STRAIGHT
[Storm fade, super dawn music]

ANNOUNCER: And the storm wore itself out during the night as Jeb Langworth and the Lone Ranger passed a peaceful night's rest. What has the coming of the Lone Ranger meant? Morning—listen!
RANGER: Much obliged for putting me up for the night, Jeb. I think I'll be on my way. I like to get an early start.
JEB: O.K. Ranger. Glad tuh to be able tuh do a good turn by yew.
RANGER: Maybe I'll be able to return the favor some day.
JEB: Don't think nuthin' of it at all.
RANGER: I was wondering, when Cal came last night, what you would say about the wet footprints on the floor.
JEB: (CHUCKLES) I reckon' I got over that all right, eh?
RANGER: Very well. Yes.
JEB: Ya see, that feller Cal Steward, he don't miss nuthin' he don't. He's got eyes like a hawk.
RANGER: Yes.
JEB: (CHUCKLES) I reckon' it rankled some in his mind that I didn't tell him whar I went an' what I went out fer eh?
RANGER: Perhaps. You don't seem to like him very well.
JEB: Aw-w he's all right, but him an' me got differn't idees, that's all.
RANGER: I see. Well, I'll say goodbye to you.

(d) *Door opens*

JEB: G'bye Ranger. Whar's yer hoss?
RANGER: I'll show you. (WHISTLE)
JEB: He must be a swell hoss.
RANGER: He is.

(e) [Single] *Horses hoofs approach*

JEB: Thar he comes right enough.
RANGER: Yes.

(e) *Hoofs stop.*
(f) *Horse whinny.*

JEB: Wal . . . G'BYE . . . RANGER . . .
RANGER: GOODBYE

(e) *Hoofs start hard and fade out.*

JEB: Wal, (TO HIMSELF) I reckon' I better git my gun hitched up an' git in tuh town. Sheriff might be wantin' me . . .

(f) *Several horses approach.*

JEB: Gosh, I guess he does want me, thar he comes now.
SHERIFF: (DISTANT) STAND RIGHT WHERE YOU ARE JEB LANGWORTH

(g) *Horses stop.*

JEB: Hullo Sheriff, Mirnin' Cal . . . What's the call fer?

CAL: I guess you know what it is Jeb. Ain't you ashamed now?

JEB: Who me? Why gosh Cal, what've I done?

SHERIFF: I'm sorry Jeb, I'll have to search yore cabin.

JEB: WHAT FER?

SHERIFF: A gun.

JEB: Who'se gun?

SHERIFF: You're actin' innocent all right, but it's yore gun I want.

JEB: Mine?

CAL: Jeb, why'd yew do it?

JEB: Say, I don't git this at all.

SHERIFF: Don't yew move! You go on in Cal an' look around.

CAL: Right. You keep him here whar he can't do no damage mor'n he's done already. (FADE BACK)

JEB: Shucks Cal. I aint aimin' tuh do no damage. Sheriff, what have I done?

SHERIFF: Jeb, it's murder. That's what it is. Dan Higgens was shot last night.

JEB: DAN HIGGENS WAS. . . ?

SHERIFF: Yep. We know that he had some gold hid away in his cabin' an' he was found dead this mornin' an' there was the box that he kept his gold in but the gold was gone.

JEB: BUT GOSH SHERIFF, YO' DON'T THINK THAT I . . .

SHERIFF: Jeb, he was shot by a thirty eight. An' there aint many men here uses anything 'sides a forty five, 'ceptin' you.

JEB: BUT I DIDN'T DO IT SHERIFF.

SHERIFF: Cal, just rec'lected that he come here last night an' found that you was out of yer cabin just afore nine o'clock.

JEB: An' when was Higgens shot?

SHERIFF: The doc says it was between quarter of nine an' quarter past.

JEB: BUT . . . I . . .

SHERIFF: WHAT'D YUH FIND CAL?

CAL: I found lots. (APPROACHING) Look . . . here's his gun all right, an' they's one chamber empty.

JEB: I NEVER SHOT IT!

SHERIFF: What's that yew got Cal?

CAL: A bag. One of the kind of bags that gold is kept in, and it's got Higgens name on it.

JEB: I never see that bag afore Sheriff. I swears I didn't.

SHERIFF: Was you out of yer cabin last night, Jeb?

JEB: I . . . I . . . Oh gosh . . . I didn't kill him, I swear I didn't. I wasn't no where's near him last night.

CAL: Maybe then, you c'n explain how it comes that we finds THIS KNIFE . . . just outside of Higgens door!

SHERIFF: Is that your knife Jeb?

JEB: That's my knife . . . sure it is . . . but I . . .

CAL: I reckon' it's a pretty bad case agin' yuh, Jeb.

JEB: It's a frame up, that's what it is, Sheriff . . . a frame up . . .

SHERIFF: If you c'n prove that you wasn't out of yer cabin Jeb, but yuh can't do it, yuh see.

CAL: I c'n prove you WAS out of yer cabin. Come on. Shall I put the cuffs on him Sheriff?

JEB: I don't need no cuffs. I'll go quiet, I'm an innocent man.

2. *INTERLUDE . . . SUSPENSE*

ANNOUNCER: So they took old Jeb Langworth to jail for the murder of his friend Higgens. Did the mysterious visit of the Lone Ranger have anything to do with the fate of Jeb? Let us look in at the office of the Sheriff . . .

CAL: Purty danged cold blooded shootin' of Jeb, the way he plugged old Higgens, Sheriff.

SHERIFF: I don' know what tew think of it, Cal. It taint like Jeb at all. He was allus the most peace lovin' feller I knowed, why I didn't ever know Jeb tuh use vi'lence of any sort.

CAL: Yuh caint never tell about these silent fellers like him. Gosh, ole Higgens was well liked too.

SHERIFF: I knows it.

CAL: I'm most afeared tuh let the news get told around about Jeb.

SHERIFF: Why?

CAL: I reckon' the boys here in Red

Rock won't wait fer a trial.

SHERIFF: Think they'll lynch him?

CAL: Wouldn't be surprised.

SHERIFF: Wal, I aint a goin' tuh stand fer no lynchin'. This here is a civilized community an' I'm fer law an' order. The law says that a man's entitled tuh be tried afore a jury, an' that's what Jeb's goin' tuh be.

CAL: I'm for it Sheriff, but yuh caint stop the boys, when they gits their minds made up.

SHERIFF: They don't know thet he's been arrested yet do they?

CAL: Nope, I done my best tuh keep it quiet about who we picked up fer the murder of Higgens.

SHERIFF: Yuh done yer best yuh say?

CAL: Yep.

SHERIFF: Did anyone get tuh know about it?

CAL: Wal, I ain't jest sure, Sheriff.

SHERIFF: WHAT D'YA mean you ain't sure?

CAL: I may've dropped a remark that give it away . . . I reckon maybe we better hustle the trial along. Just tuh be on the safe side.

SHERIFF: Seems tuh me yore pow'ful anxious tuh see Jeb get hanged fer the killin', Cal.

CAL: I'm jest anxious fer tuh see him tried an' found guilty, afore he get's lynched 'thout any trial, that's all Sheriff.

SHERIFF: He's goin' tuh be tried in the due course o' time. Not afore, an' if they's anything like a lynchin' . . . I'll shoot the man that starts it. Thems my sentiments an' yo' c'n pass 'em along to the men in town here.

CAL: Jest as you say, Sheriff.

SHERIFF: I aims to carry on a little more investigatin' on my own hook, afore I makes up my mind tew anything.

CAL: Sho' you don't think Jeb didn't do it?

SHERIFF: I'm reservin' of my opinion.

CAL: Wal, that's yer priverlage, I reckon.

(h) *DISTANT GUN SHOTS*

SHERIFF: What's that?

CAL: Shootin' . . . out in front of this here office.

RANGER: (DISTANT LAUGH)

SHERIFF: What's that laugh . . . that sounds like . . .

CAL: The Lone Ranger . . . C'mon Sheriff . . . He's out front . . .

(i) *Running feet.*

SHERIFF: (FADE BACK) D'ya see him anyplace?

CAL: Cain't see nuthin' out here . . .

SHERIFF: Whar'd he go . . .

CAL: I . . . I reckon' he's got away somewheres . . .

RANGER: I'm right here gentlemen.

CAL: HUH?

SHERIFF: How'd yew git in . . . WHAT . . . Who are you?

RANGER: I came right in the side window while you were looking out the front door. No . . . don't go for a gun!

SHERIFF: I aint aimin' tuh commit suicide!

CAL: Are . . . are you . . . the Lone Ranger?

RANGER: (LAUGHS)

SHERIFF: WHA . . . What are you doing here?

RANGER: I just dropped in to tell you that Jeb Langworth did NOT kill old Higgens.

CAL: I reckon you're the one eh?

RANGER: Wrong again.

CAL: Well, you're under arrest anyway, for the . . . the murders on that there poster. Don't try any funny tricks.

RANGER: (LAUGHS) Under arrest? ME?

SHERIFF: I reckon' he's right, Mr. Ranger, we'll have tuh put you under arrest.

RANGER: That suits me all right. Are you going to let Jeb out of jail to make room for me?

SHERIFF: He stays there, I reckon the jail is large enough for both of you.

RANGER: I just came here, Sheriff . . . to tell you to let Jeb Langworth go. He's innocent.

CAL: HUMPH!

SHERIFF: You don't think I'll do it do yuh?

RANGER: No, but I think your deputy, Cal Steward will release him, to prevent me from telling WHO the

REAL murderer of Higgens is.

CAL: HUH . . . WHY YOU . . . YOU . . .

RANGER: Don't let me tempt you into reaching for your gun, Cal, I think you've heard of the way I draw a gun and fire. That's all I have to say, Sheriff.

(j) *Heavy sound of horse thumping on wood floor.*

RANGER: You see, my horse will join me, no matter where I am.

SHERIFF: Git that hoss outta my office . . .

RANGER: I intend to . . . Turn around . . . both of you.

SHERIFF: BUT . . .

RANGER: SILVER!

CAL: Hye!—Git that hoss . . .

SHERIFF: OUCH . . . (j) *Thumping*

SHERIFF: That hoss is walkin' on me . . .

RANGER: Then turn your face to the wall as I said. I don't choose to draw my gun unless I have to.

CAL: OUCH . . . Git away yuh danged nag yuh . . .

RANGER: There, that will do, Silver.

(k) *Whinny*

RANGER: A good horse is a man's best friend. He won't frame him the way a human friend will, Cal. You'd ought to have some of the qualities of a horse.

CAL: Sheriff . . . look around an' see what he's doin' . . .

SHERIFF: Look around yerself . . . I ain't aimin' tuh git tromped down.

RANGER: Remember what I have said Sheriff . . . release Jeb Langworth because his innocence can be proved and the guilty party FOUND if you force me to do it. That's all . . . Hi Yi Silver!

(l) *HEAVY HOOF BEATS ON FLOOR FOR A FEW STEPS AND THEN ON TURF AND FADE OUT*

RANGER: (LAUGHING FADE OUT)

CAL: Is . . . is that varmint gone, Sheriff?

SHERIFF: I . . . I reckon so . . . dang him . . . whyn't yuh shoot him?

CAL: Humph! I don't draw no gun again' that feller, less his back is to me. Why didn't you shoot him?

SHERIFF: Here . . . he's left one of them silver bullets of his'n on my desk, an' a note . . . he . . . (PAUSE)

CAL: What's it say?

SHERIFF: (VERY STERN) Nuthin'. Reckon' it'll make a good hunk of paper tuh light my pipe with though.

CAL: What's that note say, Sheriff?

SHERIFF: Nothing!

3. [Music] INTERLUDE . . . TENSION [Super Crowd noise]

ANNOUNCER: The Lone Ranger has given his warning. What was contained in the note he left with the Sheriff? Let's follow Cal Steward. We enter the Bar-room as Cal says . . .

CAL: (LAUGH) Well gents, I guess four queens is a good enough hand to win the pot of any poker game aint it?

JERIMY: By Tunket, Cal, I never see sech luck with cards as yew hev.

CAL: (LAUGH) Yep, the luck's with me tonight all right, Jerimy. How about you Tim? Want tuh play any more?

TIM: Me? I'm cleaned Cal, I'd give a month's pay fer a run o' luck like yew hed tuh-night.

JOE: An' me tew. I'm washed up.

CAL: (LAUGH) Wal, boys, I reckon' I'll stroll over an' see how the prisoner is gettin' on.

JERIMY: Yuh shore thet Jeb—he done the killin, Cal?

CAL: Yuh can't say he didn't in face of the evidence, Jerimy.

TIM: I hates tew think thet Jeb'd kill a fren' like Higgens.

CAL: Higgens was a good feller, surprises me that Jeb aint been lynched fore this.

JOE: Jeb's a good feller tew, an' I reckon that one that starts any talk erbout lynchin'll hev tuh face ME!

JERIMY: An me.

TIM: An' me too, by Tunket. Wal, I got tew be gittin on.

JERIMY: Wait Tim, I'll go 'long with yew.

CAL: G'nighte boys . . .

ALL: (FADE OUT . . . "Goodnight Cal" —AD LIBS CARRY THROUGH THE SCENE UNTIL DOOR CLOSE)

RANGER: Just a minute, Steward!

CAL: Huh . . . how . . . how'd YOU get in here?

RANGER: I've been standing back watching your little poker game, that's all.

CAL: What d'yew want here? Don't yuh know that the Sheriff'll shoot yuh on sight?

RANGER: Yes, but I've got to be seen, before I SEE, and my eyes are rather good. I think I'll play some poker with you.

CAL: HUH? Play poker . . . here?

RANGER: No not here. We'll go in the little room over on the side. It's more private.

CAL: I . . . I had enough poker.

RANGER: I think you'll play a few hands with *me*!

CAL: How much money yew got?

RANGER: I don't know.

CAL: I . . . I aint a goin' tuh play!

RANGER: Come . . . Hurry now. This way. You may bring your own cards if you want to . . . I'll make the stakes high enough to interest you.

CAL: BUT . . .

RANGER: Right this way,—I find that Jeb Langworth is still in jail.

CAL: I ain't got nuthin tuh do with that. YOU'LL have tuh see the Sheriff.

RANGER: I'd much prefer to see . . . YOU. Here we are. Right in there, it's nice and private.

(n) *Door closes. Stop room noises.*

RANGER: There we are. Two chairs and one table, two men and a pack of cards. Strange things can be done with a pack of cards, Cal.

CAL: Wha . . . what d'yew mean?

RANGER: Sit down there, you can deal, shuffle and cut all by yourself.

CAL: Say, look here, Ranger, let me go, an' I won't say nuthin' about you bein' here in Red Rock.

RANGER: Oh, I don't mind, you can say all you want to say. After you get out of this room. Deal the cards.

CAL: All right, if yuh want tuh get skinned.

RANGER: You may even name the stakes.

CAL: They tells me that yuh shoots silver bullets, is that right?

RANGER: That's right. Yes. Would you like to see one?

CAL: Yuh said tuh name the stakes . . .

RANGER: Right.

CAL: All right . . . I'll bet two hundred dollars.

RANGER: BAH! I can't waste my time on stakes like that!

CAL: FIVE HUNDRED THEN.

RANGER: With it your own cut, shuffle and deal, and the cards marked the way you want them? I'm surprised. I thought you'd be willing to risk more than that.

CAL: All right . . . You name 'em! I'll meet 'em.

RANGER: LIFE!

CAL: Wha . . . what d'ya mean?

RANGER: Your life . . . against mine.

CAL: What's that mean?

RANGER: You have two guns . . . so have I. I'll bet mine against yours.

CAL: An' let me deal?

RANGER: Even knowing that the cards are marked, I'll let you deal Cal Steward.

CAL: It's a go then. Lay yer guns on the table.

RANGER: There they are.

(o) *Thumps*

CAL: (LAUGH) My, but they're nice guns . . .

RANGER: Now how about yours?

CAL: Here's mine . . . you're lookin' right down 'em Ranger . . . Stick up yer hands!

RANGER: I didn't think you'd be this much of a cheat.

CAL: Reach the ceilin' Mr. Lone Ranger! I reckon this is the time that yer fast draw won't help yuh none! (LAUGH) This is the time where brains is beatin' speed! Now I've got yew right where yew should be.

RANGER: Well, what are you going to do about it?

CAL: I'm a goin' to KILL yuh! That's what.

RANGER: Not even going to give me a trial eh?

CAL: The reward is fer yuh, DEAD OR ALIVE . . . an' I'm takin' no chances on yuh gittin' away, see?

RANGER: Yes, I see. But just a minute, Steward . . . don't you know that you don't dare to kill me? Not yet, you don't.

CAL: An' why don't I?

RANGER: Because, I've written down all about how you shot Higgens, and I've told how you came to Jeb's place the night of the murder, and sent him out for kerosene . . .

CAL: HUH?

RANGER: And how you stole his knife and his gun while he was out of the room. And I've told how you shot Higgens with Jeb's gun, and left his knife there to be found, and how you came the next day to arrest Jeb, and planted his gun in his shack, as well as the bag that held the gold!

CAL: How d'yew know all this?

RANGER: I know a lot of things you see. I've written that all down, just so you won't dare to shoot me!

CAL: WHERE IS IT?

RANGER: Well, the funny thing is that it is right in the safe in the Sheriff's office, and I guess you can't get it there.

CAL: (LAUGH) THAT IS GOOD!

RANGER: It's true isn't it?

CAL: Yes, it's true . . . an' it's true that I c'n open the Sheriff's safe an' get out that writin' . . . so yuh see you ain't so smart as yuh thought. Now I'm a goin' tuh shoot yuh!

RANGER: Just as a matter of curiosity, before you shoot me, Cal, suppose you tell me just where you put the money you stole. That's fair enough isn't it?

CAL: I don't mind tellin' yah . . .

RANGER: I'd hate to die without knowing that.

CAL: I got it hid under the floor of my cabin . . . that's where . . . An' Jeb is goin' to pay fer the crime.

RANGER: Don't you think you're going to be troubled by your conscience?

CAL: No, and what's more, none of the folks around here are going to be troubled by you any longer. I'M A GOIN' tuh kill you right now, Mr. Lone Ranger . . .

SHERIFF: (DISTANT) oh no yuh ain't Cal. Put up yer hands!

CAL: SHERIFF!

RANGER: Thanks, Sheriff!

CAL: Wait . . . The Lone Ranger—I got him here!

SHERIFF: Put your guns down, Cal—I heard all that was said, and I guess it's you that'll be tried for the murder of Higgens—not Jeb!

RANGER: You see, Cal, it takes BRAINS sometimes to out guess guns! I was so sure that you'd take advantage of me, when I was unarmed and so sure of your boasting nature, that I left a little note for the Sheriff to be by that window tonight if he wanted to hear the confession of the REAL MURDERER!

SHERIFF: You stand where you are too, Ranger . . . This is a great evening for the town of Red Rock. Go on in the winder boys and put the ropes on them two.

RANGER: Sheriff, you'll of course let Jeb Langworth go free now won't you?

SHERIFF: We ain't got nuthin' on Jeb now.

RANGER: You see, he did me a favor, and I always aim to return favors. If you're sure that he'll be free now . . .

SHERIFF: What'll you do?

RANGER: I think . . . I'll be leaving.

CAL: SHERIFF . . . HE'S GRABBED HIS GUNS . . .

(p) *Door Open and slam.*

(AD LIB SHOTS . . . RUNNING FEET . . . SHOUTS OF MEN, ETC.)

RANGER: (WHISTLE) SILVER . . . SILVER . . . HERE WE ARE OLD BOY!

(q) *HORSES HOOFS APPROACH*

SHERIFF: (SHOUTING) That's the Lone Ranger . . . Stop him boys—stop him.

RANGER: Come along Silver . . . that's the boy. Hi . . . Yi . . . (HEARTY LAUGH)

(q) HOOFS POUNDING

HARDER AND FADE OUT.

[*Hoofs up full into music*]

*********** (THEME)

CLOSING ANNOUNCEMENT Might as well try and catch the wind, as this phantom rider of the plains. The Lone Ranger has gone off into the night, not to be seen again, until he finds another occasion to take into his own hands the law of the West. This is one of a series of stories of the Lone Ranger, and his horse, Silver. These stories are presented by the Jewell Players, directed by James Jewell and come to you over YOUR station, WXYZ with studios in the Maccabees Building, Detroit.

Selected Bibliography

Aaronson, Charles S. *1963 International Motion Picture Almanac*. New York: Quigley, 1963.

Barbour, Alan G. *Days of Thrills and Adventure*. New York: Macmillan, 1970.

———. *The Thrill of It All*. New York: Macmillan, 1971.

Bickel, Mary E. *Geo. W. Trendle*. New York: Exposition Press, 1971.

Boutwell, C. B. "Hi-Yo, Silver Lining!" *Nation* (January 11, 1941).

Bryan, III, J. "Hi-Yo, Silver!" *Saturday Evening Post* (October 14, 1939).

Buxton, Frank, and Owen, Bill. *The Big Broadcast*. New York: Viking, 1966.

"Death of the Ranger." *Time* (April 21, 1941).

Everson, William K. *A Pictorial History of the Western Film*. New York: Citadel, 1969.

Fernett, Gene. *Hollywood's Poverty Row*. Satellite Beach, Florida: Coral Reef Publications, 1973.

Green, Abel, and Laurie, Jr., Joe. *Show Biz*. New York: Holt, 1951.

Gross, Ben. *I Looked And I Listened*. New York: Arlington House, 1970.

Halliwell, Leslie. *The Filmgoer's Companion*. New York: Avon, 1971.

Hanley, Loretta, ed. *Series, Serials and Packages*. New York: Broadcast Information Bureau, Inc., Volume 15: Issue 2D, 1974.

Harmon, Jim. *Nostalgia Catalogue*. Los Angeles: J. P. Tarcher, 1973.

———. *The Great Radio Heroes*. New York: Doubleday, 1967.

Harmon, Jim, and Glut, Donald F. *The Great Movie Heroes*. New York: Doubleday, 1972.

Healy, Mike. "Hi Ho Buffalo! The Lone Ranger Originally Rode From Our City." *Buffalo Courier Express* (April 14, 1975).

Lamparski, Richard. *Whatever Became of . . . ?, Third Series.* New York: Crown, 1971.

McClure, Arthur F. and Jones, Ken D. *Heroes, Heavies and Sagebrush.* South Brunswick and New York: A. S. Barnes and Co., 1972.

Mitchell, Curtis. *Cavalcade of Broadcasting.* Chicago: Follett, 1970.

Nevins, Jr., Francis M. "William Witney." *Films In Review* (November 1974).

New York Times Film Reviews, The, 1913–1968, Volume 4/1949–1958. New York: The New York Times & Arno Press, 1970.

Parish, James Robert. *Actors' Television Credits 1950–1972.* New York: Scarecrow Press, 1973.

Parkinson, Michael, and Jeavons, Clyde. *A Pictorial History of Westerns.* London: Hamlyn, 1972.

Peterson, John. "Lone Ranger Creator Reflects on Radio's Golden Age." *The Detroit News* (July 6, 1969).

"Purity Pays." *Newsweek* (February 2, 1953).

Rosenberg, Bernard, and Silverstein, Harry. *The Real Tinsel.* New York: Macmillan, 1970.

Settel, Irving. *A Pictorial History of Radio.* New York: Grosset & Dunlap, 1967.

Settel, Irving and Laas, William. *A Pictorial History of Television.* New York: Grosset & Dunlap, 1969.

Shulman, Arthur, and Youman, Roger. *How Sweet It Was.* New York: Bonanza, 1966.

———. *The Television Years.* New York: Popular Library, 1973.

Striker, Fran. *The Lone Ranger and the Gold Robbery.* New York: Grosset & Dunlap, 1939. Copyright: Lone Ranger Television, Inc.

———. *The Lone Ranger and the Silver Bullet.* New York: Grosset & Dunlap, 1948. Copyright: Lone Ranger Television, Inc.

———. *The Lone Ranger Traps the Smugglers.* New York: Grosset & Dunlap, 1941. Copyright: Lone Ranger Television, Inc.

———.*The Lone Ranger in Wild Horse Canyon.* New York: Grosset & Dunlap, 1950. Copyright: Lone Ranger Television, Inc.

Twomey, Alfred E., and McClure, Arthur F. *The Versatiles.* New York: Castle, 1969.

Weaver, John T. *Forty Years of Screen Credits Volume 2.* New York: Scarecrow Press, 1970.

Weiss, Ken, and Goodgold, Ed. *To be Continued . . .* New York: Crown, 1972.

Worth, Fred L. *The Trivia Encyclopedia.* Los Angeles: Brooke House, 1974.

Index